THE CONCEPT OF KINSHIP

THE CONCEPT OF KINSHIP
AND OTHER ESSAYS ON
ANTHROPOLOGICAL METHOD
AND EXPLANATION

ERNEST GELLNER

BASIL BLACKWELL

Basil Blackwell Ltd
108 Cowley Road
Oxford OX4 1JF, UK

Basil Blackwell Inc.
432 Park Avenue South, Suite 1503
New York, NY 10016, USA

This book was first published in 1973 as *Cause and Meaning in the Social Sciences* by Routledge & Kegan Paul Ltd.

British Library Cataloguing in Publication Data
Gellner, Ernest
    The concept of kinship: and other essays
    on anthropological method and explanation.
    1. Social sciences
    I. Title   II. Cause and meaning in the
    social sciences
    300'.1   H61
    ISBN 0-631-15287-3 Pbk

Library of Congress Cataloging-in-Publication Data
Gellner, Ernest.
    The concept of kinship.

    Originally published as: Cause and meaning in the social sciences. 1973.
    Includes index.
    1. Ethnology——Philosophy.   2. Social sciences——
    Philosophy.   3. Ethnology——Methodology.   4. Social
    sciences——Methodology.   I. Title.
    GN345.G48   1986   306'.01   86-17608
    ISBN 0-631-15287-3 (pbk.)

Printed in Great Britain by TJ Press, Padstow, Cornwall

CONTENTS

INTRODUCTION

This collection of essays is inspired largely, though not exclusively, by a concern with the problems and options facing social anthropology. These issues have not changed radically since they were written. It is still, or all the more, impossible to offer any logical and neat definition of the subject, one which would tidily demarcate its subject matter, and mark it off from neighbouring fields of inquiry. Social anthropology is not concerned only with the study of simpler societies, though it is indeed preoccupied with them: yet some perfectly legitimate anthropologists also investigate highly developed communities. Equally, it cannot be defined as microsociology, in as far as some anthropologists quite legitimately indulge in abstract theory, and some non-anthropologists also explore intimate communities.

For these and similar reasons, one must abandon the quest for any logical definition, and recognise that the subject simply is *an* inquiry into man and society, one which just happens to have its own distinctive history and tradition, a continuity of issues, and a tradition of cohesion amongst its participants, and a marked character fashioned by diverse intellectual and historical circumstances. This is how the matter stands: it would be pointless to allow some yearning for logical order to lead one to pretend otherwise.

But the circumstances which have moulded anthropology have not remained constant. When anthropology was born, shortly after the middle of the nineteenth century, two factors, above all others, determined its form: Darwinism and colonialism. The former forcefully suggested questions about our social ancestry prior to recorded history, and inspired the quest for tracing evolutionary lines. It tended to push theories of progress from a historicising to a biological idiom. At the same time, the European and North American conquests of extensive regions previously inhabited only by simpler societies inevitably inspired the idea that these populations be used as surrogate time machines, allowing us to inspect our own past. (Colonialism helped anthropology, though the charge that anthropology helped colonialism is baseless.) These questions and these data seemed destined for each other, and when they met a new subject was born.

But later, in this century, a revolution occurred in the English-speaking world, under the leadership of a Pole, a revolution which transformed the subject within the very extensive intellectual sterling zone, and at least profoundly affected it in other parts of the Western World. Only the Soviet Union, where the strong historicist tradition of pre-revolutionary thought was confirmed by Marxist orthodoxy, remained uninfluenced by this change. The revolution over which Bronislaw Malinowski presided during the two inter-war decades from the London School of Economics, which for a time then emerged as the world capital of anthropology, really was a *revolution*, a total inversion, a literal overturning of things.

The greatest pleasures are said to be overcome revulsions, and the most potent taboos are perhaps those which inhibit our most passionate impulses. Anthropology was born of an intense curiosity about the past, about human *origins*. It seemed destined to provide the naturalistic vision of the world with its Book of Genesis. It was meant to satisfy our desire to know how it had all started. And now this Pole imposed an interdict on the very intellectual passion which had inspired the subject!

His authority was such that he actually managed to impose the new prohibition on speculation about the past, and, in effect, to re-define the subject in synchronicist terms. Never perhaps since the days when the ancient Brahmin priests persuaded erstwhile cattle-herding pastoral invaders of India to treat the cow as sacred and forbidden, had there been such a volte-face in sentiment, such a stunning demonstration of the power of doctrine over feeling.

I do not know whether Hindus secretly lust after beef, and whether in consequence its internalised prohibition binds them all the more powerfully to their faith and practice. But I strongly suspect that Malinowskian anthropologists, including the Master himself, were drawn to their subject by a yearning to understand our own common antecedents, so that the self-imposed interdict on speculation about origins bound them all the more passionately to the new vision, and to the charismatic community which it came to define. Group boundaries are imposed, and powerful fraternal links forged, only by difficult beliefs, not by facile ones.

Malinowski replaced Frazer as the paradigmatic anthropologist. As in the Sacred Grove at Nemi, the new priest was the one who had slain his predecessor: Frazer suffered the very fate which, in *The Golden Bough*, he had endeavoured to explain. In style of

research, Frazer had been a brilliant magpie, assembling ethnographic loot from all over the world and fusing the elements, torn
from their contexts, in an impressive and elegant collage. The
unifying principle of the grand canvas was an evolutionary pattern.
Malinowski stood anthropology on its head on both counts:
functionalism insisted on seeing all social traits *in context*, and on
explaining them in terms of their contemporaneous role. The
manifest rationale of prolonged and intimate fieldwork was to
make possible the appropriate exploration of such milieux. The
latent function of the shared ardours of fieldwork was to bind the
anthropological community to each other, to endow it with its
famous cohesion. A powerful shared initiation reinforced the
fellow feeling, which had been engendered by the shared stifling,
within each heart, of the old sinful lust for the knowledge of
origins.

Malinowski's new ideas were for a time treated almost as if they
had come from outer space, self-generated and self-justified by
their manifest truth. Founders–Lawgivers are often seen in this
spirit. Anthropologists, who would automatically have insisted on
seeing the message of an African or Polynesian visionary in terms
of its social context, did not seem impelled to apply the same
principles to ideas excogitated in the hot-house milieu of *fin de
siècle* Cracow and Zakopane, where historical romanticism and
positivist austerity struggled with each other. (Positivism was not
yet defined as the use of facts to criticise Marxism.)

In fact, Malinowski's ideas, that distinctive blend of romanticism and positivism, can only be properly understood in terms of
his Hapsburg–Polish background. This much became evident
when the approach of the centenary of his birth provoked a
remarkable outburst of Malinowski scholarship in his native
Poland, the fruits of which are now available.[1]

This made plain and visible the chemistry by which this potent
and inspiring blend was forged. Malinowski had ample local
experience of the manner in which rival nationalisms manipulated
history and hence he had good cause to distrust explanations in
terms of the past. Ernst Mach's positivism, which had been the
subject of Malinowski's doctoral dissertation, provided him with a
powerful justification of re-interpreting the use and invocation of
history. Machian positivism teaches that all empirically *in*accessible
entities are to be seen only in terms of the services they perform
for the charting of the observable world: unobservable abstractions earn their keep by unifying observables in patterns, which
then help to predict and explain *and* justify. Their role alone
endows them with reality.

This epistemological doctrine could also be and was applied *to
the past itself* which, in one sense, is unobservable for us all, being

well and truly past, and in another sense is *specially* unobservable for an anthropologist, dealing with pre-literate and hence record-less societies. Thus was anthropological method transformed. The past is a charter of present practices, and is manipulated by current interests. The relationship between past and present is not, as Edmund Burke had taught, a noble partnership: rather, it is the relationship of con-man and dupe. But Mach also linked cognition to biology, insisting that knowledge, like other activities, was to be seen in terms of the various services it renders to the total living organism. In this way, Malinowski's Machismo vindicated his a-historical functionalism twice over, both by its anti-transcendentalist and by its biologising aspects.

This unusual blend of elements enabled him to do far more than just overturn Frazerian anthropology. It enabled him to be both a cultural nationalist and a political internationalist, a man imbued with a powerful sense of culture and its unity, but sceptical of historicist political mythologies. This was an unusual blend. Unlike those who shared his sense of culture as an interconnected and powerful tissue, he was not led by his respect for culture to a reverence for history; unlike those who shared his empiricism, he was not led to a method which is culture-blind and atomises that which it investigates. He was a romantic empiricist, and a holist anti-historicist. This new *combinazzione*, a striking reshuffling of the available cards, gave him his powerful and unique appeal.

Nearly half a century has now elapsed since he left the London School of Economics (and he died a few years later in America). The subject he left behind is still recognisably the same. But the world in which it operates has changed radically. No large central-ised colonial empires provide the researcher with an enormous reservoir of relatively insulated yet easily accessible and safe societies for investigation. Most Third World societies are under-going rapid change, and many are administered by authorities hostile to and suspicious of research, and eager to obstruct it. Their ideological commitments often make them touchy about genuine investigation, as does the corruption of their officials. Accurate observation and its publication are less than welcome. One embattled Third World movement actually announced that it had no wish to be the object of any ethnographic inquiry.

At the same time, no complacent evolutionary schemata now dominate our vision, liable to obscure and distort our perception of concrete societies on the ground. Stable societies can now only be conceptually reconstructed; directly observable societies are not stable. Hence it is rather hard to apply a functionalist vision, which had almost equated explanation with the specification of mechanics of stability, and which at the same time insisted on direct observation. You can have stability and direct observation, but you can no longer have both at the same time. Ironically, Malinowski himself, and his world, are now part of that very past which on an extreme interpretation of his views is only allowed to exist in virtue of its role in the present. In Poland, Malinowski scholarship has the not-so-latent function of needling a regime legitimated in terms of a nineteenth-century historicist mythology. What is now the balance sheet of the Malinowskian period, and which way can the subject go?

Pre-Malinowskian anthropology asked fascinating questions, and assembled suspect ethnography. Perhaps Malinowskian anthropology tended to be a bit the other way round. Its ethnography was superb, but is there not a slight suspicion that its theoretical inspiration has worn a little thin? *Structuralisme*, which tried to revive it, is a kind of Synchronicism-by-Other-Means: it replaced the guiding notion of the functional interdependence of institutions by the idea of a kind of permanent cultural core, generating cultural manifestations. That core was to be reconstructed from its recorded manifestation, though the execution of this programme is tainted by suspicion of a touch of arbitrariness and fancifulness. But it provided a new theoretical justification for carrying on in the old way, especially at a time when political structures were becoming rather less accessible to the researcher than were cultural texts. But this inspiration too seems now to have lost much of its vigour.

The cult of fieldwork, the Baptist epistemology, insisting on Knowledge-by-Total-Immersion, which had virtually come to define the subject, had an (at least) double rationale. On the one hand, it distinguished anthropologists from sociologists, who are more often inclined—perhaps because they investigate phenomena in social contexts which they think they can take for granted—to suppose that they can isolate their objects of inquiry: they are much less in awe of *context*, less inclined to feel the need to immerse themselves in it. On the other hand, the method also distinguishes anthropologists from historians and orientalists, who sometimes look as if they believed that the real is the textual. By contrast, any field anthropologist who compares his findings with that which he could have extracted from texts alone, is liable to feel strongly that a merely text-based version would not only have been poorer, but often positively wrong. If men speak to hide their thoughts, they write to hide their society. Anthropologists are the anti-scripturalists of the social sciences. This makes them specially sensitive to the social role of writing, which they do not take for granted, as those who live in a scriptural world are perhaps liable to do; and they have of late turned to this topic, with considerable effectiveness.[2] So the validity of fieldwork as *a* method (quite apart from its power to forge a community of those who have shared the experience) cannot be in doubt. But can it actually *define* a subject?

It is not for any one man to pontificate as to where the subject should now be going. It might redefine itself as micro-sociology, but to do so would be to deny many of the theoretical preoccupations which in fact pervade it. On the other hand, to restrict itself to a theory and investigation of simpler societies would, once again, fail to do justice to many of the inquiries in fact successfully pursued by anthropologists. To focus on the study of 'culture', to the exclusion or disregard of more earthy constraints on human conduct, would be quite particularly restrictive. Throughout recent decades however there has been a persistent list towards a harmful kind of idealism. Anthropologists are professionally sensitive to the way in which cultures, systems of concepts, constrain men. They are liable sometimes to slide, almost imperceptibly, from this valid perception to the misguided view that *only* concepts constrain.

One of the continuous threads of these essays is the attempt to contest that insidiously seductive view. The attraction of that doctrine has many sources. There are some who are pleased by the idea that the social sciences can establish what religion no longer provides, and show that we have souls because we recognise meanings, thus providing a demonstration of the discontinuity between man and beast; to be a kind of Spiritualism by Other Means. I doubt whether such a discontinuity can be established so simply, and also whether this doctrine leads to a sound method of inquiry.

My own guess is that the subject should retain that fine sensitivity to small and intricate social structures, that awareness of the inadequacy of documentary sources on their own, that sense of something socially far more interfused, which has become its trademark; but at the same time, in its choice of questions, it should return to those historically inspired issues which were only suppressed, but never truly exorcised, during the period which is now passing. The danger of simultaneously over-abstract and messianic mega-theories, indiscriminately and insensitively devouring ethnographic data, which haunted the nineteenth century and the earlier part of the twentieth, is no longer so very great. We are less complacent, more haunted by a sense of the complexity of things. The re-marriage of anthropological data with historical questions, and of historical findings with anthropological issues, might be the correct slogan.

Cambridge   Ernest Gellner
May 1986

NOTES

1 Grazyna Kubica and Janusz Mucha (eds), *Miedszy Dwoma Swiatami— Bronislaw Malinowski*, Panstwowe Wydawnictwo Naukowe, Warszawa, Krakow, 1985. An expanded English translation is in preparation with Cambridge University Press.

2 cf. Jack Goody (ed.), *Literacy in Traditional Societies*, Cambridge, 1968; and *The Domestication of the Savage Mind*, Cambridge, 1977.

1
EXPLANATION IN HISTORY*

The problem of explanation in history is also the problem of the nature of sociology. The views adopted in this field are held to have profound moral and political implications. We have recently often been reminded of this. The simplest argument connecting a premiss about the nature of historical explanation with political or ethical consequences runs as follows: if rigid, unchangeable, and wide-ranging generalizations are attainable with regard to historical processes, then an outlook which presupposes individual responsibility is basically misguided. Having pointed out this implication, philosophers hostile to the conclusion then devote themselves to undermining the premiss. They may do so either by pointing out that the required historical laws have not been found, or by arguing that they could not be.

I shall not directly concern myself with this matter of the existence or possibility of historical *laws*, but attempt to isolate the issues which arise here that can be stated without at any rate explicit reference to the law-like nature of history. I shall concern myself with the kind of concept or term characteristically employed when we talk of history or of societies. Notoriously the grammatical subject of sentences written or uttered by social scientists is often not a man, or enumerated or characterized men, but groups, institutions, 'cultures,' etc. The proper study of mankind is human groups and institutions.

Thus the alleged argument leading to the elimination of individual autonomy and responsibility may be stated without at least explicit and obvious presupposition of the attainment of causal generalizations in history. Those concerned with defending humanity against historicist or other mythologies—I shall call these defenders 'Individualists'—notice this fact. This gives rise to an attempt to 'eliminate' so-called 'holistic' concepts, or rather to show that these are in principle eliminable. That such an elimination should be possible seems strongly suggested by the fact that, after all, groups consist of people, and institutions are what people do, etc. A state cannot exist without citizens, nor a legal system without judges, litigants, etc. The worst obstacle such elimination could encounter, it seems, would be complexity.[1]

The matter, however, is not so simple. Arguments have been put forward to the effect that the elimination is in principle impossible.[2] Moreover, it is a weighty fact that at least some explanations in social sciences would in practice not be stated or be at all easily statable in Individualist terms.[3]

To each side in this dispute, its own position appears very nearly self-evident, and the opponents' position something that can be *said*, but not seriously practised. To the Individualist, his own position appears so true that it barely needs the confirmation of actually carried out eliminations, whilst he gleefully points out that in practice the holist can and does only approach his institutions, etc., through what concrete people do, which seems to the Individualist a practical demonstration and implicit confession of the absurdity of holism. By contrast (and with neat symmetry) the holist sees in the fact that the individualist continues to talk in holistic terms a practical demonstration of the unworkability of individualism, and he certainly does not consider the fact that he can only approach groups and institutions through the doings of individuals to be something which he had implicitly denied and which could count against him. Both sides find comfort in the actual practice of the opponent.

One should add here that the possibility of political implications cuts both ways. Individualists who attempt to save us, in the name of logic and liberty, from misconstruing our situation, are not wholly free at all times from the suspicion that a little propaganda for *laissez faire* is being hitched on to those very general issues.[4]

What is at issue is the ontological status of the entities referred to by the holistic terms. As the notion of ontological status is not as clear as it might be, I shall at some stages shift provisionally to something which is as important to the reductionist and which to him is an index of existence—namely, causation. He does not wish to allow that the Whole could ever be a cause, and to insist that explanations which make it appear that it is can be translated into others. That which is a mere construct cannot causally affect that which 'really exists'; this is, I suspect, the feeling of the Individualist, the reductionist. This, in conjunction with the truism that a whole is made up of its parts, that nothing can happen to a whole without something happening to either some at least of its parts or to their mutual relations,—leads him to the misleading conclusion that explanation in history and in social studies must ultimately be in terms of individual dispositions. The holistic counter-argument works in reverse; if something (*a*) is a causal factor and (*b*) cannot be reduced, then in some sense it 'really and independently exists.'

When we face a problem of 'reduction' in philosophy we are often confronted with a dilemma; on the one hand forceful formal arguments tend to show that a reduction must be possible, on the other hand all attempted reductions fail or are incomplete, and features can be found which suggest or prove that they cannot succeed or be complete. For instance, phenomenalism is supported not by the plausibility or success of actual reductions but by the force of the arguments to the effect that there must be a reduction, whilst at the same time the interesting arguments against it as cogently indicate that phenomenalist translation can never be completed.

The situation is similar with regard to the present problem. I consider, for instance, one particular, rather ambitious [and interesting] attempt to demonstrate that a reduction must be possible.

'All social phenomena are, directly or indirectly, human creations. A lump of matter may exist which no one has perceived but not a price which no one has charged, or a disciplinary code to which no one refers, or a tool which no one would dream of using. From this truism I infer the methodological principle . . . that the social scientist can continue searching for explanations of a social phenomenon until he has reduced it to *psychological* terms.' (italics mine)

The conclusion reached in the end is:

'Individualistic ideal types of explanatory power are constructed by first discerning the form of typical . . . dispositions, and then by demonstration how these lead to certain principles of social behavior.'[5]

As the argument also maintains that 'individualistic ideal types' are alone possible, what the conclusion amounts to is something like this: to explain a social or historical situation is to deduce it from what the individuals involved in it are disposed to do.

This contention can be broken up into two claims; that an explanation specifies *individual* dispositions, and that it specifies individual *dispositions*. In other words: (1) Statements about things other than individuals are excluded from a final explanation; (2) Statements which are not about dispositions are similarly excluded. By 'disposition' here is meant something 'intelligible,' a conceivable reaction of human beings to circumstances; not necessarily one we share, still less necessarily one we can 'introspect'; but still something opposed to what we would call 'dead' physical causation where 'anything could cause anything.'

Having broken up the requirements of reduction into two parts, we get four possibilities, of which three are excluded. Let us consider these excluded ones in turn.

(1) Holistic subject plus intelligible disposition. This is equivalent to a 'group mind' theory. I take it no one is advocating this seriously.

(2) Holistic subject without *intelligible* dispositions—*i.e.* attribu-

tions of regularity or pattern to wholes, without any suggestion that these patterns express conscious or purposive reactions.

(3) Individualistic subjects without *intelligible* dispositions. Let it be said that events explicable along the lines of alternative (3) can be excluded from history or sociology only by an inconvenient and arbitrary fiat. The destruction of Pompeii or the Black Death are historical events. It is true that the *reaction* of survivors to these 'blindly casual' events calls for explanation not in terms of 'dead' causation but possibly in terms of aims, dispositions, expectations, convictions. So be it; but the very fact that semi-deliberate and blindly casual events are so often and intimately fused in life brings out the inconvenience of excluding one kind.

Consider now exclusion of kind (2). When an historian speaks of the maintenance or growth of an institution, or a linguist about phonetic change, or an anthropologist about the maintenance of a system of kinship structure, they do not in fact always or often mention individual dispositions. The question is, *could* they?

The first step towards such a translation is easy. 'The monarchy is strong' can be translated into a disposition of subjects to have a certain set of attitudes to the monarch. Note: not necessarily all subjects or all the time, but a sufficient number of them sufficiently often, and above all at crucial times. Neither 'sufficient number' nor 'sufficiently often' nor 'crucial times' can be defined with precision, nor ultimately without referring back to the holist term 'monarchy.' The same applies to the 'set of attitudes.'

By and large, institutions and social structures and climates of opinion are not the results of what people want and believe, but of what they take for granted. Let us allow the reductionist to class tacit acceptance amongst dispositions, though I suspect we shall find the same circularity here as occurs above. Such translations would, however, be clumsy, nebulous, long and vague, where the original statement about an institution or feature of the social scene was clear, brief and intelligible.

If, however, we grant that 'in principle' this translation is possible, it in no way follows that these tacit and irregularly diffused dispositions are in turn explicable in terms of familiar, intelligible human responses. The existence of a diffused monarchical disposition was inferred logically from the truth of 'The monarchy is strong'; the dependence of the latter statement on the former, if it obtains at all, does so in virtue of logic or the truism that an institution is what people do. But the dependence of the perhaps validly inferred monarchical disposition in turn on a piece of intuitively obvious psychology would be a causal matter, and there are no reasons in logic or fact for supposing it to hold. On the contrary, in as far as such a procedure seems to assume the possibility of isolating more elementary dispositions 'as they are prior to their manifestations in a social context,' formal doubts may be raised concerning the realizability of such a program. [Need all our numerous tacit dispositions, each to one of the many facets of our social environment, be—*all of them and necessarily*—by-products or modifications of some avowable aim or attitude? I doubt whether as much could be claimed for mine, unless at any rate some of them are brought under the residual and negative classifications of 'passivity,' 'inertia,' 'imitativeness' and even 'randomness'; and these dubious dispositions will fail to explain the specific modifications of my attitudes, being essentially only indications that really good explanations in terms of aim and information are not to be had.]

There are two specific points, possibly inconclusive by themselves but worth noting, which influence the holist at this stage.

First, very small differences in individual conduct distributed irregularly over a large population, may have important consequences for the society at large without being detectable individually. The argument in favour of 'social facts' is historically connected with the presence of statistical regularities where none can be found at the molecular, individual level. The statistical regularity can be explained in terms of features of the social situation as a whole, but in practice it is seldom possible to trace the nexus in individual cases. To insist that it is always 'in principle' possible is to prejudge the issue under discussion. Moreover, something like an uncertainty principle may very well operate here, for the amount of disturbance involved in observing the individual case may very often be much larger than the small difference which accounts for the statistical result and may, so to speak, 'drown it.'

Secondly, individuals do have holistic concepts and often act in terms of them. For instance, a number of reviewers of the recently published Memoirs of Général de Gaulle have commented on the fact that de Gaulle's actions were inspired by his *idea* of France— which may perhaps have had little relation to actual Frenchmen. When the holistic ideas of many individuals are co-ordinated and reinforced by public behavior and physical objects—by ceremonials, rituals, symbols, public buildings, etc.—it is difficult for the social scientist, though he observes the scene from the outside, not to use the holistic concept. It is quite true that the fact that X acts and thinks in terms of an holistic idea—*e.g.* he treats the totem as if it were his tribe, and the tribe as if it were more than the tribesmen—is itself a fact about an individual. On the other hand, though the holistic term as used by the observer may be eliminable, as used by the participant it is not. Are we to say that a logically impeccable explanation of a social situation is committed to crediting its subjects with nonsensical thought? Perhaps we are. On the other hand, the fact that holistic terms are ineliminable from the thought of participants may well be a clue to their ineliminability from that of observers. [For, in one sense, social environments *are* the *Gestalten* projected by individuals onto reality, provided they act in terms of them and provided reality is compatible with them and contains some devices for reinforcing them, such as rituals or other symbols, e.g. public buildings, totems, etc. (It is of course open to the Individualists to maintain that I have here given a schematic *individualist* account of the holistic *illusion.* Perhaps.)]

It is perhaps unnecessary at this stage to insist on the fact that very little is gained by having individual dispositions as the bedrock of a historical or social explanation. Their 'intelligibility' is either familiarity, or, equally often, springs from the fact that dispositional terms come in clusters each of which is a more or less exhaustive crude taxonomy: such as, perhaps, for instance: 'Knowing—believing—considering—tacitly accepting—disregarding,' or 'wanting—being indifferent to—not wanting.' If with the help of such terms we characterize someone's conduct, on the analogy of the parallelogram of forces, do we thereby really approach the actual causal sequences?

It is true that this kind of diagnosis fits fairly well in the case of one social science, namely, economics. This, however, is presumably due to the fact that this science restricts itself to behavior with regard to which aims and relevant convictions and explanations are reasonably avowable and specifiable; to some extent it may be said that economic theory applies to people who have been taught to act in accordance with it. Also, the words most frequently used by economists happen to be *ceteris paribus*. Moreover, whilst an economist may explain a man's behavior in a market situation, it takes a non-economist to explain how he ever comes to be economically rational. If, for instance, one comes to explain it in terms of the mundane application of a religious notion of 'vocation,' is that transition an 'intelligible disposition?' Yes, in the sense that I see, roughly, what happens, know that it could happen to me, and if I believe it to be a regular occurrence may use it to explain particular incidents. But by those criteria any disposition can become 'intelligible.'[6]

The real oddity of the reductionist case is that it seems to preclude *a priori* the possibility of human dispositions being the dependent variable in an historical explanation—when in fact this is what they often or always are—and secondly to preclude the possibility of causes, in the sense of initial conditions, being a complex fact which is not describable in terms of the characteristics of its constituent parts alone—which again seems often to be the case.

Let it be added that in as far as the original argument is valid, it is equally valid for the non-human sciences. The fact that the natural sciences seem to be free from restrictions with regard to the kind of explanation they use does not derive from the fact that there are unobserved pieces of matter.[7] Moreover, in natural science as much as anywhere else, wholes are composed of their constituent parts. Nothing follows from this truism concerning the general nature of [the initial conditions in statements asserting a dependence. It does not restrict them to predicates which refer to dispositions of the atomic parts of a situation. Hence the 'Wholes are made up of parts' tautology is not strong enough to entail the Individualist reduction. Physicists could, presumably, use animist language if they wished— they could speak of intelligible dispositions instead of the behavior of particles. It would not add anything, but as far as I can see it is not impossible.]

The present paper is essentially an attempt to separate an indisputably true—because tautologous—proposition, (roughly 'Assertions about people are assertions about people'), from its alleged implications which are at the very least questionable and hence not tautologous, and (hence) not its implications. One might equally have proceeded in the opposite direction and tried to separate the truism 'Assertions about societies *are* assertions about society' from an alleged and mistaken consequence that societies 'exist' in the same sense as individuals, or independently of them. But the contemporary climate of opinion makes this latter exercise less necessary.

A full clarification of these issues would probably be possible only if we were clearer about what is meant by causation in social contexts. A related matter which I have not pursued is the probability that what counts as 'explanation' in history and in the social sciences is far from homogeneous in kind, any more than what counts as a 'problem.' This, over and above the particular difficulties discussed in this paper, may be a very serious objection to formal methodological arguments providing an *a priori* recipe for 'explanation.'

So far I have in this paper indicated what seem to me flaws in an attempted reduction. I have little doubt that actual procedure in historical and social explanation often is holistic, and that over and above this appeal to actual procedure, general reasons can be found, and probably stated more forcefully than I have stated them, to support the contention that this must be so. But it is equally obvious to me that this will not shake the determined individualist. Not only does he see important ethical issues hinging on his doctrine, but also some deep logical intuition with which many of us can empathize would have to be repressed by him before he could abandon his position. Indisputably, 'history is about chaps'; hence 'historical events must be explained in terms of what chaps do.' Now we all agree that repression is a bad thing; hence it is desirable to diagnose and render harmless the compulsive insight, rather than merely argue against it.

Let us try to call up this intuition in ourselves by attending to the argument of one trying to demonstrate the *im*possibility of reducing holistic social concepts to individual ones.

Mandelbaum's recent argument, restating an old point in 'language'-language, starts from the premiss that an action such as drawing money from the bank cannot be explained without the use of holistic concepts such as 'banking system.' This must be (at least tacitly) understood by the agent, and must be understood by the observer if he is to understand the action. When Mandelbaum says 'explain' he might perhaps say 'describe,' for the rules of deposit banking are all somehow implicit in the concept of cashing a cheque. (A causal explanation *might* actually be simpler and not involve any understanding of the rules of banking.)

So far, there is nothing that need upset the individualist. Individuals act guided by nebulous holistic concepts—so far so good. As far as the object connoted by the concept is concerned the Individualist is sure that it can be 'translated' in terms of what various individuals involved in banking institutions are doing. (Mandelbaum does not agree, on the grounds that the description of their activity in turn will involve use of the concept of 'banking': but let us leave that aside for the moment.)

Let us just agree—as is indeed true—that drawing a cheque is internally related to the whole banking system, that what is meant by cashing a cheque involves by its very meaning the general features of banking; that, tacitly or otherwise, the concept 'bank' is being employed by anyone describing or understanding the cashing of a cheque. I am stressing this, for the Individualist cannot but come with us this far.

It is the next step that he will refuse to take. This step emerges at the end of Mandelbaum's article, when he speaks of individuals and what he calls 'societal facts' (e.g. banking systems) *interacting*; in other words, implying that it makes sense for the object of a holistic concept to have an effect on a concrete individual. What the Individualist will here object to is the inference from an holistic concept, somehow abstracted from the concrete behavior of concrete individuals, being then able to figure in the antecedent of a causal sentence. He will refuse to admit this even if he concedes the ineliminability of the holistic concept in description. This seems indeed, he feels, to endow an abstraction with flesh and power; and we can easily feel this with him.

Of course, he isn't denying that causal statements of this kind are meaningfully and truthfully uttered. He only wishes to insist that the antecedent must in such cases be translatable into individualistic terms. Surely the insubstantial cannot constrain the substantial? I think we can provisionally agree to this principle; (though earlier we *seemed* to have contradicted it when uttering the truism that a cause may be as complex an event as we wish—as indeed it can). At the same time Mandelbaum's central point, that holistic concepts cannot be eliminated, stands. Here is a dilemma indeed.

Attempted Diagnosis. Consider the following two series:

(1) Jones is going to Germany. All members of the platoon are going, etc. All members of the company are going, etc. All members of the battalion are going, etc.

(2) Jones. That Platoon. The Company. The Battalion.

The first series begins with a singular proposition, and continues with general ones of increasing generality. The second series is one of terms or concepts [or things, in which at each stage the preceding is or designates a part of the subsequent one].

Concerning series (1) it is obvious that each subsequent proposition can only be true in virtue of a set of propositions of the earlier kind being true. Propositions of the latter kind can, unless their subjects are open classes, be 'reduced' or translated into conjunctions of propositions of the preceding kind. To talk of the more general propositions causing, constraining etc., those of lesser generality subsumed under them is nonsense.

Series (2) lists parts and wholes in such a manner that an earlier member of the series is always a part of a latter member. Latter members depend for their existence on the existence of earlier members, though not necessarily any definite list of them. *But*: there is no reason in logic or fact why causal sentences should in their antecedent clauses (or consequent clauses, for that matter) be restricted in their subjects to items of the kind that would only appear at the beginning of the series. If 'complexity of causes' obtains, which it often seems to, causal sentences will have to have later members of the series as parts of their subjects.

The cause, or at any rate one of the central causes, of the general dilemma under discussion is the attribution of obvious features of series (1) to the series (2), concerning which they are certainly not obvious and probably not true.

For when we speak of societies we mean partly (*a*) generalizations about classes of human individuals which indeed are true only in virtue of propositions about those individuals, and can be 'reduced' to them, but also (*b*) groups, complexes, constellations of facts. These latter can indeed exist only if their parts exist—that is indeed the predicament of all wholes—but their fates *qua* fates of complexes can nevertheless be the initial conditions or indeed final conditions of a causal sequence.

The powerful disinclination to allow social or general causes arises from the confusion of (*a*) and (*b*). Jones is not caused to go to Germany by the general fact that all other members of the battalion are going; the general proposition merely *says*, amongst other things, that Jones is going. But there is no reason whatever for excluding *a priori* the possibility of unanimity of his comrades, *qua* unanimity, influencing Jones to volunteer to go. That all members of the unit feel the *esprit de corps* is a generalization; but to say that *esprit de corps* has influenced an individual is not to say that he has been influenced by isolable individuals or their acts.

It should now be clear that the following three propositions are *not* incompatible:

A generalization is true only in virtue of the truth of singular propositions.

A whole is made up of its parts.

No *a priori* legislation is possible concerning the complexity of links in causal chains.

The error of the Individualist is to conclude from the first two propositions, which are analytic, to the falsity of the third, through the confused identification of the hierarchy of propositions in terms of generality with the hierarchy of things in terms of complexity and inclusiveness. Let us illustrate this with another example. If I say 'All the men in the square were excited' I may simply mean a generalization to the effect that each of the men there was excited; in such a case it would make no sense to speak of the generalization as being an independent fact, less still a causal factor.

If, on the other hand, I say 'There was an atmosphere of tension in the square,' though this cannot be true without some of a nebulously defined and large set of propositions about the men in the square being true, and *a fortiori* it cannot be true unless there are men in the square, there is yet no way of interpreting this as a mere conjunction. We cannot even describe the state of mind of typical individual participants in the situation without referring back to the situation as a whole. This to some extent throws light on a fact mentioned earlier, namely that whatever the logical rights and wrongs of the case, individuals do think in holistic terms. What this amounts to— amongst other things—is the kind of patterns they are capable of isolating in their environment and react to. The pattern isolated, however, is not 'merely abstracted' but is, as I am somewhat sheep- ishly tempted to say, 'really there.'

For any individual, the *mores*, institutions, tacit presuppositions, etc., of his society are an independent and external fact, as much so as the physical environment and usually more important. And if this is so for each individual, it *does* follow that it is so for the totality of individuals composing a society. Of course, societies not being en- dowed with group minds, the question doesn't arise for 'the totality'; *just because* the Individualist is in one sense right and 'there is no such *thing*' as the 'totality,' the question of the externality and independence of social facts does not arise for it. But it can and does arise for the observer, who may of course be simultaneously a member of the society in question. And though he may in some cases account in some way for the social facts in terms of the interaction of individual decisions with prior 'social facts,' any attempt to eliminate these altogether will only lead to a regress and possibly to an irrelevant genetic question of the hen-and-egg kind. The important thing about 'hen-and-egg' is not that we do not know, but that if we did know it would not throw much light on either hens or eggs.

It might be objected that too much is being made of this matter of causation. Complexity of causes is a familiar phenomenon; it does not follow from its occurrence that the constituents of a complex cause make up a 'whole.' My suggestion is that if perceived as a whole, referred to as such, etc., they do. It might again be objected that this merely shows that there are Social *Gestalten* incorporated in the perception by individuals of their social environment. But these *Gestalten* are so to speak veridical and efficacious; their objects, individual ways of behaving, conform to them and often act as their sanctions, as reminders to the perceiver of the *Gestalt* that its object is there and must be reckoned with. These re-inforcing acts are indeed acts of individuals; but they in turn are led to behave along suitable lines by their perception of the same or similar 'social fact.'

The existence of a complex concept, parts of which are logically inseparable, is after all a familiar thing. For example, a mountain summit *entails* a slope, and so on. The complications which arise with regard to the present problem are two; first, that of the two constituents which appear to be so connected, i.e. individual men and their social context, one is tangible, the other not. (Of course, it is not 'man' and *any* social contact that is so connected, but individual acts, and their contexts.) This leads to the desire to 'reduce' the latter to the former, on the misguided assumption that unless this is done one would have to concede that the latter is similarly tangible. The reductionist indeed points both to the intangibility and necessary connection ('Without men and their doings, no society, institutions, etc.'), and then mistakenly infers that a reduction must be possible. The second complication arises through the fact that in these subjects we are dealing with conscious men, in other words objects aware of things in the same way as the observer. Hence the complex concepts are met with twice over—once in the mind of the observer, and once *in re* as the dealings of the men with things and each other.

The confusion of the hierarchy of propositions graded by generality and of groups graded by size and inclusiveness leads to what might be called the Picture or Mirror theory of explanation.[8] The merits and otherwise of the picture theory of meaning and propositions is a familiar story, but the reappearance of this tempting model with regard to explanation deserves special treatment.

What seems to happen is something along the following lines. Take as an example a generalization such as 'The committee decided to appoint Jones.' This means, amongst other things, that each of the members of the committee came in the end to accept a certain conclusion, and if this were an important or interesting event, the historian or sociologist concerned with explaining it might be very happy if he could give an account of the ways by which each of the committee members came to reach his conclusion. This is indeed the paradigm of explanation as conceived by the Individualist—the feared Whole has evaporated in a series of partial biographies and character studies.

It is of course perfectly true that generalizations and abstractions do not give us additional facts; but it does not follow that all propositions whose subjects seem to include the 'atoms'—whatever they may happen to be—of a particular discourse, are therefore necessarily generalizations, abstractions or somehow constructs. A failure to see this is the defect often attributed to 'atomism' in other spheres, and sociological reductionism seems to be a related species.

In as far as the proposition used as an example is only a generalization of the form 'All members of the committee . . .' the alleged explanation, the paradigm of all explanations, is merely a verification and not an explanation at all. If this were all that could be done, explanation in history and the social sciences would be identical with the gathering of confirming evidence. To explain would be to illustrate; to illustrate fully, to provide the complete picture, would be to give the best explanation. But is this so?

Of course, the Individualist feels that something more should be involved in explanation than illustration, but he seeks it in broader generalization about each of the committee-men involved; 'broader' meaning either more persistent, or 'simpler' in a sense to be indicated. There are what might be called simple disposition-types,—sloth, pursuit of gain, of power, or security, etc., of which the more idiosyncratic dispositions of individual men may perhaps be interpreted as variants or combinations.

An example of this kind of approach would be, for instance, the eighteenth-century attempt to explain moral feelings as combinations of sympathy and vengefulness: vengefulness on behalf of sufferers other than oneself, whose sufferings had been imaginatively re-lived, produces, say, a sense of justice. (This kind of approach, incidentally, is not *always* unfruitful; I am only arguing against the contention that historical or social explanation must always employ it.)

It is difficult to see how this attempt to bring in explanation which is more than illustration differs from what has sometimes been called psychologism.[9] The objection to it is that there is no way in general of isolating these pure or more persistent dispositions from the social context in which they occur. We have indeed two impossibilities here, one causal and one logical. Popper's argument against psychologism makes use of the former, Mandelbaum's of the latter. As a matter of causal fact, our dispositions are not independent of the social context in which they occur; but they are not even independent logically, for they cannot be described without reference to their social context.

What the Individualist is demanding might be described [,from the viewpoint of an institution,] as the translation from the Active into the Passive Voice; the translation of statements such as 'such and such a kind of family organization tends to perpetuate itself' into statements such as 'As a result of such and such aims, convictions, dispositions, etc., of individuals, this kind of family organization continues.' (To the Individualist it seems, of course, that the translation is *into* a 'really' Active Voice, on the general ground that institutions, etc., being constructs from individual behavior, *must* 'really' be passive.) But the undesirability of such a translation in some cases follows partly from various considerations already stated such as the diffused, individually imperceptible nature of some of these dispositions, or the fact that they refer back to the institutional context, and also from the fact that they may be utterly uninteresting because obvious. The only relevant dispositions may be, to take the example of the permanence of a kind of family organization, the normal sexual, security and reproductive aspirations which do not distinguish people in that social context from others. The *differentia*, which as the distinctive component in a complex set of conditions will be worthy of the investigator's attention may well be something institutional and not psychological. It is perfectly possible, for instance, that there are no psychological differences of any importance between two European countries of widely divergent institutions, and that to explain the differentiation is only possible in sociological, not in psychological terms. Of course, psychological differences *may* be significant. The harm done by the kind of Individualism discussed, if taken seriously by investigators, is that it leads to a conviction that such differences must always be present and be significant. The danger of this pre-conception seems to me graver at present than the one which worries the Individualist, namely that of 'reifying' abstractions.

In fact, some historical or sociological explanations—as when, for instance, an historian explains the growth of an institution, or an anthropologist the self-maintenance of a social structure—will do this in terms of features of the relevant institution or structure without explicit mention of any individual dispositions.

At this point the Individualist will no doubt protest that despite the absence of explicit mention of individual dispositions, implicitly they are present; ultimately, every social event must have its habitat in the individual psyche. Now this must be conceded: if Individualism is to degenerate into what could be called social Monadism, the desperate incorporation of complex and diffuse relations into the related terms or individuals, then it must be admitted to be true 'in a sense.' 'Algy met a bear, the bear was bulgy, the bulge was Algy'; the individual may consume what Durkheim and others have called social facts, but he will bulge most uncomfortably, and Algy will still be there.[10] I suspect that actual investigators will often, though perhaps not always, prefer to have Algy outside the bear.[11]

The uselessness of Monadism-at-all-costs can be illustrated thus: certain tribes I know have what anthropologists call a segmentary patrilineal structure, which moreover maintains itself very well over time. I could 'explain' this by saying that the tribesmen have, all or most of them, dispositions whose effect is to maintain the system. But, of course, not only have they never given the matter much thought, but it also might very well be impossible to isolate anything in the characters and conduct of the individual tribesmen which *explains* how they come to maintain the system (though of course conduct *illustrating* how the system is being maintained will be found).

The recipe for reduction which we are considering does not commit the older errors of inventing dispositions *ad hoc* for each social thing to be explained, or of deriving social conduct from alleged pre-social, pure dispositions. It claims as its explanations low-level generalizations about the conduct of individuals.

But: these dispositions are not always relevant; sometimes or often they are not isolable without this affecting the possibility of explanation; they are not independent variables, but usually depend on highly generalized social factors; and they are often not statable without reference to social facts. If Individualism does not deny all this, perhaps nothing remains to disagree with it about; but if indeed it does not deny this, its programmatic implications for historians and social scientists no longer hold.

Perhaps, in the end, there is agreement to this extent: (human) history *is* about chaps—and nothing else. But perhaps this should be written: History is *about* chaps. It does not follow that its explanations are always in terms of chaps. Societies are what people do, but social scientists are not biographers *en grande série*.

APPENDIX: REPLY TO MR WATKINS

Watkins suggests that discussing the issue in terms of the existence of social *facts* rather than *laws* empties it of most of its interest. I doubt whether in fact anyone argued in favor of irreducible social facts just in a *l'art pour l'art* spirit. To insist on social facts is, if you like to put it that way, a manner of saying something about sociological laws: namely, that they cannot all have a certain form, that they cannot invariably be psychological laws or the corollaries of psychological laws or statements.

Watkins says he is at a loss to understand how I came to conclude that what Popper calls psychologism is indistinguishable from methodological individualism as more fully worked out by Watkins. This is the way I came to that view. Methodological individualism insists that individual dispositions, etc., alone must be the ultimate elements by which a social situation is explained. It is not denied that a situation results from the interaction of an individual and a social context, but it is maintained that this context itself must be similarly explicable. The defect in this is, to my mind, the unending regress involved; a new social milieu has to be mentioned each time the individualistic explanation is taken one stage further. But this precisely is Popper's objection against psychologism. My conclusion regarding the difficulty of distinguishing the two doctrines resulted, therefore, from their being open to the same criticism. If this doesn't entail their identity it at least suggests that they overlap at crucial points.

The regress that seems to me involved can be illustrated in terms of the example Watkins takes over. The impact of rules and how tribesmen come to accept them can indeed be explained individualistically —to that extent I agree—meaning by this that a description of what is happening to individuals is always involved; but not without a reference to the social background as a factor, and to that extent I disagree, at least with what I take methodological individualism to be saying.

This abstract problem has its empirical, heuristic counterpart even if standpoints on the latter are not strictly entailed by standpoints on the former. The attitude encouraged by individualism is either a methodology which encourages *deduction* from simple psychological premises (e.g. economic theory), or research into social variation of the *psyche* by projection tests, etc. Both neglect institutions, and neither seems to me as fruitful, in some contexts at least, as the study of institutions.

Finally, I should like to say that I still find the problem confusing, that my criticism of what seems to me over-simple reduction is not an argument for a *mystique* of the social whole, and that my guess is that the solution may be found in more careful distinguishing of the way in which whole-and-part, generalization-and-instance, premiss-and-conclusion, cause-and-entity and perhaps other dichotomies enter into statements one can make about men and groups; and that clarification of the issue, rather than a trial of two protagonists assumed to have rival and incompatible claims, is called for with regard to this problem.

NOTES

* Passages enclosed in square brackets do not appear in the original Aristotelian Society 1956 version of this chapter, but in the reprint in Patrick Gardiner (ed.), *Theories of History*, Free Press, 1959. [eds]

1   There is one foreseeable objection to both my arguments and those I criticize, namely, that a 'naming' theory of meaning underlies both the approaches contemplated. For instance, Mr R. Wollheim in his review of Mr Weldon's *Vocabulary of Politics* in *Mind*, n.s. **64**, 1955, 410–20, makes a point of this kind in a similar context. Now this type of currently fashionable general appeal to the heterogeneity of meaning does not seem to me to cut much ice; perhaps because the 'naming theory' of meaning has not been adequately exorcized from my mind, but perhaps for better reasons. These might be along the following lines: not all reductions are impossible, but on the contrary some are both possible and salutary. The general acceptance of the great variety of ways in which words have meaning does indeed leave us with the baby, but also with much undesirable bath water. It does not by itself give us any insight into how various concepts are used. We gain that, amongst other ways, by trying to reduce some concepts to others. For instance, the Individualist is quite right in insisting that a rising marriage rate is not the kind of thing which could be the cause of an individual marriage. It only records the fact that more such marriages occur. At the same time when reductions fail, the fact that they do and the reasons why they do, give us some understanding of the nature of the unreduced concepts.
2   Cf. Maurice Mandelbaum, 'Societal Facts,' *British Journal of Sociology*, **6**, 1955, 305–17.
3   Cf. M. Ginsberg, 'The Individual and Society' in *The Diversity of Morals*, London, 1956.
4   As Ginsberg says: 'Similarly those who refuse to accept methodological individualism . . . are not committed . . . to a totalitarian view of political action. They are well aware . . . of the dangers

of concentrated power. But they deny that the only choice open to us is between a spontaneous competitive order on one hand, and a system of all-pervading control on the other. It is odd that those who attack what they call scientism should feel able to predict with certainty that any form of socialism must necessarily lead to cultural and political totalitarianism . . . In any event, "logicism" is no improvement on "scientism."' Op. cit., pp. 161–2.
5   J. W. N. Watkins, 'Ideal Types and Historical Explanation,' *British Journal for the Philosophy of Science*, 3, 1952–3, 22–43. See also discussion of his own paper by the same author in the following issue of the same *Journal* ('The Principle of Methodological Individualism,' *BJPS*, 3, 1952–3, 186–9).
   When in this paper I say 'Individualism' I mean 'methodological individualism,' roughly along the lines outlined in those two articles.
6   Having criticized the notion of 'intelligibility' of human dispositions and in particular the accompanying suggestion that it gives us double access or confirmation of human reality, once through social appearance and secondly through dispositions as psychological things-in-themselves, I do not wish to be interpreted as denying the importance of *Einfühlung*, of sympathetic understanding. But the nature and value of this method or heuristic device seems to me the very opposite to what is supposed by the reductionist. It lies in the familiarization with alien reactions and dispositions, not in forcing on them interpretations making them into variants of what is familiar anyway. This last may perhaps be the practice of economic theorists— but just that may help to explain the unreality of that discipline outside certain limits.
   Collingwood's celebrated doctrines concerning this matter seem to amount perhaps to not much more than this: history like other disciplines uses the hypothetico-deductive method, and in history the hypotheses are usually about what people attempted to do. Stated thus, the doctrine becomes less startling. It also ceases to be open to the two

criticisms normally levelled against it, namely that Collingwood took the Ghost in the Machine too seriously, and secondly, that he misinterpreted an heuristic device as an essential characteristic of historical knowledge.

Further, 'hypothetico-deductive method' is a misnomer. One can only speak of *method* where there is an alternative. But the only alternative to *this* way of studying things is not another way, but not studying them at all. For this 'method' really means only thinking about things and then seeing whether what one had thought is true.

7 Evidently Watkins himself no longer holds this proof valid. He explains in the Discussion note (op. cit.) that he considers a counter-example to the principle of methodological individualism to be conceivable; so that the principle can hardly be susceptible of formal proof. But the counter-example envisaged by him is of the 'group mind' type—dispositional interpretation predicated of social wholes, in my scheme—such as he thinks might be suggested by some facts from the social life of insects. My arguments against the Principle are quite independent of any such possibility. I am more than willing to concede that no phenomena calling for a 'group mind' occur.

8 'Its overt characteristics (i.e. those of a "complex social situation") may be *established* empirically, but they are only to be *explained* by being shown to be the resultants of individual activities.' Watkins, op. cit. (italics his). This might be called the Stock Exchange theory. The opposite could easily be maintained; though I prefer merely to deny the second part of the statement. The temptation to believe that overt general features can be observed but must then be explained by something individual may spring from the fact that, for instance, the economist gets his empirical material pre-digested by the statistician. An index or a price level looks like a general fact. The field-worker is less tempted to believe that it is the overt feature of the social situation which he *observes*, whilst he only concludes about the individual. On the contrary, he is in close contact with the individuals with whom he passes the time of day, and if the explanations were *there*, he'd have his explanation as soon as he'd gathered his material, or at worst as soon as he had explored the character of the individual. But this is not what happens. It cannot even be said that his task is the exploration of long-term and unforeseen consepuences of individual dispositions. It is the consequences of social features that he is after.

9 Cf. K. Popper, *The Open Society and Its Enemies*, London, Routledge, 1945, Chapter 14. In this chapter Popper refers to both 'psychologism,' which he condemns, and 'methodological individualism,' which he commends. When, in the articles discussed, 'methodological individualism' is worked out more fully than is the case in Popper's book, it seems to me indistinguishable from 'psychologism.'

10 Social phenomena have always been most suggestive of the Principle of Internal Relations. This principle is frequently being re-discovered by social scientists.

11 The Individualist maintains that Algy always was in the bear. Yes, if you like. But the bear isn't Algy, though the bulge is Algy.

2
CONCEPTS AND SOCIETY

1. This paper is concerned with the application of Functionalism to the interpretation of concepts and beliefs.

Concepts and beliefs are themselves, in a sense, institutions amongst others; for they provide a kind of fairly permanent frame, as do other institutions, independent of any one individual, within which individual conduct takes place. In another sense, they are correlates of *all* the institutions of a society: and to understand the *working* of the concepts of a society is to understand its institutions.[1] Hence, a discussion of the application of Functionalism to interpretation (of concepts and beliefs), rather than Functionalism as such, is not really much of a restriction of the subject-matter.

Concepts and beliefs are, of course, of particular concern to social anthropology. Sociology can sometimes be a matter of ascertaining facts within an institutional framework which is taken for granted. The anthropologist can virtually never take anything for granted in this way. But anthropology is also the discipline most associated with Functionalism. The connection is not fortuitous.

2. Nevertheless the problem of the *interpretation* of concepts is almost as important within sociology—in the narrower sense in which it excludes Social Anthropology. For instance, the problem which is one of the mainsprings of sociological theory and which remains at the very centre of sociology—the question concerning the impact of theological doctrines on the emergence of economic rationality—hinges in large part on how one *interprets* the relevant theological concepts and arguments. Is one merely to take what the recorded theological text says and explicitly recommends? In that case, the connection seems very tenuous. Or is one to take what the text says *and* interpret its meaning, for the people influenced by it, in the light of what they actually *did*? In that case, the explanation of behaviour in terms of doctrine risks becoming vacuous and circular. There must, one hopes, be some middle way, which allows interpretation, which allows some but not all of the context to be incorporated into the meaning of the concept, thus avoiding both an unrealistic literal-minded scholasticism, and yet also escaping circularity of explanation.

The problem concerns the rules and limits of the invocation of social *context* in interpreting the participants' concepts.

Consider as an example one of the most recent contributions to this debate, Professor Kurt Samuelsson's *Religion and Economic Action* (London, 1961; Swedish edition, *Ekonomi och Religion*, Stockholm, 1957). This work is an onslaught on the Weberian thesis. '. . . our scrutiny of Puritan doctrine and capitalist ideology . . . has rendered untenable the hypothesis of a connection between Puritanism and capitalism . . .' (p. 153). Samuelsson employs a battery of arguments to support his conclusion, and some of these are highly relevant to the present theme. For one, he refers (p. 153) to ' . . . the impossibility, in the last resort, of correlating concepts as broad and vague as those in question'. Here he seems to mean primarily the sociologist's own concepts (Puritanism, capitalism), but indirectly the alleged breadth and vagueness of these reflects the vagueness of Puritan or capitalist notions themselves. But it would be an absurd requirement to restrict sociological interpretation to clear and distinct concepts: these are historically a rarity, and there is nothing to make one suppose that vague and broad notions, whose logical implications for conduct are ill-determined, do not in fact have a powerful and specific impact on actual behaviour. We are faced here with the unfortunate need to *interpret* just what the concepts in question meant to the participants—and the problems connected with such interpretation are the theme of the present paper.

Samuelsson is not content with a declaration of the impossibility 'in the last resort' of establishing such correlations at all, but also specifically tries to refute the correlation by adducing contrary evidence. This counter-evidence largely consists, reasonably enough, of examining just what the Puritans actually said, and the kind of conduct they actually commended. Considering this, Samuelsson concludes (p. 41) that 'unquestionably, this ought to have impeded rather than promoted a capitalist trend'. He then considers counter-objections to this, such as Tawney's: these consist of arguing that the 'Christian casuistry of economic conduct', which *logically* should have impeded capitalism (i.e. if one considers what the statements in the text actually entail), in fact, in virtue of what they *meant* to the people concerned, 'braced the energies' and 'fortified the temper' of the capitalist spirit. In other words, he convicts Tawney of claiming to know better than the texts what Puritanism really meant to its devotees. Samuelsson appears to have a great contempt for such implicit claims to access to hidden meanings: it is (p. 41) 'a somersault in the best Weberian style'. With irony he comments (p. 42, italics mine) that on the view he opposes, the capitalist spirit 'was the *true and genuine* Puritan spirit' (as opposed to the spirit actually found in the texts), and that thus 'Puritanism *in some other and more capitalist sense* . . . becomes the capitalistic spirit's principal source of power . . .'

I am not concerned, nor competent, to argue whether Samuelsson's employment, in this particular case, of his tacit principle that one must not re-interpret the assertions one actually finds, is valid. What is relevant here is that if such a principle is made explicit and general-ised, it would make nonsense of most sociological studies of the relationship of belief and conduct. We shall find anthropologists driven to employ the very opposite principle, the insistence on rather than refusal of contextual re-interpretation.

3. This is where Functionalism is relevant. The essence of Func-tionalism is perhaps the stress on context (rather than origin or overt motive) in the explanation of social behaviour. Formulated as an extreme doctrine, it asserts that each social institution is ideally suited to its context. The paradigm of explanation then becomes an account of just how a given institution does ideally fit its context, which means presumably just how it serves the survival and stability of the whole better than would any available alternative.

One of the charges made against this doctrine is that it is 'teleo-logical', that it explains the present behaviour in terms of its conse-quences in the future, i.e. in terms of the manner in which those consequences *will* be desirable from the given society's viewpoint.

It seems to me that it is not difficult to answer this particular charge. All that is required is that each 'functional' explanation be as it were *read backwards*. The 'explanation' of institution X is not really the proper, causal explanation of *it*, but of the manner in which it contributes to the society as a whole. The 'real' explanation of X is provided when the functional account of the *other* institutions is given—of all of them, or of a relevant subset of those of them which contribute towards the maintenance of X—which jointly make up a 'real', causal explanation of X itself (just as the 'functional' account of X figures in *their* causal explanation). This of course implies that good and proper explanations can only be had when a whole society is seen as a unity, and that partial studies of institutions in isolation are incomplete, and only a step towards proper understanding. But such a stress on societies seen as unities is indeed a part of the 'Functional-ist' syndrome of ideas.

But there cannot be many people today who hold Functionalism in its extreme form.[2] What needs to be said about that has been most brilliantly and succinctly said by Professor Lévi-Strauss:

'Dire qu'une société fonctionne est un truisme; mais dire que tout, dans une société, fonctionne est absurdité.'

Anthropologie Structurale. (Paris, 1958, p. 17.)

The thesis of social adjustment is not really a theory: it is a promise of a theory, a promise that somewhere along the spectrum between an absurdity and a truism there is a point where truth without triviality is to be found. Until the precise point along that spectrum is located, it will not be a theory, and as far as I know no one has attempted to locate it, and it is difficult to see how one could. The corollary of the doctrine in its *extreme form*, the claim of perfect stability and self-maintenance of societies, is plainly false. The requirement that societies be seen as unities is unsatisfiable for most societies in the modern world, in view of their size, complexity and in view of the difficulties of delimiting 'societies'.

But whilst, for these reasons, 'strong' Functionalism is dead or moribund, moderate Functionalism, or Functionalism as a method rather than as a theory, is happily very much alive. Lévi-Strauss is perhaps right when he speaks of

'. . . cette forme primaire du structuralisme qu'on appelle fonctionnalisme.'

op. cit. (p. 357).

The exploration of social structure is one of the main preoccupations of sociology. It must require of the investigator of any one institution an awareness of its context, of the 'structure' within which that institution finds itself.

But if moderate Functionalism is justifiably alive, its application to the interpretation of concepts and doctrines is particularly relevant. It consists of the insistence on the fact that concepts and beliefs do not exist in isolation, in texts or in individual minds, but in the life of men and societies. The activities and institutions, in the context of which a word or phrase or set of phrases is used, must be known before that word or those phrases can be understood, before we can really speak of a *concept* or a *belief*.

4. The particular application of the functional, context-stressing method to concepts is nothing new. It can be found above all in the work of Emile Durkheim which is one of the fountainheads of Functionalism in general, in *Les Formes Elémentaires de la Vie Religieuse*. I think that less than justice is done to Durkheim when he is remembered as the author of a doctrine to the effect that primitive societies or societies in general really 'worship themselves'. The real essence of his doctrine in that remarkable work seems to me to lie elsewhere, in the view that concepts, as opposed to sensations, are only possible in a social context[3] (and a fortiori that they can only be understood when the social context is known), and that important, categorial concepts, on which all others depend, require ritual

if they are to be sustained. It tends to be forgotten that Durkheim's main problem, as he saw it, was not to explain religion but to explain conceptual thought and above all the *necessity*, the compulsive nature of certain of our general concepts. This is a Kantian problem, and Durkheim claimed to have solved it in a way which resembled Kant's, but differed from it in various important ways.

Above all, it differed from it in two ways: the machinery, so to speak, which was responsible for the compulsive nature of our categorial concepts was collective and observable, rather than hidden in the backstage recesses of the individual mind; and secondly, it did not, like a Balliol man, function effortlessly, but needed for its effective working to keep in training, to be forever flexing its muscles and keeping them in trim—and just this was Durkheim's theory of ritual, which for him was the method by which the intelligibility and compulsiveness of crucial categories was maintained in the minds of members of a given society. Ritual and religion did publicly what the Kantian transcendental ego did only behind the impassable iron curtain of the noumenal. It was thus Durkheim who paved the way for modern anthropological fieldwork: it was his view that in observing (say) the rituals associated with a clan totem, we were privileged to observe the machinery which explains the conceptual, logical and moral compulsions of the members of *that* society, compulsions similar, for instance to our inability to think of the world outside time. Much later, a linguistic philosopher commenting somewhere on transcendental beliefs, hinted that their source lay in language by saying that men needed a god of time as little as they needed a god of tenses. Durkheim's much more plausible point was precisely this in reverse: in order to have and understand tenses, we need first of all to have or to have had (something like) a god and a ritual of time . . .

Our contemporary invocations of the functional, social-context approach to the study and interpretation of concepts is in various ways very different from Durkheim's. Durkheim was not so much concerned to defend the concepts of primitive societies: in their setting, they did not need a defence, and in the setting of modern and changing societies he was not anxious to defend what was archaic, nor loth to suggest that some intellectual luggage might well be archaic. He was really concerned to explain the compulsiveness of what in practice did not seem to need any defence (and in so doing, he claimed he was solving the problem of knowledge whose solution had in his view evaded Kant and others, and to be solving it without falling into either empiricism or apriorism). Whether he was successful I do not propose to discuss: for a variety of reasons it seems to me that he was not.[4]

By contrast, the modern user of the Functionalist approach to concepts is concerned to defend, rather than to explain a compulsion. In anthropology, he may be concerned to defend the objects of his particular study from the charge of absurdity or pre-logical thought; in philosophy he may be concerned with applying the crypto-Functionalist theory of language which is the basis of so much contemporary philosophy. And behind either of these motives, there is, more potent than either, the consideration springing from our general intellectual climate—the desire to assist or reinforce the tacit *concordat* which seems to have been reached between intellectual criticism and established concepts in the middle of the twentieth century.

5. The situation, facing a social anthropologist who wishes to interpret a concept, assertion or doctrine in an alien culture, is basically simple. He is, say, faced with an assertion S in the local language. He has at his disposal the large or infinite set of possible sentences in his own language. His task is to locate the nearest equivalent or equivalents of S in his own language.

He may not be wholly happy about this situation, but he cannot avoid it. There is no third language which could mediate between the native language and his own, in which equivalences could be stated and which would avoid the pitfalls arising from the fact that his own language has its own way of handling the world, which may not be those of the native language studied, and which consequently are liable to distort that which is being translated.

Naïvely, people sometimes think that *reality* itself could be this kind of mediator, and 'third language': that equivalences between expressions in different languages could be established by locating just which objects in the world they referred to. (If the objects were identical, then so were the expressions . . .) For a variety of powerful reasons, this is of course no good. Language functions in a variety of ways other than 'referring to objects'. Many objects are simply not there, in any obvious physical sense, to be located: how could one, by this method, establish the equivalences, if they exist, between abstract or negative or hypothetical or religious expressions? Again, many 'objects' are in a sense created by the language, by the manner in which its terms carve up the world or experience. Thus the mediating third party is simply not to be found: either it turns out to be an elusive ghost ('reality') or it is just one further language, with idiosyncrasies of its own which are as liable to distort in translation as did the original language of the investigator. Using it only multiplies the probability of distortion by adding to the number of conceptual middlemen, and in any case the procedure involves a vicious regress.

This situation is described, for instance, in a recent important study of primitive religion: '(The) unity and multiplicity of Divinity causes no difficulty in the context of Dinka language and life, but it is impossible entirely to avoid the logical and semantic problems which arise when Dinka statements bearing upon it are translated, together, into English,' in Godfrey Lienhardt, *Divinity and Experience: The Religion of the Dinka* (Oxford, 1961, p. 56).

Or, as the same author puts it in the context of a general discussion of anthropology, in *The Institutions of Primitive Society*, by various authors (Oxford, 1954, chapter VIII):

'The problem of describing to others how members of a remote tribe think then begins to appear *largely as one of translation*, of making the coherence primitive thought has . . . as clear as possible in our own.' (p. 97, italics mine.)

The situation facing the historical sociologist is not very different. Samuelsson says (*op. cit.*, p. 36): 'Neither in St. Paul nor in Baxter do the texts . . . form coherent chains of reasoning . . . The source material, in both cases, consists of a few sentences, statements made on isolated occasions . . . often clearly contradictory and not infrequently framed with such oracular sophistry that it is impossible for the reader of a later age to determine with certainty the "intrinsic meaning". . .'

The problem is analogous, though there are differences. One is that if the historical sociologist's material is disjointed and fragmentary, there is less he can do about it than the anthropologist confronting a still continuing culture. Another difference is that this particular sociologist is not over-charitable in attributing coherence to the authors of his texts, whilst the anthropologist cited appears to make it a condition of a good translation that it conveys the coherence which he assumes is there to be found in primitive thought. Such charity, or lack of it, is a matter of fashion in various disciplines. Most anthropologists at present are, I think, charitable: in sociology the situation is not so clear, and there is no reason to think that Samuelsson is similarly typical.[5]

One main stream of contemporary philosophy is inclined towards similar charity towards the concepts of the philosopher's own society. Mr R. Wollheim, for instance, in *F. H. Bradley* (Penguin Books, 1959, p. 67) observes: '. . . there are those (philosophers) who think that . . . what we think is far truer, far profounder than we ordinarily take it to be . . .' and goes on, correctly, to cite as the contemporary origin of this charitable view the later Wittgenstein. But Wittgenstein is also the author of the insistence on seeing the meaning of utterances as their use, and on seeing language as a 'form of life': in anthropological terms, on interpreting them in the light of their function in the culture of which they are a part. This influential movement is of course liable to confirm anthropologists in their attitude, and at least one of them, in a brilliant essay,[6] has drawn attention to the parallelism. Time was when neither philosophers nor anthropologists were so charitable.

6. Thus the basic situation is simple. I am schematising it below. Indigenous or textual sentence S faces a long or infinite column of all possible (say) English sentences. The investigator, with some misgivings, locates the nearest equivalent of S in the column.

7. Having done this, the anthropologist simply cannot, whether he likes it or not, and however much he may strive to be *wertfrei*, prevent himself from noticing whether the equivalents found in his own language for S are sensible or silly, as assertions. One's first reaction

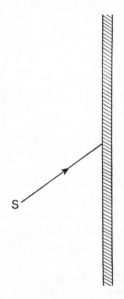

to assertions in one's own language, inseparable from appreciating their meaning, is to classify them in some way as Good or Bad. (I do not say 'true' or 'false', for this only arises with regard to some types of assertion. With regard to others, other dichotomies, such as 'meaningful' and 'absurd' or 'sensible' and 'silly' might apply. I deliberately use the words 'Good' and 'Bad' so as to cover all such possible polar alternatives, whichever might best apply to the equivalent of S.)

So in terms of our diagram, we have two boxes, G(ood) and B(ad); and having located the equivalents of S in his own language, the anthropologist willy-nilly goes on to note whether these equivalents go into G or B. (He may of course think that he is doing this purely in his own private capacity, and not professionally as an anthropologist. No matter, he does do it.) So the schema becomes slightly more complex. Let us assume in this case that the anthropologist judges the equivalents of S to be silly, B(ad). The schema now is:

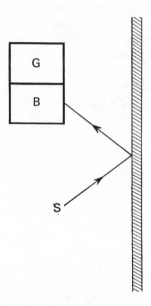

8. But what the preceding diagram describes is, as an account of contemporary interpretations, unrealistic. On the contrary, it describes a state of affairs much more characteristic of an earlier period, of what may almost be called the pre-history of anthropology. To come out with an interpretation of the indigenous sentence which classifies it as B(ad), as false or irrational or absurd, or at any rate to do it often, is a sign of *ethnocentricity*. Ethnocentricity is a grave defect from the viewpoint of the standards of the anthropological community.

Like members of other tribes, anthropologists are socialised by means of legends. These legends of course need not be false: indeed the one I am about to describe has much truth in it. Nevertheless, it is their socialising, indoctrinating function rather than their historical accuracy which is relevant. The legend by means of which a new anthropologist is moulded runs something as follows: Once upon a time, the anthropological world was inhabited by a proto-population who were *ethnocentric*. They collected information about primitives mainly in order to poke fun at them, to illustrate the primitive's inferiority to themselves. The information collected, even if accurate (which it often wasn't) was worthless because it was torn out of context.

The pre-enlightenment anthropologist, struck by the frequency with which the interpretations resulted in assertions which were

B(ad), and crediting this to the backwardness of the societies whose beliefs were being described, tended to explain this in terms of one of two theories: (a) Primitive Mentality theories, or (b) Jacob's Ladder (Evolutionist) theories of moral and intellectual growth. The former theory amounts to saying that savages get things wrong and confused so systematically, rather than being just occasionally in error, that one can characterise their thought as 'pre-logical'. The latter theory is somewhat more charitable and supposes that the savages are on the same ladder as we are, but so far behind that most of what he believes, whilst resulting from the application of the same logical principles as our own, is also an example of so unskilled an application of them that it is all too frequently wrong. Neither of these theories is much favoured at present.

For, one day the Age of Darkness came to an end. Modern anthropology begins with good, genuine, real modern fieldwork. The essence of such fieldwork is that it does see institutions, practices, beliefs etc. *in context*. At the same time, ethnocentrism is overcome. It is no longer the aim of studies to titillate a feeling of superiority by retailing piquant oddities. The two things, the seeing of institutions etc. in context, and the overcoming of ethnocentrism, are of course intimately connected. The schema which now applies is somewhat different:

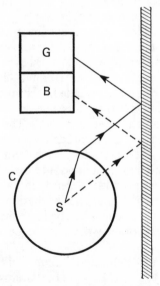

The circle C around the original indigenous assertion S stands for its social context. The context so to speak refracts the line of interpretation: with the aid of context, one arrives at a different equivalent in English of the original sentence S. And, lo and behold, if one *then* asks oneself about the merit of the newly interpreted S, one finds oneself giving it a high mark for sensibleness, truth or whatnot. One ends at G(ood) rather than B(ad). The earlier, bad old practice is indicated on this diagram by a dotted line.

9. There are various motives and/or justifications for the new, contextual approach. One of them is simply that it contains a good deal of validity: one does indeed get incomparably better appreciation of a doctrine by seeing its setting and use. But there are other motives. One of them is the laudable desire to be tolerant, understanding and liberal, to refrain from an uncomprehending and presumptuous superiority in one's attitude to other (notably 'primitive') societies.

In the modern world, this can be an urgent concern and connected with the need to combat racialism. A notable example of this use of anthropological sophistication is Professor Lévi-Strauss' *Race and History* (UNESCO, Paris, 1952). In a chapter entitled 'The Ethnocentric Attitude' he describes the widespread tendency to discount and despise members of other cultures as savages or barbarians, and speaks of it (p. 11) as 'this naïve attitude . . . deeply rooted in most men' and adds that 'this [i.e. his] booklet . . . in fact refutes it'. The main method he employs here to dissuade us from ethnocentricity is to point out that ethnocentrism characterises above all just those whom one would describe as savages. 'This attitude of mind, which excludes as "savages" (or any people one may choose to regard as savages) from human kind, is precisely the attitude most strikingly characteristic of those same savages.' One may be worried by the fact that the second occurrence of the word *savages* in the preceding sentence does not occur in inverted commas: in other words, that Lévi-Strauss is attempting to dissuade us from speaking of 'savages' by warning us that *savages* do so. Does he not here presuppose their existence and a condemnation of them? The liberal is in great danger of falling into paradox: either he condemns the ethnocentrism of savages and thus his tolerance has an important limit, or he does not, and then he at least condones *their* intolerance . . .

The paradox emerges even more clearly in an aphoristic definition he offers a little later (p. 12) of the 'barbarian'. 'The barbarian is, first and foremost, the man who believes in barbarism.' What makes one a savage, in other words, is the belief that some others *are* such.

Let us follow out this definition, taking it literally. A barbarian is he who believes that some others are barbarians. Notoriously, there are such people. They, therefore, are barbarians. We know they believe it. Hence, we believe they are barbarians. Ergo, we too are barbarians (by reapplication of the initial definition). And so is anyone who has noticed this fact and knows that *we* are, and so on.

Lévi-Strauss' definition has the curious property that, by a kind of regression or contagion, it spreads barbarism like wildfire through the mere awareness of it . . .

This paradox follows logically from Lévi-Strauss' innocuous-seeming definition. But this is not merely a logical oddity, arising from some quirk or careless formulation. It reflects something far more fundamental. It springs from a dilemma deep in the very foundations of the tolerant, understanding liberalism, of which sophisticated anthropology is a part, and it goes back at least to the thought of the Enlightenment which is the ancestor of such liberalism. The (unresolved) dilemma, which the thought of the Enlightenment faced, was between a relativistic-functionalist view of thought, and the absolutist claims of enlightened Reason. Viewing man as part of nature, as enlightened Reason requires, it wished to see his cognitive and evaluative activities as parts of nature too, and hence as varying, legitimately, from organism to organism and context to context. (This is the relativist-functional view.) But at the same time in recommending life according to Reason and Nature, it wished at the very least to exempt this view itself (and, in practice, some others) from such a relativism.

This dilemma was never really resolved in as far as a naturalistic or third-person view of beliefs (individual or collective) leads us to relativism, whilst our thought at the same time makes an exception in its own favour. We are here only concerned with the working out of this dilemma in anthropology. What characteristically happened in anthropology is rather like that pattern of alliances, in which one's neighbours are one's enemies, but one's neighbours-but-one are one's allies. Anthropologists were relativistic, tolerant, contextually-comprehending vis-à-vis the savages who are after all some distance away, but absolutistic, intolerant vis-à-vis their immediate neighbours or predecessors, the members of our own society who do not share their comprehending outlook and are themselves 'ethnocentric' . . .

The anthropologists were roughly liberals in their own society and Tories on behalf of the society they were investigating: they 'understood' the tribesman but condemned the District Officer or the Missionary. A bitter and misinformed attack on this attitude occurs in A. J. Hanna's *European Rule in Africa* (London, 1961, p. 22): 'The rise of social anthropology did much to foster (the) attitude (of trying to perpetuate tribalism) . . . exploring with fascinated interest the subtle and complex ramifications of tribal structure, and disdaining to mention . . . murder, mutilation, torture, witch-hunting (sic), cattle-raiding, wife-raiding . . . A . . . psychological tendency led the anthropologist to become the champion not only of the tribe whose customs he studied, but of its customs themselves.'

It is interesting to note, however, that the pattern of alliances, as it were, has changed since the days of the liberals who were, in a relativist spirit, tolerantly understanding of the intolerant absolutism of the distant tribesman, but less so of the absolutist beliefs in their own society. Nowadays, more sociological students of religion are themselves believers: in other words, contextual charity ends at home.

10. My main point about the tolerance-engendering contextual interpretation is that it calls for caution: that as a method it can be rather more wobbly than at first appears. Let us return to the diagram. What the last diagram expressed—the diagram schematising context-respecting, enlightened investigation—can involve some self-deception. What really happens, at any rate sometimes, is this:

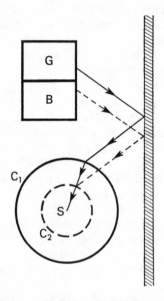

This diagram differs from the preceding one partly in the direction of the arrows. What I mean is this: it is the *prior* determination that S, the indigenous affirmation, be interpreted favourably, which determines just how much context will be taken into consideration. The diagram shows how different ranges of context—C_1 or C_2—are brought in according to whether the starting point is charitable or not . . . The context 'refracts' the line of interpretation: take a little more, or a little less, (as in the dotted lines), and a different interpretation of S in English will result. Or rather, the prior disposition concerning what kind of interpretation one wishes to find, determines the range of context brought in. (Apart from varying the range, there will also be different views of what the context is, either empirically, or in the way it is described and seen. A believing and an agnostic anthropologist may have differing views about what contexts there are to be seen.) The dotted circle represents a different—in this case, smaller—range of context taken into consideration.

It may be that the sympathetic, positive interpretations of indigenous assertions are not the result of a sophisticated appreciation of context, but *the other way round*: that the manner in which the context is invoked, the amount and kind of context and the way the context itself is interpreted, depends on prior tacit determination concerning the kind of interpretation one wishes to find . . . After all, there is nothing in the nature of things or societies to dictate visibly just how much context is relevant to any given utterance, or how that context should be described.

Professor Raymond Firth has remarked in *Problem and Assumption in an Anthropological Study of Religion* (Huxley Memorial Lecture, 1959, p. 139), 'From my own experience, I am impressed by the ease with which it is possible to add one's own personal dimension to the interpretation of an alien religious ideology, to raise the generalisations to a higher power than the empirical content of the material warrants.' My point is, really, that it is more than a matter of *ease*—it is a matter of necessity: for interpretation cannot be determinate without assumptions concerning the success or failure of the interpreted communication, and the criteria of such success are not manifest in the 'content of the material' itself. One has to work them out as best one can, and it will *not* do to take the short cut of reading them off the material by assuming that the material is always successful, i.e. that the statements investigated do satisfy and exemplify criteria of coherence, and hence that interpretation is not successful until this coherence has been made manifest in the translation. The logical *assessment* of an assertion, and the identification of its nearest equivalent in our language, are intimately linked and inseparable.

11. But this formal argument may carry more conviction if illustrated by concrete examples. The first I shall take is Professor Evans-Pritchard's treatment of Nuer religion, notably in Chapter V, 'The Problem of Symbols', of *Nuer Religion* (Oxford, 1956). Evans-Pritchard's main theoretical concern in this book is to refute Lévy-Bruhl's thesis concerning 'pre-logical mentality'. Evans-Pritchard's method in the pursuit of this aim is to take Nuer assertions and doctrines which, on the face of it, would indeed provide excellent evidence for a doctrine of the 'pre-logical mentality' of primitives, and then to proceed with the help of contextual interpretation to show that in fact they do not.

Evans-Pritchard begins his discussion as follows (p. 123): 'Our problem . . . can be simply stated by the question: What meaning are we to attach to Nuer statements that such-and-such a thing is *kwoth*, spirit? The answer is not so simple.' For the point is that the Nuer do make assertions which, prima facie, support a Lévy-Bruhl-type theory of 'primitive mentality', as Evans-Pritchard himself admits and stresses:

'It seems odd, if not absurd, to a European when he is told that a twin is a bird as though it were an obvious fact, for Nuer are not saying that a twin is like a bird but that he is a bird. There seems to be a complete contradiction in the statement: and it was precisely on statements of this kind recorded by observers of primitive peoples that Lévy-Bruhl based his theory of the prelogical mentality of these peoples, its chief characteristic being, in his view, that it permits such evident contradictions—that a thing can be what it is and at the same time something altogether different' (p. 131). Or again, 'When a cucumber is used as a sacrificial victim Nuer speak of it as an ox. In doing so they are asserting something rather more than that it takes the place of an ox' (p. 128).

But this is not the only kind of apparently odd assertion in which the Nuer indulge. This kind of statement appears to be in conflict with the principle of identity or non-contradiction, or with common sense, or with manifest observable fact: human twins are *not* birds, and vice versa. But they *also* make assertions which are in conflict with good theology, or at any rate with the theology which, according to Evans-Pritchard, they really hold. '. . . Nuer religious thought . . . pre-eminently dualistic'. '. . . there is . . . a duality between *kwoth*, Spirit, which is immaterial . . . and *cak*, creation, the material world known to the senses. Rain and lightning and pestilences and murrains belong to this created world . . .' (p. 124).

Nevertheless, Nuer do make assertions which appear to be in conflict with this theology as well. '. . . certain things are said, or may be said, "to be" God—rain, lightning, and various other natural . . . things . . .' (p. 123). 'They may say of rain or lightning or pestilence "*e kwoth*", "it is God". . .' (p. 124).

What is the solution? How are the Nuer saved for both common-sense *and* for dualistic theology, when their assertions appear to convict them of self-contradiction *and* of a doctrine of the immanence of the Deity in the world?

I shall present the solution in Professor Evans-Pritchard's own words. Concerning the apparent contradiction in Nuer thought, arising from the identification of twins, and birds, it appears (p. 131) that 'no contradiction is involved in the statement, which, on the contrary, appears quite sensible and even true, to one who presents the idea to himself in the Nuer language and within their system of religious thought. . . . *They are not saying that a twin has a beak,*

*feathers, and so forth. Nor in their everyday relations as twins do
Nuer speak of them as birds or act towards them as though they
were birds.'* (Italics mine.)

One may ask here—but what, then, *would* count as pre-logical
thought? Only, presumably, the behaviour of a totally demented
person, suffering from permanent hallucinations, who *would* treat
something which is perceptibly a human being as though it had all
the physical attributes of a bird. But could Lévy-Bruhl conceivably
have meant this when he was putting forward the doctrine of pre-
logical mentality? He knew, and could hardly have helped knowing,
that savages like everyone else are capable of distinguishing objects
which are so unlike physically as a human being who happens to be
a twin, and a bird. (In as far as there is nothing about the physical
appearance of a human being who happens to be a twin—unless
perhaps some socially significant markings, but Evans-Pritchard does
not say that Nuer twins have something of this kind—to distinguish
him from other human beings, the Nuer capacity to distinguish him
from a bird follows from their very capacity to distinguish humans
in general from birds, a capacity which can hardly be in doubt . . .)
This being so, Lévy-Bruhl's thesis can hardly with fairness be interpreted as entailing that errors such as the confusion of human and
bird bodies is genuinely committed by primitives. He could not have
meant this: or rather, we may not attribute this doctrine to him if
we extend to *him* too the courtesy or charity of contextual interpretation, which requires that we do not credit people with beliefs—
whatever they *say*—which are plainly in conflict with what they can
be assumed to know in the light of what they actually do. (E.g.—
Nuer cannot believe twins to be birds as their conduct distinguishes
between the two.)

If it be adopted as a principle that people cannot mean what at
some level (e.g. implicitly, through their conduct) they also know
to be false or absurd, then this principle must be applicable to Lévy-
Bruhl too . . . The trouble with the principle is, of course, that it is
too charitable: it absolves too many people of the charge of systematically illogical or false or self-deceptive thought.

It is worth considering just why the principle is so indiscriminately charitable. It insists, as Evans-Pritchard does when applying
it, on interpreting assertions in the light of actual *conduct*. But no ongoing viable system of conduct—and any society, and also any sane
surviving man, exemplifies such a system—*can* be self-contradictory.
Assertions, doctrines, can easily be illogical: conduct, and in particular the conduct of a *society* which is, by definition, a human group
persisting over time, cannot easily be illogical. The object of anthropological inquiries are precisely human groups persisting over time.
Their very persistence entails that they are reasonably viable: and

this viability in turns ensures that a 'context' is available for the sympathetic interpretation which will make sense of the local doctrines and assertions, however odd they may seem on the surface. This hermeneutic principle, tacitly employed by Evans-Pritchard, is too strong, for it ensures that no reasonably viable society can be said to be based on or to uphold absurd or 'pre-logical' doctrines. The trouble with such all-embracing logical charity is for one thing, that it is unwittingly quite *a priori*: it may delude anthropologists into thinking that they have *found* that no society upholds absurd or self-contradictory beliefs, whilst in fact the principle employed has ensured in advance of any inquiry that nothing may count as pre-logical, inconsistent or categorially absurd though it may be. And this, apart from anything else, would blind one to at least one socially significant phenomenon: the social role of absurdity.

12. But before proceeding with this general consideration, one should also look at Evans-Pritchard's second re-interpretation of Nuer assertions. The first one was to save them for common sense or consistency from the charge of self-contradiction. The second was to save them for a dualist theology and from an immanentist one. Again, it is best to present the case in Evans-Pritchard's own words. Referring to the fact that Nuer appear to speak of certain things—rain, lightning etc.—as being God (as quoted above), in contradiction of the dualist theology with which he credits them, Evans-Pritchard comments (pages 123 and 124):

'There is here an ambiguity, or an obscurity, to be elucidated, for Nuer are not now saying that God or Spirit is like this or that, but that this or that "is" God or Spirit.'

In interpreting this crucial sentence, a good deal depends on just what Evans-Pritchard meant by putting the final occurrence of the word *is* in inverted commas. He might simply have wished to accentuate it, by contrast to the expression *is like* in the preceding clause. But there are two good objections to this interpretation: had this been his intention, he might simply have italicised it, as is more customary, and secondly, he should have given the same treatment, whether inverted commas or italicisation, to the contrasted expression *is like*. In fact, I interpret him as saying that the Nuer do not really say that these things are God, but merely that they 'are' God. They mean something other than what they say.

And indeed, we are told (p. 125), 'When Nuer say of rain or lightning that it is God they are making an elliptical statement. What is understood is not that the thing in itself is Spirit but that it is what we could call a medium or manifestation or sign of divine activity in relation to men and of significance for them.' And no doubt, elliptical statements are common in all languages. What is at issue are the procedures for filling in the gaps left by ellipses.

It is important of course that the Nuer themselves being illiterate do not put any kind of inverted commas around their word for *is*, nor do they adopt any kind of phonetic equivalent of such a device. (Evans-Pritchard at no point suggests that they do.) Hence the attribution of the inverted commas, of the non-literal meaning, is a matter of interpretation, not of direct observation of the utterance itself.

And what is the logic of this interpretation? How are the gaps filled? In part, the argument is based on the assumption that the Nuer *cannot* mean the assertion literally because (their notion of) Deity is such that this would make no sense. 'Indeed it is because Spirit is conceived of in itself, as the creator and the one, and quite apart from any of its material manifestations, that phenomena can be said to be sent by it or to be its instruments' (p. 125). But to argue thus is of course to assume precisely that they do have such a self-sufficient, substantial-Creator notion of Spirit as they are credited with, *and* that they follow out the implications consistently. Indeed one may doubt whether and in what sense the Nuer can be said to possess a notion of the One, self-sufficient substance and Creator, independent of His material manifestations, etc., difficult notions which, explicitly formulated in this way, seem to presuppose the context of scholastic philosophy. It is something like this that Schoolmen have done for God: can the same be meaningfully said of the Nuer God, the Nuer having no Schoolmen?

But the position is supported not only by this argument, but also by some good independent evidence. One argument is that '. . . Nuer readily expand such statements by adding that thunder, rain, and pestilence are all instruments . . . of God or that they are sent by . . . God . . .' (p. 125). This is indeed a good and independent piece of evidence. Another argument is from the irreversibility of the judgments which claim that those certain mundane manifestations 'are' God: God or Spirit cannot in Nuer be said to 'be' them. This does not seem to me to be so valid a point. It is of course difficult for one who speaks no Nuer to judge, but in English it is possible, in some contexts, to say that A is B without the statement being reversible, but at the same time implying that A is a part of B and in that sense identical with it (or rather with a part of it). To someone who inquires about my suburb, I may in some contexts say that Putney is London, (it is not Surrey): and I cannot say that London is Putney. It could be that for Nuer, rain etc. is in this sense (part of) the deity, and this would then indicate that the Nuer view of God is at least in part an immanent one, and not as severely transcendent as Evans-Pritchard seems to be arguing. (' . . . God not being an observable object, [the situation could scarcely arise] in which Nuer would require or desire to say about him that he is anything', p. 125.) Again one may also wonder whether Nuer can be credited with so firm a theological position on a question which they can hardly have explicitly posed in such terms.

I do not wish to be misunderstood: I am *not* arguing that Evans-Pritchard's account of Nuer concepts is a bad one. (Nor am I anxious to revive a doctrine of pre-logical mentality *à la* Lévy-Bruhl.) On the contrary, I have the greatest admiration for it. What I am anxious to argue is that contextual interpretation, which offers an account of what assertions 'really mean' in opposition to what they seem to mean in isolation, does not by itself clinch matters. It cannot arrive at determinate answers (concerning 'what they mean') without doing a number of things which may in fact prejudge the question: without delimiting just which context is to be taken into consideration, without crediting the people concerned with consistency (which is precisely what is sub judice when we discuss, as Evans-Pritchard does, Lévy-Bruhl's thesis), or without assumptions concerning what they can mean (which, again, is precisely what we do not know but are trying to find out). In fairness, one should add that Evans-Pritchard is aware of this, as just before he severely rebukes Lévy-Bruhl and others for their errors, he also remarks (p. 140): 'I can take the analysis no further: but if it is inconclusive it at least shows, if it is correct, how wide of the mark have been . . .' (Lévy-Bruhl and some others.)

13. To say all this is not to argue for a scepticism or agnosticism concerning what members of alien cultures and speakers of alien languages mean, still less to argue for an abstention from the contextual method of interpretation. (On the contrary, I shall argue for a fuller use of it, fuller in the sense of allowing for the possibility that what people mean is sometimes absurd.)

In a sense, Evans-Pritchard's saving of the Nuer for a dualistic theology is a more difficult exercise than is his saving of them from a charge of pre-logical mentality. We know anyway, without field-work, that they could in conduct distinguish birds from men and bulls from cucumbers, and to argue from these premises to the absence of pre-logical thought does not perhaps really advance the question of whether pre-logical thought occurs. On the other hand nothing prior to field-work evidence could give us any reason for having views about whether Nuer theology was or was not dualistic.

14. It is interesting at this stage to contrast Evans-Pritchard's use of the method with that of another distinguished practitioner of it, Mr Edmund Leach.

We have seen how Evans-Pritchard takes Nuer statements which, on the face of it, violate common-sense and also others which go counter to a dualistic theology which separates a transcendent deity from the immanent world, and how, by holding these statements to be metaphorical or elliptical, he squares them with common sense and an acceptable theology. Mr Leach, in *Political Systems of Highland Burma*, London, 1954, copes with other odd statements, made by Burmese Kachins.

Again, these statements are odd. It appears (p. 14) that a Kachin found killing a pig and asked what he is doing may reply that he is 'giving to the nats'. The oddity arises simply from the non-existence of nats. On the face of it, we might accuse the Kachins, if not of 'pre-logical mentality', at any rate of populating the world with imaginary creatures in their own image. Indeed, this seems to be so, for Leach tells us (p. 173) that nats are 'magnified non-natural men', and that 'in the *nat* world, as in the human world, there are chiefs, aristocrats, commoners and slaves'.

Nevertheless, Leach does not, like Evans-Pritchard, intend to give us a picture of what that supernatural world is like. (Evans-Pritchard gave us a picture of the Nuer vision of the supernatural which was sufficiently determinate to exclude some superficially plausible interpretations of some Nuer assertions.) On the contrary, he tells us (p. 172) 'it is nonsensical to discuss the actions or qualities of supernatural beings except in terms of human action'. 'Myth . . . is not so much a justification for ritual as a description of it.' Or (p. 13) 'Myth [and] . . . ritual . . . are one and the same'. '. . . myth regarded as a statement in words "says" the same thing as ritual regarded as a statement in action. To ask questions about the content of belief which are not contained in the content of ritual is nonsense.'[7] '. . . a very large part of anthropological literature on religion [is] a discussion of the content of belief and of the rationality or otherwise of that content. Most such arguments seem to me scholastic nonsense.'

Or again (p. 14), when a Kachin is killing a pig and says he is giving it to the nats, 'it is nonsense to ask such questions as: "Do nats have legs? Do they eat flesh? Do they live in the sky?"' (Given the fact that they are 'magnified non-natural men' and that they are 'chiefs, aristocrats, commoners and slaves', it seems odd that it should be nonsense to credit them with legs, a diet, and a habitat . . .)

Concerning his own procedure, Leach tells us (p. 14): '. . . I make frequent reference to Kachin mythology but I . . . make no attempt to find any logical coherence in the myths to which I refer. Myths for me are simply one way of describing certain types of human behaviour . . .' And, later, not only are myth and ritual one, so that it makes no sense to ask non-contextual questions about the former, but also (p. 182) '. . . it becomes clear that the various nats of Kachin religious ideology are, in the last analysis, nothing more than ways of describing the formal relationships that exist between real persons and real groups in ordinary Kachin society'.

It is possible to discern what has happened. Leach's exegetic procedures have also saved the Kachins from being credited with meaning what they *appear* to be saying. Their assertions are reinterpreted in the light of the author's disregard for the supernatural, in the light of the doctrine that myths simply mean the ritual which they accompany and nothing else, and that the ritual in turn 'means', symbolises, the society in which it occurs. The 'Social' theory of religion appears to have, in our society, the following function (amongst other, possible): to enable us to attribute meaning to assertions which might otherwise be found to lack it.

Again, I am not concerned, nor indeed inclined, to challenge Leach's specific interpretations of the Kachins; though one wishes that some enterprising teacher of anthropology would set his students the task of writing an essay on *kwoth* as it would be written by Leach, and another on *nats* as it would be written by Evans-Pritchard. The point with which I am concerned is to show how the range of context, and the manner in which the context is seen, necessarily affect the interpretation. Both Evans-Pritchard and Leach are charitable to their subjects, and neither allows them to be credited with nonsense: but in the case of Leach, the 'sense' with which they are credited is identified by means of an essentially *social* doctrine of religion, a doctrine which is also precisely that which Evans-Pritchard strives to refute with the help of *his* interpretations.

15. The crux of the matter is that when, in a sense rightly, the interpretation of people's assertions must be made in the light of what they do and the social setting they do it in, this requirement is profoundly ambiguous. Two quite different things may be intended (though those who postulate the requirement may have failed to be clear in their own minds about this). The distinction between these two things can best be brought out, at any rate to begin with, by means of a simplified imaginary social situation.

Assume that in the language of a given society, there is a word *boble* which is applied to characterise people. Research reveals that *bobleness* or *bobility* is attributed to people under *either* of the following conditions: (a) a person who antecedently displays certain characteristics in his conduct, say uprightness, courage and generosity, is called *boble*, (b) any person holding a certain office, or a certain social position, is also ipso facto described as *boble*. One is tempted to say that bobility (a) is a descriptive term whose operational definition consists of tests for the possession of certain attributes (and might consist of seeing how large a portion of his income he distributed as largesse, how he behaved in danger, etc.), whereas (b) is simply an ascription, depending on the will or whim of those in authority, or on the social situation, but not in any reasonably direct or identifiable way dependent on the characteristics of the person in question. But the point is: the society in question does not distinguish *two concepts*, boble (a) and boble (b). It only uses one word, boble *tout court*; and again its theories about bobility, expressed in proverbs, legends or even disquisitions of wise elders, only know bobility, one and indivisible. As a first and simplified approximation, the logic of bobility is not an unrecognisable model, perhaps, of some familiar concepts in our own languages.

But what is the observer to say about bobility-like, so to speak semi-operational concepts? Bobility is a conceptual device by which the privileged class of the society in question acquires some of the prestige of certain virtues respected in that society, without the inconvenience of needing to practice it, thanks to the fact that the same word is applied either to practitioners of those virtues or to occupiers of favoured positions. It is, at the same time, a manner of reinforcing the appeal of those virtues, by associating them, through the use of the same appellation, with prestige and power. But all this needs to be said, and to say it is to bring out the internal logical incoherence of the concept—an incoherence which, indeed, is socially functional.

What this shows, however, is that the over-charitable interpreter, determined to defend the concepts he is investigating from the charge of logical incoherence, is bound to misdescribe the social situation. To make sense of the concept is to make nonsense of the society. Thus the *uncharitable* may be 'contextualist' in the second, deeper and better sense.

It seems to me that anthropologists are curiously charitable to concepts. They are not unduly charitable to individuals. On the contrary, they are all too willing to describe how individuals 'manipulate' each other and the rules of the local game: indeed the word 'manipulation' has a certain vogue and is encountered with very great frequency. But why should concepts not be similarly open to manipulation? Why should it not be a part of their use that the ambiguity of words, the logically illicit transformation of one concept into another (like a spirit appearing in diverse forms) is exploited to the full by the users of what seems to be 'one' concept?

Excessive indulgence in contextual charity blinds us to what is best and what is worst in the life of societies. It blinds us to the possibility that social change may occur through the replacement of an inconsistent doctrine or ethic by a better one, or through a more consistent application of either. It equally blinds us to the possibility of, for instance, social control through the employment of absurd, ambiguous, inconsistent or unintelligible doctrines. I should not accept for one moment the contention that neither of these things ever occurs: but even if they never occurred it would be wrong to employ a method which excludes their possibility a priori.

16. It may be worth illustrating the point further with a real rather than schematised example, amongst central Moroccan Berbers, and I shall draw on my own field-work for this. Two concepts are relevant: *baraka* and *agurram* (pl. *igurramen*). *Baraka* is a word which can mean simply 'enough', but it also means plenitude, and above all blessedness manifested amongst other things in prosperity and the power to cause prosperity in others by supernatural means. An *agurram* is a possessor of *baraka*.[8] The concept *baraka* has been explored before, notably by Westermarck's *Ritual and Belief in Morocco* (London, 1926, Chapters II & III). The concept of *agurram* has not to my knowledge previously been properly explored.

Igurramen are a minority in the wider tribal society of which they are a part. They are a fairly privileged and influential one, and they perform essential and important functions as mediators, arbitrators etc. amongst the feuding tribal population around them. They are selected from a range of potential *igurramen*, who are defined by descent—roughly speaking, to be one it is necessary that one's ancestors or at least some of them should have been *igurramen* too. The crucial questions is—*how* are they selected?

The local belief is that they are selected by God. Moreover, God makes his choice manifest by endowing those whom he has selected with certain characteristics, including magical powers, and great generosity, prosperity, a consider-the-lilies attitude, pacifism, and so forth.

The reality of the situation is, however, that the *igurramen* are in fact selected by the surrounding ordinary tribesmen who use their services, by being called to perform those services and being preferred to the rival candidates for their performance. What appears to be *vox Dei* is in reality *vox populi*. Moreover, the matter of the blessed characteristics, the stigmata of *agurram*-hood is more complicated. It is essential that successful candidates to *agurram* status be *credited* with these characteristics, but it is equally essential, at any rate with regard to some of them, that they should not really possess them. For instance, an *agurram* who was extremely generous in a consider-the-lilies spirit would soon be impoverished and, as such, fail by another crucial test, that of prosperity.

There is here a crucial divergence between concept and reality, a divergence which moreover is quite essential for the working of the social system. It is no use saying, as has been suggested to me by an advocate of the hermeneutic method which I am criticising, that the notion of divine selection of *igurramen* is simply the local way of conceptualising a popular election. This interpretation is excluded for a number of reasons. For one thing, the Berbers of central

Morocco are perfectly familiar with *real* elections. In their traditional system, they also have, apart from the *igurramen*, lay tribal chiefs, (*amghar*, pl. *imgharen*) who are elected, annually, by tribal assembly. In these real elections the tribesmen do indeed hope for and request divine guidance, but they are quite clear that it is they themselves who do the electing. They distinguish clearly between this kind of genuine annual election, and the very long-drawn-out process (stretching over generations) by which *igurramen* are selected, in fact by the tribesmen, but ideally by God. But it would be presumptuous and blasphemous for tribesmen to claim to appoint an *agurram*. Secondly, it is of the essence of the function of an *agurram* that he is given from the outside: he has to be a neutral who arbitrates and mediates between tribes. If he were chosen, like a chief or an ally, by the tribesmen, or rather if he were seen to be chosen by tribesmen (as in fact he is), for a litigant to submit to his verdict would be in effect to submit to those other tribesmen who had chosen the *agurram*. This, of course, would involve a loss of face and constitute a confession of weakness. Tribesmen sometimes do choose lay arbitrators: but they then know what they are doing and the point of invoking *igurramen* is the invoking of *independent* authority. Submission to a divinely chosen *agurram*, is a sign not of weakness but of piety. Not to submit to him is, and is explicitly claimed to be, *shameful*. (This illustrates a point which seems to me enormously important, namely that concepts generally contain *justifications* of practices, and hence that one misinterprets them grossly if one treats them simply as these practices, and their context, in another dress. The justifications are independent of the thing justified.)

It might be objected that my unwillingness to accept the indigenous account at its face value merely reflects my theological prejudices, i.e. my unwillingness to believe that the deity interferes in the political life of the central High Atlas. But this kind of objection does not have even a prima facie plausibility with regard to the other social mechanism mentioned. There is nothing in my conceptual spectacles to make me unwilling to conceive that some people might be generous and uncalculating, nor should I be unwilling to describe them in these terms if I found them to be so. It is just that field-work observation of *igurramen* and the social context in which they operate has convinced me that, whilst indeed *igurramen* must entertain lavishly and with an air of insouciance, they *must* also at least balance their income from donations from pilgrims with the outgoings from entertaining them, for a poor *agurram* is a no-good *agurram*. Here again, we are faced with a socially essential discrepancy between concept and reality. What is required is not disregard for social context, but, on the contrary, a fuller appreciation of it which is not wedded a priori to find good sense in the concepts.

One might sum up all this by saying that nothing is more false than the claim that, for a given assertion, *its use is its meaning*. On the contrary, its use may depend on its lack of meaning, its ambiguity, its possession of wholly different and incompatible meanings in different contexts, *and* on the fact that, at the same time, it as it were emits the impression of possessing a consistent meaning throughout —on retaining, for instance, the aura of a justification valid only in one context when used in quite another.

17. It is worth exploring this in connection with the other concept mentioned, *baraka*. I shall not say much about it, as the literature concerning it is already extensive (E. Westermarck's *Ritual and Belief in Morocco*, London, 1926, Chapters II & III). Suffice it to say that the concept is a source of great joy to me, for it violates, simultaneously, no fewer than three of the major and most advertised categorial distinctions favoured by recent philosophers. It is an evaluative term, but it is used as though it were a descriptive one: possessors of *baraka* are treated as though they were possessors of an objective characteristic rather than recipients of high moral grades from their fellow men. And in as far as it is claimed to be an objective characteristic of people, manifest in their conduct, it could only be a dispositional one—but it is treated as though it were the name of some *stuff*: apart from being transmitted genetically, it can also be transmitted by its possessor to another person by means of spitting into the mouth, etc. Thirdly, its attribution is really a case of the performative use of language, for people in fact become possessors of *baraka* by being treated as possessors of it—but nevertheless, it is treated as though its possession were a matter wholly independent of the volition of those who attribute it. (This has already been explained in connection with the account of *agurram*, the possessor of *baraka*, and it has also been explained how this deception is essential for the working of the social system in question.)

In other words, the actual life of this concept goes dead against the celebrated work of recent philosophers. One may well speculate that the society in question could be undermined by acquainting its members with the works of Ryle, Ayer, Stevenson and J. L. Austin. The question is somewhat academic, for in its traditional form the society is virtually illiterate (that is, illiterate but for a small number of Muslim scribes whose range is severely circumscribed) and not amenable to the persuasion of external teachers, and by the time it has ceased to be illiterate and unreceptive, it shall have been disrupted anyway.

But this does illustrate a number of important points. I have already stressed that it is no use supposing that one can deal with this by claiming that the indigenous societies always live, as it were, in a conceptual dimension of their own, in which our categorial boundaries do not apply. On the contrary, we can sometimes only make sense of the society in question by seeing how the manipulation of concepts and the violation of categorial boundaries helps it to work. It is precisely the logical *in*consistency of *baraka* which enables it to be applied according to social need and to endow what is a social need with the appearance of external, given and indeed authoritative reality.

18. There are, both in philosophy and the wider intellectual climate of our time, considerable forces giving support to the kind of Functionalism which makes good sense of everything. In philosophy, it springs from the doctrine which identifies *meaning* with *use*, and there is already in existence at least one work by a philosopher about the social sciences in general—Mr P. Winch's, cited above— which elaborates (and commends) the consequences of this doctrine. A proper discussion of the philosophic questions involved would of course take longer.

In the world at large, there is much incentive to paper over the incoherence, and inconveniences, of current ideologies by emulating this anthropological technique. How many ideologists treat their *own* beliefs with a technique similar to that employed by anthropologists for tribesmen! I for one do not feel that, in the realm of concepts and doctrines, we may say that *tout comprendre c'est tout pardonner*. On the contrary, in the social sciences at any rate, if we forgive too much we understand nothing. The attitude of *credo quia absurdum* is *also* a social phenomenon, and we miss its point and its social role if we water it down by interpretation to make it just one further form of non-absurdity, sensible simply in virtue of being viable.

19. One major charge against Functionalism in the past has been the allegation that it cannot deal with social change. With regard to Functionalism in general this charge has now little relevance, as it only applies to strong or extreme formulations of it, and these are held by few. But with regard to the Functionalist approach to interpretation of concepts, it applies very strongly. For it precludes us from making sense of those social changes which arise at least in part from the fact that people sometimes notice the incoherences of doctrines and concepts and proceed to reform the institutions justified by them. This may never happen *just* like that: it may be that it invariably is a discontented segment of society, a new rising class for instance, which exploits those incoherences. But even if this were so, and the discovery of incoherences were never more than a contributory rather than a sufficient cause, it still would not be legitimate for us to employ a method which inherently prevents any possible appreciation of this fact. When anthropologists were concerned primarily with stable societies (or societies held to be such), the mistake was perhaps excusable: but nowadays it is not.

In the end, it is illuminating to return to one of the sources of the functionalist approach, Durkheim. Durkheim is sometimes accused of overrating the cohesion-engendering function of belief. In the *Elementary Forms of Religious Life*, which is the object of these charges, he did also put forward, albeit briefly, a theory of social change.[9] This theory he sums up in one brief passage, and it is a theory plainly parallel to his theory of social cohesion.

> Car une société (est) constituée . . . avant tout, par l'idée qu'elle se fait d'elle-même. Et sans doute, il arrive qu'elle hésite sur la manière dont elle doit se concevoir: elle se sent tiraillée en des sens divergents . . . ces conflits, quand ils éclatent, ont lieu non entre l'idéal et la réalité, mais entre idéaux différents. . . .
>
> *Les Formes Elementaires de la Vie Religieuse* (1925) edition, p. 604).

This theory, the germ of which is contained in Durkheim, has been elaborated by Mr E. R. Leach's *Political Systems of Highland Burma* (London, 1959, esp. pp. 8–9). My main point here is that there was no need for Durkheim to look even that far for a theory of social change. He apparently thought that if the one set of ritually reinforced and inculcated concepts explained social stability, then it took the presence of *two sets* to account for social change. But ironically, such a refinement is not necessary. Some social change may be accounted for precisely because *one* set of ideas has been inculcated too well, or has come to have too great a hold over the loyalties and imaginations of the members of the society in question, or because one of its subgroups has chosen to exploit the imperfect application of those ideas, and to iron out the inconsistencies and incoherencies. Overcharitable exegesis would blind us to this.

Contextual interpretation is in some respects like the invocation of ad hoc additional hypotheses in science: it is inevitable, proper, often very valuable, and at the same time dangerous and liable to disastrous abuse. It is probably impossible in either case to draw up general rules for delimiting the legitimate and illegitimate uses of it. In science, the best safeguard may be a vivid sense of the possibility that the initial theory which is being saved may have been false after all; in sociological interpretation, an equally vivid sense of the possibility that the interpreted statement may contain absurdity.

20. There remains the issue in the wider society outside the social sciences, the question of the justifiability of 'Functionalist' whitewashing of concepts and doctrines. Professor Evans-Pritchard sternly rebukes Durkheim at the end of his book *Nuer Religion*, p. 313: 'It was Durkheim and not the savage who made society into a god.'

Perhaps, but it is ironic that if the savage did not, modern man *does* seem to worship his own society through his religion.[10]

My plea against charity did not have as its aim the revival of a 'pre-logical primitive mentality' theory. On the contrary: I hope rather we shall be less charitable to ourselves. I agree entirely with Mr Leach's point in his contribution to *Man and Culture*, that when it comes to the general way in which concepts are embedded in use and context, there is no difference between 'primitives' and us. There is no need to be too charitable to *either*.

My own view of Durkheim is that at the core of his thought there lies not the doctrine of worshipping one's own society, but the doctrine that concepts are essentially social and that religion is the way in which society endows us with them and imposes their hold over us. But, consistently or not, he did not combine this with a static view of society and intellectual life. It would be ironic if neo-Functionalist interpretation now became the means by which our own concepts were ossified amongst us.

NOTES

1 It is however very important not to misunderstand this point. For it is *not* true to say that to understand the concepts of a society (in the way its members do) is to understand the society. Concepts are as liable to mask reality as to reveal it, and masking some of it may be a part of their function. The profoundly mistaken doctrine that to understand a society is to understand its concepts has a certain vogue and has recently been revived and argued, for instance, in Mr P. Winch's *The Idea of a Social Science*, London, 1958. Some of the reasons why this view is false are discussed below.
2 But they do still exist. Consider Professor Ralph Piddington's essay, 'Malinowski's Theory of Needs', in *Man and Culture*, edited by Professor Raymond Firth, London, 1957, esp. p. 47.
3 *Much* later, L. Wittgenstein was credited with just this discovery.
4 Somewhat to my surprise, Mr D. G. MacRae appears to think that he was: '. . . Durkheim *showed* . . . how time, space, causality and other fundamental categories . . . are in great measure social products . . .' *Ideology and Society*, London, 1961, p. 83. (Italics mine.)

Much depends of course on how great a measure 'great measure' is. Durkheim was concerned to explain the compulsiveness of categories. He succeeded in showing, I think, how our power of *apprehending* them depended on society. He did not explain why, once they are in our possession, we cannot escape them.

The distinction is important. Precisely the same is also true of Durkheim's (quite unwitting) follower and successor, Wittgenstein, who also supposed categories were validated by being parts of a 'form of life' and who, incidentally, like Durkheim also vacillated between supposing all concepts could be validated in this manner, and restricting this confirmation to categories.

I am quite prepared to believe that at the root of our ability to count, to relate things along a time series or spatially, is a social order which exemplifies and 'ritually' brings home to us the concepts involved. But I do not think this accounts either for their compulsiveness or for occasional lapses from it. There is something comic about this idea. Are we to say that Riemann and Lobachevsky were inadequately exposed to those rituals of Western society which make the Euclidean picture of space compulsive to its members?
5 For instance, Dr W. Stark, in *The Sociology of Knowledge*, London, 1958, recommends almost universal charity in this respect, with the help of arguments which differ both from Durkheim's and from those of Functionalists. See also 'Sociology of Faith', *Inquiry*, 1958, 1, 247–52; below pp. 213–18.
6 E. R. Leach, in 'The Epistemological Background to Malinowski's

Empiricism', in *Man and Culture*, ed. R. Firth, London, 1957, p. 119.

7   If Mr Leach meant this quite literally, he should of course give us only the Kachin expression itself plus a description of the ritual and of the society—and *not*, as in fact he does, *translations* of the ritual statements.

8   The term *baraka* is in use throughout North Africa by Arabs and Berbers, and also elsewhere. The term *agurram* is only known among Berbers, and not among all of these. It is used in central and southern Morocco, but not among the northern Berbers of the Rif mountains. It is also used by Algerian Berbers, but I do not know how extensively.

9   The work also contains some other suggestions on this subject, not so relevant to my argument here.

10   Cf. Will Herberg, *Catholic-Protestant-Jew*, New York, 1955.

3
WINCH'S IDEA OF A SOCIAL SCIENCE

Peter Winch's *The Idea of a Social Science* [London: Routledge & Kegan Paul, 1958] formulates, in a laudably uncompromising form, an extreme position concerning the study of man and human societies: that human societies can only be understood as it were 'from the inside', through their own concepts, and hence, as these concepts are generally quite distinct from those of natural science and causal explanation, that therefore we can consider ourselves free from the bogey of causal determinism. The book is, however, important for philosophers rather than for social scientists, for a variety of reasons; its manner of conveying its message will not make it easily intelligible to non-philosophers, and the content of that message, in as far as it is true, will not be so novel for them either.

Mr Winch is an enthusiastic disciple of Wittgenstein. Amongst the central preoccupations of Wittgenstein and his school there was a concern with what it was to *understand* something (say a concept or a procedure), what it is to follow a rule (socially, or in mathematics), and so on. The sophistication about these problems was bound sooner or later to spill over and stimulate a new look in a whole class of questions in the social sciences: issues such as, for instance, the invocation of subjective and objective factors in economics (marginalism and all that), in sociology (concerning, e.g. the inner and outer aspects of class), the methodological status of introspection, of explanations in terms of conscious and of unconscious motivation, and so forth. Mr Winch's book can be seen as one of the first fruits in this predictable harvest, although he sets his sights somewhat higher: he believes that a new and, at long last, correct understanding of the social sciences as such follows from the Wittgensteinian insights. The book is, as the title says, about the *idea* of a social science (in the singular): Mr Winch clearly believes that by analysing this idea he can establish significant conclusions for the benefit of the practitioners of the social sciences. He checks his conclusions by arguments, interesting and often penetrating, with the general methodological and programmatic views of major figures in the thought *about* the social sciences. But the social sciences are also a *reality*, and one which, however imperfect, did not wait for recent philosophic revelations for permission to actualize itself. To this reality Mr Winch in his rather Platonic procedure does not pay much attention. Had he done so, his arguments and conclusions might have profited and he would at the very least have avoided the somewhat awe-inspiring posture of a philosophic Superman flying in from outside and setting things right for the earthbound social scientists. Mr Winch's concern, however, is not *only* with telling social scientists what they are really about: he also wishes to tell philosophers what *they* are about, and he considers the two tasks to be identical. Concerning philosophy, he rejects the view that philosophy is a kind of preliminary tool-sharpening, concerned with concepts as opposed to reality: and he rejects it for the important reason that our crucial concepts and reality are inseparable, the concepts as it were *making* the reality. Moreover, concepts are essentially social. And concerning the social sciences, his central idea is that societies are, in turn, so to speak *made* by the ideas of the men participating in them: institutions and concepts are essentially correlative. (The concepts we have do not exist prior to the social contexts, but in turn are necessarily dependent on them. This, the inescapably social nature of concepts, is presumably the Wittgensteinian seed from which the book grew.)

Thus, for Mr Winch, philosophy and sociology (in a broad sense) are very similar, if not almost identical: they both deal with a subject-matter in which concepts and things are inextricably fused. They are both concerned with learning to understand concepts. He seems to think (p. 114) that the difference between the philosopher and the sociologist—both concerned (only?) with the way in which concepts are enmeshed in reality—is that existing between the therapist and the ordinary investigator. The implicit corollaries of this are curious: that philosophy is really applied sociology, and (in conjunction with other premisses about the neutrality of accounts of concepts to which he openly subscribes), that both sociology and philosophy must be conservative.

With regard to philosophy, I find Mr Winch's conclusions attractive. It would be nice to see Wittgensteinian philosophers really following up the doctrine of the essentially social nature of thought and language, instead of merely using it as a stick with which to beat empiricism, and to take a good look at concrete social contexts, rather than doing it in a very general way and inventing their examples *ad hoc* and without check in the course of discussion with each other. But whilst sympathizing with his conclusions here, one must add that he does not stick to them consistently: he frequently lapses into facile invocation of the distinction between 'conceptual' and 'substantive' issues, and moreover, there is a pragmatic contradiction between what perhaps he says and the way he has written his book at all: the book itself is, plainly, an attempted 're-tooling' by an 'under-labourer' of the kind he condemns. . . .

For sociology, his conclusions seem to me far less useful. The Wittgensteinian idea of the correlativeness of activities (or institutions) and concepts—even assuming that Wittgenstein had solved the problems involved—cuts both ways: it implies not merely that in order to understand outer facts we have to know the ideas which give them life, but also that, in order to understand those ideas, we have to look at the outer goings-on which give them substance. And this is precisely what very many social scientists are doing anyway. Moreover, there are many important aspects of societies which can, and must, be investigated without bothering overmuch with *verstehen*: to understand the class structure of a society one must not only know what rank, etc., means in it, but also how many people occupy each grade, and this is a matter of counting, not understanding. Again, a very crucial part of a sociological analysis is that dark area of discrepancy between the ideas of a society (in the sense of that part of behaviour which could be inferred from the account of avowed concepts) and the generally diverging reality of behaviour (which, indeed, can *also* be 'understood') but which may have no ratification in official concepts, and which has to be detected by the investigator in a way which is quite different from learning to handle a concept as a member of a society.

In brief, what Mr Winch has to tell the sociologist is not new; it is stated in a way which makes it difficult for him to see just what is being claimed; and it does not deal with difficulties adequately. For instance, it will not do simply to condemn the possibility of comparative studies (p. 106 et seq.) by appealing to the essential connection between a social feature and its general context. Mr Winch seems too excited by discoveries which are new to him, to see that the methodological issues which hinge on them must by now be discussed with reference to concrete work rather than by formal argument alone. Again, his treatment of causation is somewhat cavalier. (Incidentally, on p. 116 he opposes the notion of *function* not on the usual grounds that it is teleological and insufficiently causal, but because it *is* causal.)

Mr Winch's book ends with the curious assumption—curious anyway, and doubly odd in a disciple of that Wittgenstein who wanted to 'show us differences'—that the various social sciences are sufficiently similar not to call for special treatment in connection with the issues he deals with. It is doubtful whether this is true, but it is certain that it would have to be supported by argument.

4

THE NEW IDEALISM—CAUSE AND
MEANING IN THE SOCIAL
SCIENCES

Anthropomorphism is not a live issue in the natural sciences. On the whole, the freedom of natural scientists does not need to be protected from people insisting that the picture presented by the results *must* conform to some human image—that it must resemble man, make room for him, underwrite his purposes, be compatible with his self-image, or with some doctrine concerning these matters. There are notorious exceptions to this generalisation, such as for instance the interference with Soviet biologists or even physicists in the interests of supporting an extrapolated version of a social theory: but these are, happily, exceptions. In an important and extended sense, the Copernican revolution is well established: humanity is known not to be at the centre of things; human requirements are not allowed to limit, or even create presumptions in, the sphere of scientific theory. (Moral philosophers are proud of the autonomy of ethics: this is one point on which a large proportion of professional practitioners of the subject are agreed. They do not quite so often note that the autonomy of ethics only followed on the autonomy of science, the exclusion of the argument from morals to fact, *from* 'ought' *to* 'is', of the form 'This must be true, otherwise our life would not make sense', or 'This cannot be true, otherwise our life would make no sense'.)

In social or human studies or sciences, however, the question of anthropomorphism—though not under this name—is by no means dead. The plea for a *humanist* psychology or sociology is frequently heard. The philosophy of mind has recently witnessed a sustained and interesting attack on the view that individuals have 'privileged access', cognitively, to their *own* minds. But there has been no corresponding attack on the view, which might at least superficially seem parallel, that we have, *collectively*, a privileged access, through our shared human concepts, to the understanding of the social life and institutions of humanity. On the contrary: philosophers associated with the school responsible for the attack on the *individual* 'privileged access' view, have at the same time been prominent in putting forward versions of what I call the collective privileged access theory—that we understand social life through human concepts.

The general motive or attraction of anthropomorphism, in any sphere, is fairly obvious. Anthropomorphic doctrines enlist the world on the side of our values or aspirations. If, to take an example with with which I am familiar, the deity or supernatural beings arrange floods, droughts, or other disasters in a way such that these sanctions strike perjurors and their lineages, this provides a convenient underpinning for a legal system. A centralised and effective state may have neither the need, nor indeed be willing to tolerate, the handing over of punishment to the supernatural: but where such a centralised law-enforcing agency is absent, and Nature apparently allows itself to be used in so moral a manner, this makes possible trial by collective oath—a very common institution in anarchic or semi-anarchic tribal contexts. The rain does *not* fall on the just and the unjust alike.

Those concerned with defending anthropomorphism, in any sphere, can do so positively or negatively, or perhaps one should say in an offensive or a defensive spirit. A positive anthropomorphism, one that is on the offensive as it were, puts forward a specific doctrine, a doctrine which if true restores a 'meaningful moral order' to the area which it is meant to cover.

A negative or defensive anthropomorphism is not concerned with putting forward a specific positive picture, but merely with demonstrating that theories which necessarily make the world 'meaningless', which inescapably exclude meaningful visions, *cannot* be true. How can this be shown? Most commonly, perhaps, we show that a class of theories is false by establishing that some other theory, incompatible with all the members of that class, is true. But negative or defensive anthropomorphism (by definition) does not put forward any specific theory of its own. It has an alternative way, and one which we may (in accordance with the terminology of its propounders, I think), call epistemological. It argues that the very nature of knowledge, in the sphere in question, is such that no non-anthropomorphic theory can possibly be true. This leaves the field open for anthropomorphic theories, without however at the same time positively singling out any one of them.

The present argument will be concerned with these negative or defensive, epistemologically based anthropomorphisms. It would be an exaggeration to say that positive anthropomorphic theories are absent from the intellectual scene. They do exist, in social theory, on the fringes of medicine, in psychotherapy, and perhaps elsewhere. One of the appeals of psychotherapeutic techniques is, I suspect, precisely that they restore a kind of moral order: people find it more tolerable to believe that the fault is in themselves, than that they have been struck arbitrarily, accidentally, for no purpose whatever. In the joke, the psychiatrist tells the patient: 'The reason you feel inferior is that you *are* inferior. That will be 20 guineas.' In fact, he does not say anything as brutal. He tells the patient that his suffering is the corollary of something else, and has its roots within him. The manifest advantage of this is that it makes the suffering manipulable, but the latent, and perhaps more important advantage, one which survives the possible failure to manipulate and remove the misery, is that it makes it meaningful, and at least quasi-deserved. I think we prefer to be guilty, rather than the objects of entirely accidental 'punishment' which, somehow, is *more* humiliating.

In brief, positive, moral-order-preserving anthropomorphic doctrines do exist, even in the field of 'modern' theories, i.e. those formulated in our time and in a contemporary idiom. But within philosophy we find more commonly the negative, defensive versions, which defend a whole class of meaningful visions against a whole class of, as it were, inhuman ones. The 'meaningfulness' defended need not be a crude picture in which sinners are punished and virtue prevails. It is rather a world in which things happen and are understood in human terms, in some sense to be clarified further. These thinkers are not concerned or able to demonstrate that the human world is a *moral* tale, with justice and truth vindicated and some noble purpose attained: but they are concerned to show that it is, at least, a *human* tale. They wish to defend *the anthropomorphic image of man* himself.

This aspiration is by no means self-evidently absurd. The requirement that human activities and institutions should be interpreted in human terms does not have the offensiveness which nowadays immediately attaches to the requirement that *nature* be seen in human terms. *That* requirement offends both our tacit autonomy of nature principle, and our rejection of a-priorism. (These two might be considered in conflict, but anyway, I think we hold them both.) Hence modern anthropomorphism is doubly transformed, it has undergone two shifts: it has shifted its area (from nature to man), and its grounds (from substantive to epistemological). The *in*human interpretations against which the negative, defensive anthropomorphist guards us may be various, but some of their forms are very notorious: materialistic, mechanistic, deterministic, 'external' causal explanations.

Anthropomorphic or idealistic thought (as we may call it with reference to its contrast, and in order to bring out a certain continuity) has undergone another interesting development, in addition to the shift from nature to man and from substantive to epistemological considerations. This development concerns the *terms* in which the contrast with matter, to mechanical causation, etc., is conceived. Roughly: idealism has moved first from stuff to subject, and then from subject to meaning.

Throughout, the requirement is always to establish a *dis*continuity, between the area abandoned to mechanism or what have you, where anthropomorphism is abandoned, and the redoubt area where the human is to be preserved. But the redoubt is conceived differently at the various stages. Descartes' thinking substance is conceived as substance, in the image of extended substance, and somehow parallel to it and co-ordinate with it. Kant has no truck with a substance-self (a paralogism, this), but for him it is the cognising and acting subject who provides a bearer for those crucial human characteristics (freedom, responsibility, validity of thought), for which there is no room in nature.

The recent form of idealism with which I am now concerned does not attempt to reassure us by telling us that, as cognisers and agents, we may be allowed a kind of inner emigration from nature: it tells us, instead, that meaningful action, as such, is exempt from nature, in the sense that it is not susceptible to the kind of explanation held to be appropriate in nature, with its attendant moral inconveniences. The outstanding and most uncompromising formulation of this view is found in the work of Mr Peter Winch, notably in *The Idea of a Social Science*, London, 1958.

This book is, and is intended to be, the working out of the implications of L. Wittgenstein's mature philosophy for the social sciences. It is in fact meant to be more than this, in as far as Winch believes that these implications are not something marginal or tangential to that philosophy, but on the contrary are altogether central to it. (In that I think he is entirely right.) Likewise, he does not consider these implications to be marginal or tangential for the social sciences either: on the contrary, he believes that they reveal the central and most important features of those sciences. Winch's book has certainly made an impact on those concerned with the philosophy of the social sciences.

All this gives it a double interest. The central part of what he has to say about social sciences and hence (whether he intends this or not) about actual societies, seems to me profoundly and significantly wrong. Hence it has the interest of an influential and well-formulated expression of an (in my view) mistaken theory. But it also has another interest. It constitutes the best, most elegant and forceful, if quite unintended, refutation of Wittgenstein—one far more forceful than any stated by a deliberate critic. If WM is to stand for

'Wittgenstein's mature philosophy', and ISS for the position argued in Winch's book, the situation is roughly as follows:

$$WM \to ISS \qquad (1)$$
$$\text{but ISS is absurd} \qquad (2)$$

therefore WM is absurd.

When I say that ISS is absurd, I mean that it stands in blatant and manifest contradiction with obvious and salient features of both human societies and the practices of social scientists.

Mr Winch does not think that he is doing methodology at all, and would deny that he is interfering with the specific methodology of social scientists. He would, on the contrary, maintain that he is merely clarifying what the social sciences in general amount to, something they share at an abstract level, and that this does not affect the specific research strategies which may be adopted locally in this or that subject, or for this or that problem. This image of his own position and its implications seems to me quite mistaken. For one thing, Winch does say harsh things about some, at any rate, methods or aspirations of social scientists, e.g. the use of the comparative method or the pursuit of causal explanations. A theory cannot be all at once a condemnation of some methods, *and* methodologically neutral.

What underlies Winch's wrong assessment of his own position at this point is simply a preconception, an *a priori* philosophic idea that one can clarify what social knowledge is in general without prejudice to its specific tools. But this preconception has no intrinsic authority: it must be judged in the light of whether in fact Winch's position does or does not have methodological implications, and if it does, the preconception must be withdrawn. The preconception must not be invoked as a reason for why the methodological difficulties must be based on a misinterpretation of his position! In fact, methodological implications, negative and positive, do follow. And more than this: not merely a mistaken methodology, but also quite mistaken substantive beliefs about concrete societies, do follow from Winch's position.

If this is so, and if proposition (1), on which he and I agree, be granted, one should have thought that only a critic of Wittgenstein would have gone out of his way to establish that WM entails ISS. But this, interestingly, was not Winch's case. He is anxious to establish (1).

The steps condensed into (1) are, however, of some interest.

Wittgenstein's central doctrine was the account of meaning in terms of use. Meaning was not reference to an entity, be it transempirical (various forms of Platonism), be it a range of actual or possible sensations (various forms of empiricism): it was, on the contrary, the employment of an expression in diverse concrete contexts. These contexts were endlessly diversified, and were parts of 'forms of life'.

This is the form in which the doctrine first made its impact, and, as indicated, it was in this form aimed primarily against rival theories of meaning, notably those contained in either transcendentalism or empiricism. It does not in this form *seem* to have any particular relevance to the social sciences.

Winch's interest is that he was the first, at any rate from within the movement, to read the doctrine in the reverse direction and work out fully its implications. If 'meaning=use', then 'use=meaning'. Of course, no one actually formulated the first equation *as* a formal equation (which would give us the premise for the second, reverse order reading), and in any case, it is not very clear what the thing means when formulated in reverse order. Nothing in the present argument hinges on this: I use this merely as a kind of expository device, to bring out the underlying pattern of Winch's argument.

The inference obtained by inverting the order, as it were, reads roughly as follows when expanded into more intelligible English: if the meaning of expressions is their employment, then, in turn, it is of the essence of the employment of expressions (and by an independent but legitimate extension, of other social behaviour), that it is meaningful. This gives us a kind of mnemonic device for understanding the genesis of Winch's position. We can see why, all at once, he can claim (rightly, in my view), to be following the Master, and yet find in a hitherto apparently unsociological doctrine, *the* 'Idea of a Social Science'. Where Wittgenstein taught philosophers not to ask for the meaning but for the use, Winch advises social scientists not to look for the cause, but for the meaning. Social behaviour is essentially meaningful: to understand it is to understand its meaning. It cannot but have meaning: the fear that understanding might reveal it to be the slave of antecedent causes (thus being 'explained' by them) turns out to be an error, and one demonstrably such in *all* cases: one, it appears, arising from a fundamental error concerning the very nature of social understanding. This is where the idealism comes in: remove this one error, and we are freed forever, by an omnibus proof, of the bogies of determinism, mechanism and so on.

'One appears to be attempting an impossible task of *a priori* legislation against a purely empirical possibility. What in fact one is showing, however, is that the central concepts which belong to our understanding of social life are incompatible with concepts central to the activity of scientific prediction' (ISS, p. 94).

What, incidentally, *is* it for an action to 'have meaning', or, in as far as this is meant to be a defining characteristic of an 'action', for an event to become an action through possessing meaning? I think it corresponds roughly to what we would, in unselfconscious unsophisticated moments, describe as 'being lived through consciously from the inside, as it were'; but Winch, of course, in accordance with the principles and customs of his movement, does not operate with notions such as 'consciousness', 'inside', etc. Instead, an event acquires meaning through the fact that it is conceptualised by the agent with the help of shared concepts—and for Winch all concepts are necessarily shared[1]—and that the conceptualisation is essential to the very recognition of the event. Example: a man 'gets married' not merely by going through certain motions in church or registry office, but by possessing the concept of what it is to be married. If the concept were lacking, the same physical movements, in the same places, simply could not be classified as 'marriage'. For Winch, it follows from the fact that an event 'has meaning' that it cannot be caused.

The manner in which this position is extracted from Wittgensteinian premises is interesting and throws light both on those premises and on Winch's idealism. One crucial step has already been stressed: it consists of reading backwards the tie up between meaning and social behaviour, and instead of invoking this connection to destroy both Platonic and empiricist theories of meaning, using it instead to establish that 'meaningfulness' is an essential attribute of social conduct, *and* that this excludes causal, mechanical explanation. But there are other crucial steps.

Winch himself highlights these crucial Wittgensteinian premises. On page 40 of his book, he quotes from Wittgenstein's *Philosophical Investigations* 'What has to be accepted, the given, is—as one could say—forms of life.' The first wave of Wittgensteinians, including the Master himself, using this perception merely to beat rival theories of language, did not worry much about the fact that 'forms of life' (i.e. societies, cultures) are numerous, diverse, overlapping, and undergo change. Which of them is to be accepted? All of them? Or each of them, on the principle 'When in Rome do as the Romans do'? But what happens when these 'forms' are in conflict, or when one of them is in fundamental inner conflict?

These questions, obvious though they be, did not seem to have been raised in the course of what I called the first wave of the movement. The significance of Winch is that he has pondered on the fact that others (i.e. social scientists) have also taken an interest in 'forms of life', and tried to bring their concern in contact with the invocation of 'forms of life' in philosophy. The oddity of Winch is that he has used this connection not in a *reductio ad absurdum* of Wittgenstein, but in an attempt to set right the social sciences. Because: the multiplicity, conflict (inner and outer), and change, all undergone by 'forms of life', present a crucial, indeed on its own terms insoluble, problem for a philosophy which would treat them as something 'to be accepted', as 'the given'. For the point about forms of life is that they do not always, or even frequently, accept themselves as given, as something to be accepted. On the contrary, they often reject their own past practices as absurd, irrational, etc. Hence the recommendation of acceptance becomes internally incoherent. It has the form—'Accept whatever X says as true', when, in fact, (a) there is a number of mutually inconsistent sources called X, and (b) some Xs say: 'What I have said in the past is false'. (There are interesting historical precedents for this incoherence. In the seventeenth century conflict between the Papacy and the French Crown, the Papacy in the end ordered its French supporters to accept the authority of the Crown. Hence the acceptance of the authority of Papacy entailed . . . its rejection. During the Second World War, the leader of the American Communist Party instructed the members to 'embrace capitalism'. Hence the acceptance of the authority of Moscow entailed its rejection. Similarly, the acceptance of the ultimacy of 'forms of life' has just this paradoxical consequence.)

Both the argument from plurality and the argument from self-rejection or self-criticism is disastrous for the general position. The early Wittgensteinians simply did not think about societies and social change, and *given* this, it is at least in some measure understandable, why they did not notice this decisive weakness in their position. (What is not intelligible is how any man, in the mid-twentieth century, can be oblivious of social diversity or change.) The oddity of Winch is, as stated, that he is aware of both—and in particular of diversity— and still holds on to the initial premisses.

Let us take the problem of plurality first. Like the other problem (of social self-criticism), it imposes a dilemma on anyone holding the initial premisses, a dilemma neither of whose horns is acceptable. But Winch is clearly aware of this particular dilemma, and firmly embraces one of the available alternatives. Hence to explain the dilemma is also to explain the genesis of Winch's position.

The initial position is: 'forms of life' are ultimate, they cannot be criticised from some external viewpoint, by some independent standard. There is no such standard. There is no external reality in terms of which forms of life, 'languages', could be judged, for the distinction between that which is real and that which is not only occurs within a language, a form of life.[2]

The first dilemma is this: does this acceptance embrace *all* cultures, or only one?

Either answer entails intolerable consequences. Suppose that only one (or, for that matter, a limited set) is 'accepted': it necessarily follows that it must be selected by some principle of selection. This must be stateable and some reasons should be available for preferring it to other principles or selections. There is of course nothing absurd about this position as such (and I happen to believe that something like this is true), but it is in blatant contradiction with that central Wittgensteinian doctrine, taken over by Winch, to the effect that one cannot seek external and general criteria for the validation of linguistic or conceptual custom. If *selection* is to take place, then it follows that some principle is being employed. This means, in turn, that philosophy must return to the place which in my view it should never have left—the attempt to formulate and defend criteria which are more than mere descriptions of *de facto* custom.

Winch firmly commits himself to the other alternative. The trouble with this branch of the fork is quite different from the first: it does not, at least immediately, lead us to the implicit assumption of extra-cultural norms and hence the contradiction of the initial assumption. It leads us to recognise a multiplicity of 'forms of life', each with its own criteria of distinguishing the real from the unreal, and none of them competent to judge the others. Repeatedly, this is the picture Winch sketches and to which he commits himself. In other words, he commits himself to a profound conceptual relativism: contrary to what, for instance, Sir James Frazer and most of us think, scientific language is not to him superior to the witchcraft language of (say) the Azande, even when they appear to be explaining the same type of phenomenon. 'Reality is not what gives language sense. What is real and what is unreal shows itself *in* the sense that language has' (italics Winch's). Later, in the same article,[3] the Wittgensteinian premiss is made very clear: 'Oracular revelations (among the Azande) are not treated as hypotheses and, *since their sense derives from the way they are treated in their context*, they therefore *are not* hypotheses' (first set of italics mine, the second Winch's).

Winch does, it is true, reject *individual* relativism (quite consistently with his position—indeed his position strictly requires this): '. . . it is *within* the religious use of language that the conception of God's reality has its place, though, I repeat, this does not mean that it is at the mercy of what anyone cares to say . . .' (italics Winch's). A use of language, it appears, does convey reality, though not through the agency of 'anyone', i.e. not, presumably, through any one individual. (We shall have very significant trouble with the question of how many individuals, or under what conditions of differentiation, constitute *a* use of language. A single atheist—or, to strengthen the case, a single logical-positivist—denying that the term 'God' has any meaning, makes no difference. But how about the Soviet Union?)

He also rejects, more obscurely, 'an extreme Protagorean relativism, with all the paradoxes that involves'. No indication is given how such an 'extreme' kind differs from the kind he actually puts forward (without claiming the name, though I do not believe he would repudiate the title 'conceptual relativism'). The paradoxes certainly are not avoided.

There can be no doubt about this relativism itself. Concerning the Zande acceptance of witchcraft and the European rejection of it, Winch says '. . . it is clear . . . that [Evans-Pritchard] would have wished to add . . . the European is right and the Zande wrong. This addition I regard as illegitimate . . .'[4] In other words, witches or the processes alleged to occur according to witchcraft belief, are, like the deity, though not apparently at the mercy of *individual* belief, at the mercy of a whole style of thought. For the Azande they exist, as scientific entities exist for us, and no one is entitled (or rather: no one can meaningfully) to judge between the two!

As Winch does not surreptitiously return to some hidden standard by which to sort out valid language from invalid, but accepts all languages as valid—by their own lights, and there are for him no others—we must consider why such relativism is untenable. It is worth noting that it is intuitively repellent to pretend that the Zande belief in witchcraft is as valid as our rejection of it, and that to suppose it such is a philosophical affectation, which cannot be maintained outside the study. I should not myself urge this point against a position—at least, not in isolation. But it ought to worry Winch, who belongs to a tradition in which the fact that a given belief can be held by the philosopher in the study, but not in life, is held to be a serious, or crucial, or indeed *the* crucial, objection to a belief. Such a state of philosophic schizophrenia is held to be an indication that the philosopher in question divorces, in his study, some terms which he uses, from their real (and hence authoritative) use in his real life, and is of course incapable of carrying this divorce over into his real life. Had he but remembered the real use, *and* the fact that this is what gives those terms sense, he would not have embraced the schizophrenia-engendering doctrine. There is thus a pragmatic contradiction within Winch's position.

There is another objection which is frequently urged against any kind of relativism, and that is that it leads to a paradox when applied to itself.

This objection is not applicable to Winch, or at any rate not immediately, for he gives us no warrant to apply his relativism to his own argument. He makes an exception, not merely for himself, but for philosophy in general. (Presumably for sociology as well, in view of its near identity, in his view, with philosophy.) This view involves its own and very considerable difficulties, but it does at any rate exempt Winch from the conventional and facile charge to which relativists are often exposed.

We are arguing that Winch's account of the social sciences is incompatible with certain conspicuous and important features both of the methods of social sciences, and of societies themselves. The latter class of objections—the contradiction between what Winch says and social reality itself—can be made very concrete. Here again there are two subclasses: the contradictions which arise from certain features internal to individual societies, and those which arise from the existence of a multiplicity of societies and their mutual relations.

Let us take the former. Consider certain crucial events/ideas/forces in Western history, events without which quite obviously no adequate account of Western society can be given: Christianity, the Reformation, the Enlightenment. All these have something in common with each other and with other movements or systems of ideas which could be added to the list: they are inherently, essentially, committed to proselytising and to a kind of exclusiveness. In this they may be wrong, intellectually or morally: but there can be no doubt about the beliefs themselves. These are not, as it were, tribal deities, willing to accommodate tribal deities of neighbouring communities on terms of tolerance and equality. On the contrary, they contain a claim to unique, exclusive and absolute truth.

For Winch, philosophical theories of meaning, and substantive beliefs of concrete societies, are as it were at different levels and do not, cannot, come into conflict. In fact, however, absolutist and exclusive and proselytising faiths do come into conflict with his contextualist theory of meaning and its appendage, the contextualist theory of truth. Take the example of a Reformer. He says, in substance, that the Divine Will is revealed and accessible in a set of Scriptures, and that its meaning is accessible to the individual conscience. If social practice, the ongoing tradition which claims allegiance to those scriptures, the organised church, is in its real activities at variance with the content of the independently knowable Word—well, then those practices, that church are in error and must be reformed.

That, at any rate, is what the Reformer claims. My argument does not require the Reformer to be right: it merely requires Reformers to be an important social phenomenon—and this can hardly be denied. And what is true of Reformers is *mutatis mutandis*, true of proselytisers of Christianity itself, of believers in Natural Law, of rationalists of various kinds, and of many of the more radical kinds of secular reformers.

An agent of the Counter Reformation, equipped with philosophic prescience, might have replied to our ideal-typical Reformer as follows: but your insistence on the independent meaning of Scripture and its alleged divergence from the actual practices of the Church betrays, on your part, an illusion concerning the nature of meaning. If the sacred formulae seem to you in conflict with practice, ought you not to remember that what gives formulae meaning is the real social context in which they occur? It is *your interpretation* of the formulae, and not reality, which is at fault! Thus, an infallibility of the real social context, of e.g. the concrete church, could easily be deduced from a theory of meaning . . .

I do not know whether any of the theoreticians of the Counter Reformation employed variants of this argument. But the secularised descendants of the Reformers, the thinkers of the Enlightenment, certainly encountered it from romantic and conservative political theorists. Rationalist rejection of superstition had the same logic, in this respect, as Protestant rejection of idolatry.

In brief: a very important segment of the *subject matter* of the social scientist, (i.e., certain civilisations, broad movements, etc.) holds beliefs which are themselves in contradiction with the principles which, according to Winch, must guide the social scientist. If whole societies believe that what they believed in the past is profoundly absurd, then Winch, who is committed to excluding the possibility of a whole society being wrong in its belief, is caught out, either way: either the pagans were wrong, or the Christians were (*in supposing the pagans to be wrong*); either the pre-Reformation Church was wrong, or the Reformers were, in supposing *it* to be wrong; either those addicted to superstition were wrong, or the rationalists were wrong . . . One way or the other, *someone* must be wrong!

It is instructive to observe Winch's attempts at coping with this question, crucial for his position, and in my view quite insurmountable. He makes a number of attempts:

(1) A shift from a descriptive or analytical position to a normative or prescriptive one. He says, in effect: Yes, there are proselytisers, missionaries, who attempt to interfere in the customs and beliefs of other societies, and remould them in the image of an abstract ideal. But they are *wrong*. They *ought not* to do this.[5]

It is difficult to see how this shift to a normative viewpoint can be either justified or squared with the general purpose of Winch's argument. That he should consider this possible at all is connected with his assumption of a philosophical vantage point outside and above all concrete societies and their beliefs. The fact that from this vantage point certain social trends—notably missionaries, proselytisers—should become open to a supposedly neutral, dispassionate condemnation, makes one suspicious of the alleged neutrality of that viewpoint. This Instant Olympus looks rather like a camouflage for one of the concrete beliefs (for a certain romantic traditionalism), and its neutrality is quite spurious.

One could deal with his whole argument here in summary fashion and say that the social sciences are just as concerned with intolerant exclusive beliefs as with tolerant tribal ones, with reformers as much as with traditionalists, with rationalists as much as with believers: a methodology which cannot explain one side of this antithesis, and turns into an ethic, is useless.

But we need not be quite as summary as this. A small dose of normativism might be tolerable even in an analysis or a methodology.[6]

Above all, this would be in total harmony with Winch's general Wittgensteinian position.

That position can be summed up as follows: men speak and live their lives and pursue their manifold interests in the context of 'forms of life', cultural/linguistic traditions, and the concepts they employ derive their validity from, and only from, possessing a place in these forms of life. It is not the task of philosophy to interfere with these traditions. But from time to time misguided philosophers (of the old kind) arise, who, under the mistaken and generally tacit belief that concepts are all of some simple kind, and that they can possess a universal and as it were extra-cultural justification, try to judge, and in effect misinterpret, those actually used concepts, in terms of those supposed external norms. It *is* the task of philosophy to neutralise this error, to protect actual traditions from such misguided interference.

Given such a picture, a small amount of normativism does indeed follow: the philosopher is neutral vis-à-vis cultural traditions proper, (and indeed, this is Winch's view), but he is professionally entitled, or obliged, to castigate that small minority of transgressors, e.g. missionaries, who would interfere with other cultures, or their own, in the name of a supposed universal norm, of a kind of validity which is more than the recognition of a place of a concept in a culture.

The trouble is, however, very simple: *these transgressors are not a minority.* They are the majority. They are not deviants. They are the mainstream of at least one important tradition. Missionaries are not foolish and redundant excrescences from e.g. the Christian tradition: they are of its essence. It is not a contingent, but an essential feature of Christianity, that the Gospel should be spread!

In other words, the normativism does not come in a small dose, but is, in effect, overwhelmingly large. Think away the missionaries who spread Christianity over Europe, the Reformers who reformed it, the Rationalists who secularised it—and what is left of the European tradition?

(2) A second, and equally desperate way out for Winch is to claim that the offensive doctrines—the absolutism, exclusiveness, universalistic claims—whose proscription would, absurdly, exclude most of the European tradition from the European tradition, are not really part of it at all, but 'about it': that, for instance, the belief that some god is the only true god is not part of the belief in him, but a belief

about the belief—a philosophical accretion, as it were: something which only occurs to the theoretician looking at the belief from the outside, not to the real, practising believer.[7]

There may well be tribal religions concerning which something of this kind is true. The believer subscribes to certain ritually consecrated formulae which, interpreted naturally—i.e. on the assumption that the words employed here have the same meaning as they do on other similar occasions—convey a certain meaning: for instance, that the deity created the first man X, where X is also known to be the general tribal ancestor, descent from whom defines membership of the tribe and the moral community. Taking this belief literally, it has certain strange consequences: either, that all men are descendants of X, as the first and only created man, and hence that all men are also members of the tribe—which in fact is in contradiction with the practice of treating foreigners as non-members—or, alternatively, that foreigners are non-human. In fact, and in contradiction of the implications of the legend, the actual practice of the tribe recognises foreigners as humans who at the same time are not members of the tribe.

In this case, it could certainly be false to credit the tribe with holding the manifest implication of its proclaimed belief (i.e. that either all humanity can lay rightful claim to its tribal membership, or that some beings normally considered human are not really such). The context in which the initial belief is asserted is one which does not lead the believers to ask themselves which of the alternative implications they accept. Hence they cannot really be credited with holding either implication.[8] Only an outsider to the usual practice would ask the question. He might, I suppose, be a member of the tribe acting in, as it were, a different capacity, but the question and its answer cannot really be credited to the tribesmen themselves. (But, as we have noted in connection with Winch's device (1), if the questioner is also a member of the tribe, the supposition that the questioning is only done in a kind of external capacity, as an honorary outsider, as it were, becomes quite absurd when the inner questioners become numerous, a real force within the society, or even the majority!)

But whilst the treatment of theoretical questions concerning the belief—concerning, to take the crucial example, its exclusive validity, for instance—can generally be credited to a real or honorary 'outsider' in the case of *some* tribal religions, it becomes quite absurd to do so in the case of the literate, scriptural world religions. Consider the following news item:

Pope Paul's ruling on Eucharist
    . . . Pope Paul yesterday published an encyclical letter upholding traditional Catholic doctrine on the Eucharist. . . . the Pope

reasserted . . . that the body and blood of Jesus Christ 'are truly and substantially present' in the consecrated bread and wine during Mass. The 6500-word document is believed to be the Pope's reply to a group of West European Catholic theologians who expressed the view that the bread and wine of the Eucharist were purely symbols . . .

(*Observer*, 12 September 1965)

At a pinch, one might perhaps allow Winch to say that the views of the group of 'West European Catholic Theologians' were 'about', and not 'within', their faith. But Pope Paul's encyclical letter, whilst as a reply to the theologians it must be on the same logical level as their error, is manifestly also an event, a pronouncement, *within* the Faith itself. This merely illustrates something terribly obvious, but something also in blatant contradiction with Winch's position: in the Western tradition (amongst others), a dialogue between the 'beliefs *within*' and the 'theories *about*' religion has become part of religion and belief itself.

Or take another example, crucial for Winch: the exclusiveness of the Muslim deity. The stress on Its exclusiveness, the classification of un-believers, the prescriptions for their treatment, all this is manifestly *part* of the religion itself, not a piece of speculation added on from outside by theoreticians.

(3) Winch's third device for coping with the fact that cultures themselves indulge in self-correction and self-condemnation is to assert that the corrections themselves *emanate from inside*, from the practice of the tradition itself, and thus do not lead to the paradoxes with which his critic would saddle him.[9]

But the paradox cannot be avoided where the self-correction also involves the view that the previous practice was radically irrational— the view, roughly, which the Reformers have of the mediaeval Church, or the Rationalists of the preceding periods of religious faith. The point of Winch's claim that the corrections somehow arise from within the practice is meant to be that each tradition still fails to rise above that collective solipsism, that private enclosure, with which in his view they are all credited.

But the view that the correction and its norms arise from inside is ambiguous and, on either of two possible interpretations, untenable. The two possible interpretations are: (a) that the corrections or their norms arise from within the society, *as opposed to other societies*, and (b) that they arise from within society as such, *as opposed to some extrasocial realm which houses norms of rationality*.

Taking interpretation (a): as a generalisation, this is simply false in the most straightforward, empirical sense. Sometimes, indeed, social change and new standards are endogenous. But, for instance, the diffusion of Christianity in early mediaeval Europe, or the diffusion of industrial-scientific society throughout the world in the modern period, to take two events which have made the world what it is, have, both of them, meant the transformation of societies by ideas and standards which were in no way the fruits of an inner development, but which, on the contrary, arrived from outside.

But let us interpret Winch's point here in the second sense. There is, I suppose, no way of forcing Winch out of that strange collective subjectivism, if he is determined to hold it. Some criteria of rationality seem to me quite independent of any social tradition, but I don't quite see how I could go about establishing this. But here we return to device (2) and the paradox to which Winch finds himself committed: societies themselves, when reforming their previous practices and beliefs, believe themselves to be acting under the guidance of an external, independently valid principle of rationality, and not merely externalising something emanating from their own nature. So— either they were systematically wrong in their earlier, rejected belief, or they are wrong in their new stance and their belief in its absolute justification. Either way, they contradict Winch. His only way out here is to claim that they speak with a different voice when they claim absolute justification, from the healthy voice in which they assert what are, in Winch's account, more basic, first-order beliefs. But this doctrine of the Two Voices and its total inapplicability to the major literate traditions has already been discussed.

Winch's theory can be destroyed either by appealing to the way in which the major and most interesting traditions actually view themselves, as in the above arguments, or equally by appealing to the multiplicity of existing traditions. This second line of attack, however, calls for some elaboration. Winch's theory and attitude would be, for practical purposes, an acceptable one, *in a certain kind of world*. (It would still be, in an ultimate sense, false, in as far as even in a world designed to fit it, our actual world would remain a possibility.) But it is instructive to sketch out such a world. Ironically, it is a world in which there would be no room for Winch. But no matter: let us nevertheless imagine this world, Winch-less but observed and recorded by a for-the-sake-of-the-argument-Winch. What would this world look like?

Imagine a world populated by a set of fairly small tribes, discontinuous enough to have fairly little to do with each other and—here is an important characteristic of this imaginary world—of roughly equal cognitive power. Not one of these small, fairly discontinuous tribes possesses an understanding of its environment which would, numerically or in power, put it at a decisive advantage vis-à-vis the others.

For the sake of the argument we must now imagine at least two

philosophers in such a world. One of them is a bad, pre-Wittgen-
steinian thinker. The other is a kind of proto-Winch. The bad one
has succeeded, by luck, accident, or endeavour, in travelling from
one of the tribes to another, and his reflections have been stimulated
by the differences he has observed. He tries to judge the practices of
one tribe by the standards of another; or he tries to attain speculatively some standards independent of either; or he tries to combine
premises drawn from diverse traditions, or to convert members of
one tradition to the beliefs of another, etc.

At this point, he encounters the Ur-Winch, who expostulates:
'My dear friend—you are quite misguided. You are doing nothing
but mischief by trying to convert tribe A to the rituals and doctrine
of tribe B. The doctrines and rituals of tribe B developed in the
natural and social context of tribe B, where they make good sense and
perform a valuable role. But transplanted into the quite different
social context of A, they make no sense at all. There is no one reality
and one set of norms, for all tribes: there are different forms of life,
and each of them generates, or contains as an essential part of itself,
its own way of distinguishing the real from the unreal, the good from
the bad. And do not be misled by the fact that the traditions themselves change! They do, under the impact of new norms emanating
from their own practice; but it would be a total misunderstanding to
infer from this to suppose that they can or should change under the
impact of some outer standard.'

In an ultimate and fundamental sense, the Ur-Winch is still mistaken—because, as indicated, even in this hypothetical world, our
real world remains a possibility—but for most practical purposes,
in that kind of a world, he would be right.

But it is a fact of very considerable interest, that our world is
quite unlike this imaginary world. The world we do live in is one of
countless, overlapping, interacting traditions—so much so that, for
sociological purposes, it is extremely difficult to decide which units
are to be isolated for purposes of comparison. (This is, notoriously,
one of the crucial problems of the 'comparative method'.) Not small,
discontinuous, and roughly equal (in size and in cognitive and real
power) tribes: but overlapping civilisations of quite unequal cognitive and technical power.

We have seen how the Winchian collective solipsism, derived from
the Wittgensteinian treatment of 'forms of life' as ultimate and not
susceptible to external validation, is refuted through the fact that
some forms of life themselves refuse to treat themselves as ultimate.
It is equally refuted by the fact that, in the world as it is, we simply
do not have—and have not had for a very, very long time, if indeed
we ever did have—those self-contained units, which could be their
own standards of intelligibility and reality (and of everything else).

What we do have is a set of traditions so complex, so differentiated internally, that we do not know how to delimit our units—indeed any delimitation is largely arbitrary; and these traditions are so sophisticated, so systematically aware of conceptual and moral alternatives, so habituated to interaction, that it is quite meaningless to advise them to turn inwards.

Winch's philosophy illuminates the world we really do live in by sheer contrast; the real contemporary world illuminates Wittgenstein's position by drawing out its crucial implications. These two illuminations are closely connected. It is useful to approach them through considering the strange role of relativism in Winch and Wittgenstein.

For most modern thinkers, relativism is a *problem*: for Winch and Wittgenstein, it is a *solution*. Other thinkers start from the fact of the diversification of belief and morals, and try to find the touchstone of correct belief, etc. This, I think, is the general form of the mainstream of modern Western thought. (For instance: empiricism is, essentially, a theory of the touchstone of truth, or, in later forms, of meaning itself. Materialism is used in a similar way. The various forms of evolutionism claim to have a touchstone which grades degrees of validity, and which is moreover as it were democratically elicited from the specimens to be graded, instead of operating in the material from outside.)

But Wittgenstein and Winch *arrive* at relativism, they don't start out from it, and they arrive at it as a solution to quite another problem, the problem of meaning. Meaning, they say, is not an echo, a reduplication, a structural mirroring of the thing meant, aided perhaps by the struts of a formal framework (*this* was the rejected theory of Wittgenstein's youthful *Tractatus*): it is the possession of a place, a role, in a 'language', a 'form of life', a culture. Wittgenstein arrived at this solution in too exhausted a state to perceive that it raises further enormous problems, given the kinds of complex, interlocking, competing, internally diversified, and rapidly changing cultures which in fact make up our world. Nor did he seem to perceive the terribly obvious truth that *this* problem provides most of philosophy with its content: for had he noticed this, he could not have seen his own particular arrival at a position, which is a solution to him and a problem for almost everyone else, as *the* paradigm of philosophy, or as its euthanasia.

It is both characteristic and profoundly revealing that, despite the enormous importance which the notion of a 'form of life' plays in his philosophy, Wittgenstein in *The Philosophical Investigations* gives *no* example of it. Is *English* a form of life? Or only subcultures within the great world of English-speakers, such as, for instance, that of Cambridge dons, of the Gorbals, of West African patois?

Or must we, on the contrary, go to some larger *Kulturkreis*? Or would only self-contained tribes do?

As far as Wittgenstein himself is concerned, it is quite manifest from his writings that he did not bother to ask himself this obvious question. He had found a solution to his particular problem, the problem of how words come to have meaning: this solution was in terms of a highly abstract model, i.e. the possession of a role in a 'form of life', and although 'forms of life' were the cornerstone of this model, he felt no need to provide examples of them. In this, he was entirely true to himself. In his youth, he had elaborated a philosophy of meaning in terms of an abstract model in which notions such as that of a 'fact' or 'thing' played crucial parts. No examples at all were given: and the philosophy collapsed when he and others tried to find some examples, failed, and had the grace to ask themselves why they failed. The philosophy was then replaced by a new model, that of 'forms of life'. But once again—no examples! It is deeply ironic that Wittgenstein's general diagnosis of faulty philosophy is the conceptual intoxication with an abstract model, unchecked by comparison with real examples. His diagnosis certainly has at least one correct application.

The importance of Winch lies in the fact that he does try to relate the abstract model which he has inherited, to concrete examples.

If what matters is cultures, and these are the objects of the studies of social scientists, it follows that philosophy and social sciences have the same subject matter, and that the correct method in the one field is also the correct method in the other. From this, he tries— quite mistakenly, in my view—to inform social scientists of the correct method in their field, by deduction from what he considers the correct method in philosophy; whilst the proper procedure is, it seems to me, to argue the other way, and conclude to the mistaken nature of the method in philosophy, from its inapplicability to the concrete objects of the social sciences.

The importance of Winch lies in his attempt to relate the abstract model to reality; his error lies in doing great violence to reality in the process, instead of correcting the model by reference to reality. Some of the features of the real world which are incompatible with the model have already been stressed. One crucial one which remains to be stressed is this: in the world as we know it, cultures are extremely unequal in cognitive power. Some possess concepts and methods which enable them to attain some degree of understanding of their environment, and some possess such an understanding only to a minimal degree. To deny this cognitive inequality is an affectation, which can at most be sustained in the study, but not in real life. (Here is another profound irony of Wittgensteinianism: it fails the philosophic test which it has itself popularised, namely, whether a view can really be held, in the business of living, as opposed to being held merely in the special conditions of a kind of philosopher's licence. This is closely connected with the irony mentioned above: the reason why a view cannot be held outside the context of real life, is of course connected with a failure to look at real instances of the abstract model.) No one, least of all those who are deprived of it, has any doubts about the superior cognitive effectiveness of the 'scientific outlook'.

Similarly, no one really has any doubts about the cognitive inferiority of the pre-scientific outlook. It is in this obverse form that the situation comes to the notice of the anthropologist, of course: he frequently has to report beliefs of the form 'ox equals cucumber', 'wine equals blood', 'witchcraft causes death', etc. Are beliefs of this kind to be described as false and inferior?

Winch, quite consistently with his symmetrical relativism ('symmetrical' in the sense of being egalitarian as between cultures, refusing to judge any of them in terms of another or in terms of a supposedly external norm), rejects this condemnation. In the context of the practices and institutions in which they occur, these assertions—he holds—are *not* absurd. It is the interpretations which find them so which are at fault.

The first thing to note about this is that this 'principle of invariably benevolent interpretation' is in conflict both with the actual practice of social scientists, and with *any* possible practice on their part. In fact, they continue to translate or give account of the belief of distant cultures in terms which often make them plainly absurd. Cucumbers are not oxen, the laying-on of royal hands does not have any therapeutic effects, etc., etc. Why do we not admonish anthropologists, historians, etc., who come back with such reports, for translating so badly (or, perhaps, for translating at all!) as to give us the impression of absurdity? It is supremely noteworthy that Winch himself does not admonish Professor Evans-Pritchard, whose account of Azande witchcraft he uses, for misdescribing, or mistranslating, Azande beliefs; he merely criticises him for his tendency to suppose those beliefs false. Yet *if* Evans-Pritchard is basically at fault in being tempted to suppose Azande beliefs to be false (as we are all tempted, including, I believe, contemporary Azande), then surely his mistake occurred earlier—in his account of the beliefs, which seems to imply that Azande have faith in the causal connectedness of magical practices and certain consequences.

But, in fact, one cannot avoid these translations, which give the game away and highlight the strangeness of the belief. Many things over and above the belief in a causal connection may be involved—and, indeed, generally are—but that belief is *also* involved. Evans-Pritchard's account, which is left unchallenged by Winch, consists in large part of showing how these beliefs survive falsification. This would be redundant and irrelevant, if they were not in fact frequently falsified! The anthropologist's account, far from being committed to respect the truth, in its context, of the belief, as Winch claims, is in fact based on a recognition of its falsehood. Anthropologists do not generally give complex accounts of how a tribe manages to sustain the faith in fire burning, wood floating, etc.: indeed, it would require an anthropological account if the tribe managed to sustain a *denial* of these.

Nor is the anthropologist at liberty simply to seek some other, non-absurd translation. It is part of the role of witchcraft beliefs that it is held possible to *cause* harm in certain ways. Winch's 'principle of universal benevolent interpretation' would exclude, quite *a priori*, important social phenomena such as the social use of absurdity, ambiguity, etc. An absurd formula may, for instance, be used to highlight the solemnity of an occasion. A translation which emptied it of its absurdity, treating it, for instance, simply as the announcement of impending solemnity, would miss the fact that the absurdity is used as a means of conveying that something special is happening, and hence must be present, *as* absurdity.

The example of transsubstantiation is instructive and useful, particularly as it is drawn from the local culture and thus does not call for specialised knowledge for the appreciation of the issues involved. As we have seen, the recognised authority within the religion himself solemnly excludes 'symbolic' interpretations of it, such as the benevolent-anthropological one. Perhaps Winch would not accept the papal ruling, holding it to be an event *within* the 'form of life', and as such not binding on an outside philosophic observer. But surely any adequate account of the Catholic form of life must include a recognition of the fact that, whatever subtleties are present in the interpretation of a Catholic intellectual, to a peasant the doctrine means just what it says, which is highlighted by the fact that, as the papal letter stresses, the simple believer is distressed when encountering the sophisticated interpretations within the fold itself.[10] And let us remember: the point about miracles is that they are *miracles*. They are such not merely to the unsympathetic observer but also, and above all, to the participants.

Let us return to the interesting and illuminating question of relativism. For Wittgenstein, as indicated, it was a solution and not a problem. It was a rather special kind of relativism, with as it were only one term: in the abstract, a general relativism of 'forms of life' was formulated, but in application, only one form of life was considered—that of the academic philosopher himself, and his disciples. (This was the main basis of the appeal of this philosophy: it provided a justification for a 'form of life' which in fact was threatened by the implications of scientific revisions of our world-view. The philosophy in question provided an omnibus justification of the old view, and facilitated the discounting of the new implications by calling them 'metaphysical', and maintaining that they had the same root as quite artificial, genuinely 'metaphysical' revisions which were re-invented, as straw men, for the purpose.)

Winch has considered other forms of life and the implications of their existence and investigation (though not the implications of the fact that they live non-isolated lives and interact intensely and violently with each other and with our own 'form of life', however that is to be delimited). Consequently he *does* face relativism as a problem, not merely as a solution. He accepts it. This acceptance can be usefully considered a kind of solution. It is—and this is important for the purposes of my argument—a most *symmetrical* solution. It does not favour one form of life over another. It treats them all as equal.

My main contention here is that *no* symmetrical solution of this problem is acceptable. (The evolutionists had a symmetrical solution, which was the main source of the appeal of their doctrine: it 'overcame' relativism by seeing various forms of life as members of one great series, such that later or superior members of the series incorporated all or most of the merits of earlier members, whilst adding something more. In this way, all forms of life had some validity, but there was some over-all yardstick all the same. This solution is no longer available, if only because forms of life cannot be arranged into any neat and unique series in this manner.) Winch's solution is not merely symmetrical, like that of the evolutionists, but also rather static; all forms of life are equal. Even if they are credited with change, they all go their own ways. The starting point of one is not the terminus of another, they form no grand series.

When formulated in a very abstract manner, I doubt whether the problem of relativism has a solution. In this it may resemble the problem of solipsism, of which indeed it may be seen as a special variant, one in which cultural collectivities replace individual islands of consciousness. But if one considers the world as it really is— something which Winch refrains from doing—we see that there is a kind of solution.

The philosophical significance of the scientific–industrial 'form of life', whose rapid global diffusion is the main event of our time, is that for all practical purposes it does provide us with a solution of the problem of relativism—though a highly unsymmetrical one. (It is for this reason that no symmetrical solution can be entertained.) The cognitive and technical superiority of one form of life is so manifest, and so loaded with implications for the satisfaction of human wants and needs—and, for better or worse, for power—that it simply cannot be questioned.

If a doctrine conflicts with the acceptance of the superiority of scientific–industrial societies over others, then it really is out. This must not be misunderstood.[11] The cognitive and technical superiority does not imply or bring with it superiority in any other field. What it does is to bring along the *possibility*—no more—of a certain material liberation. On any moderately realistic estimate of human nature, as long as the price of decent behaviour was, in effect, total self-sacrifice (which was the case in the conditions of scarcity which characterise pre-industrial society), the prospects of decent behaviour were negligible. But thanks to the cognitive and technical effectiveness of industrial society, the *possibility*, though no more, is now present.

This effectiveness of scientific industrial civilisation and its diffusion are the central facts of our time. It must be accepted, but it does not uniquely determine the other aspects of our existence. The first task of thought is to understand and perceive the limits within which we operate, and the alternatives they offer.

For this reason, any symmetrical solution of the problem of relativism—which automatically ignores the crucial asymmetry of our situation—is erroneous and harmful. If in addition it obstructs social understanding by making sympathetic acceptance an obligation for all interpretation, by excluding the very possibility of false consciousness, in a quite *a priori* manner, then so much the worse. Wittgensteinianism proper led to a narcissistic and sterile observation of the alleged conceptual customs of one's own 'form of life'—sterile because, in fact, philosophic questions are *not* generated by misunderstandings of the working of concepts. The more thorough and realistic—but not realistic enough—application of this philosophy by Winch leads to a misunderstanding both of the real social situation—of the way real 'forms of life' are related to each other in history and notably in the twentieth century—and of the methods really employed by social scientists.

APPENDIX: ANTHROPOMORPHISM

I find myself in very substantial agreement with both the general position and the specific arguments put forward by Cohen and Watkins.[12] Consequently no very detailed additional comments are really called for.

Still, there is one point at which I am not too sure of my agreement with Watkins. It is perhaps ungracious for me to bite the hand which was raised in my support, for Watkins' argument is, as he states, put up to reinforce my own. My apology for this ungracious conduct is two-fold. First, the issue which may divide us seems to me intrinsically interesting, and well worth clarifying, irrespective of whether Watkins or I be right on this point. The interest of the issue is greater than the obligation of reciprocity, if such an obligation be admitted in scholarly matters at all. Secondly, I am not at all clear in my own mind what the correct answer is on this point, and find myself pulled in contrary directions in different contexts. Hence my observations are less in the nature of a polemic, than a fairly impartial exploration of an inner doubt.

To begin with, some comments on Watkins' summary of my own position. This does not seem to me entirely correct, and misleading in a way relevant to the issue I wish to raise. Watkins says (summing up my position): 'Let us agree that the study of nature should not be anthropomorphic and that the study of man can hardly avoid being anthropomorphic. Then what about the study of *society*—to which side should it incline?'

It is *not* obvious to me that 'the study of man can hardly avoid being anthropomorphic'. The fact that, tautologically, the subject matter of the 'study of man' is indeed *man* does not seem to me to entail that the *explanatory* concepts invoked must also be, in some sense further to be defined, *human*. The position of, let us say, behaviourists, to the effect that certain very human concepts ('consciousness') must be excluded, whether true or false, does not seem to me self-evidently absurd. There is one fairly straightforward sense in which the study of man can be 'non-human' in form: if it consists of causal explanations of human behaviour, in which the antecedents are events outside the range of ordinary human experience, and only accessible to the scientists with special equipment (for instance, microscopes).

Interestingly enough, on an earlier occasion Watkins himself held such a position,[13] allowing *psychology* to be possibly non-human in this sense, though not sociology. At that point, he seemed to consider the asymmetry between sociology and psychology to be the very reverse of what, by implication, he considers it to be in the present note.

In practice, however, my own doubts about the applicability of human explanations of human conduct are not inspired by a preoccupation with neurological or similar explanations. For the purposes of my present concern, there is no asymmetry between psychology and sociology. Neither, I suspect, is bound to be anthropomorphic; and sociology does not occupy some middle position, liable to incline either to the non-anthropomorphism of science or the anthropomorphism of psychology. From the viewpoint of my present concern, psychology and sociology stand or fall together.

My concern can be stated very simply. Our life is lived in terms of ideas drawn from the common stock of the society in which we find ourselves, or rather, from the over-lapping number of societies in which we are involved. For a variety of obvious reasons, we cannot avoid using those ideas. For one thing, we have to use *some* ideas. For another, whilst we might possibly introduce some innovations at one or two points, it is beyond the powers of any individual to re-fashion the lot.

These ideas which we take over have theories built into them and often presuppose a good deal about the nature of the world. These ideas and presuppositions can be false, and I believe they frequently are false or vacuous. (They may nevertheless be viable.) *Yoh-hee-hoh* contains little information about the social organisation of the Volga boatmen. Many conceptual accompaniments of activities contain no more.

It seems to me an interesting feature of modern life that a certain awareness of this is extremely pervasive. People both act on 'commonsense notions', and are at the same time aware that these 'commonsense notions' are cognitively inadequate and second rate. This is reflected in a number of well-known characteristics of modern life: the invocation of the expert when important decisions are taken, the expectation that the expert's language shall be specialised and unintelligible, the prestige of any unintelligibility when it suggests expertise, the artificial manufacture of such unintelligibility for the purpose of acquiring such prestige, the invention of ideologies whose appeal hinges on a claim that their concepts, underlying assumptions, and so on, are cognitively superior to those of commonsense. The fact that many such claims are spurious in no way undermines the plausibility of the under-lying feeling, to the effect that life takes place at two quite distinct levels: those of the concepts of daily life, which we cannot but use but which are grossly inadequate if not positively misleading, and another set of concepts which are accessible, at most, to some genuine experts, but which are cognitively adequate.

The ideological relevance of Winch is of course that he tries to reassure himself and others that this feeling is mistaken. Watkins' argument against Winch is meant to show that Winch may be right in those cases when all is well with some ongoing activity, but that it may become inapplicable, or requires great refinement, when that activity undergoes a cataclysm. In terms of his example, the concepts of cricket can be invoked to explain a cricket game which is proceeding satisfactorily, but not a situation in which the spectators pelt the umpire with beer bottles. My own doubts about the invocation of concepts internal to the activity itself extend *equally* to both situations, to stability and cataclysm.

It may be worthwhile to digress for a moment on the question of just what it is that makes concepts 'human' or 'non-human'. One can be a relativist or an absolutist about this. A relativistic position would be: concepts become 'human' simply through familiarity. Psycho-analytic or cybernetic concepts began by being 'non-human' when they were unfamiliar, explaining familiar concepts in terms of quite unfamiliar notions, but now that those concepts have become popularised and many people commonly use them to describe their own or others' behaviour, they have become 'human'. That is all there is to it. The distinction does not amount to much. Alternatively, one can treat the distinction as permanent and absolute. For instance, one can consider concepts such as 'purpose', 'consciousness' or 'responsibility' to be inherently and permanently human, whilst considering the concepts connected with causal determination as inherently inhuman. If moreover the two sets of concepts are mutually incompatible, and if one set of them is cognitively powerful and inherent either in the results or in the methods of science, whilst the other is a precondition of value, choice and responsibility, we are led to a very familiar philosophic problem.

Winch attempts to provide an omnibus validation and justification of the human concepts. It is instructive to compare him on this point with Kant. The difference is that Winch thinks that his aim can be achieved easily, that it is fairly obvious and that there is a straightforward mistake on the other side. Kant thought that it was terribly difficult, that the human concepts could only be saved at the cost of utmost philosophic exertion and of making the most difficult assumptions, which assumptions, though justified by this one important purpose, would otherwise not be justifiable. Winch thinks they are easily justified in themselves, irrespective of need. Secondly, Winch thinks he can save *all* human concepts, whatever they be, whereas Kant thought he could only save a very small number, the minimal and ultimate prerequisites of value, freedom and responsibility.

My own reaction to this endeavour is the following: much as one might wish to save our humanity from the corrosive effect of scientific or sociological explanation, I doubt whether we can do it in this way, either wholesale or selectively.

If we attempt to do it wholesale, we tend to finish up in a self-contradictory position: by trying to save *all* our notions, we at the same time, and self-contradictorily, condemn those of our common notions which themselves condemn the others. (We condemn that strong and important element in our shared consciousness which *accepts* the inadequacy of commonsense.) But I also doubt whether we can do it selectively, whether we can insulate and guarantee a re-doubt of both crucial and unimpugnable human notions.

This brings me back to my tentative disagreement with Watkins. If I understand his position correctly, he is a selective humanist, as opposed to the Winchian omnibus variety. His selective humanity, however, is different from Kant's. It does not select a minimal set of notions on the basis of their being the absolute prerequisites of responsibility etc. The basis for a selection is to be found in methodology, not in ethics (at least, not directly). The sociological explanation must be reintegrated into the model associated with the suggestive slogan of the 'logic of the situation'. This does not give us (at least immediately) responsibility and freedom, but it does give us *aim* and *belief* as the essential and irreducible elements of the human situation. An explanation in terms of the 'logic of the situation' is an explanation which shows us, given certain aims, given a certain environment, and given certain beliefs about that environment, how the behaviour which is to be explained naturally follows. If all sociological explanation ultimately has this form, it follows that we shall never need, for sociological reasons, to revise at least one variant of the 'human' view of human life, namely one which sees it as the resultant of the interplay of *purpose* with both environment and *belief* about environment.

The consideration which, at this point, tends to swing me over to Watkins' viewpoint is that indeed, the most satisfying kind of explanation in the social sciences is one which shows, given fairly crude and simple and recognised human aims, how these get canalised by existing circumstances into the social situation which requires explanation. The considerations, on the other hand, which sway me in the other direction are two-fold:

(1) Is it the aims and beliefs *as conceived by the participants* which matter?

(2) If it be granted, as I think it is, that there is a kind of regress here, that the explanation of one social situation invokes the assumption of a further *social* context in which the agents were operating, should the stress be on the ever *un*completed nature of this regress or on the fact that we are impelled to undertake it? Only the latter alternative favours Watkins' position.

Roughly: the general characteristics of societies, their culture and their language, which enable their members to conceptualise aims and beliefs about environments, and which consequently are presupposed by special explanations, are not perhaps correctly represented by the beliefs of those members themselves.

This is a big theme, and clearly cannot be dealt with here. But if this suspicion is correct, then the human interpretation of human beings cannot be vindicated in Watkins' selective manner, any more than in Winch's totally unselective one. Moreover, it is not the case that stable and customary situations are more open to 'inner' explanations than cataclysmic ones. It is true that in stable customary ones, customary notions are more easily accepted by participants (by definition, in effect), but this in no way indicates that those notions are veridical. On the contrary: harmony and consensus may provide opportunities for indulgence in wild ideological fantasy, or vacuity. Who will bother to check the ideologists, when all is going well?

NOTES

1 In a sense, Wittgenstein went beyond Durkheim: for Wittgenstein *all* representations are collective.
2 Cf. the formulation of this position in P. Winch, 'Understanding a Primitive Society', *American Philosophical Quarterly*, 1, 1964, 307–24.
3 ibid.
4 ibid.
5 Cf. for instance, a statement of Winch's in a broadcast on the Third Programme, 'Men and Things', 2 May 1961: '. . . this is a way of thinking which I wouldn't support at all . . . I am not generally in favour of missionary activities . . .' These are his comments on the universalist claims of some faiths, claims not mindful of cultural boundaries.
6 Hume was guilty of precisely this in his ethics. He gives a certain account of the basis of moral valuation— roughly, in terms of human convenience —and when he comes across *ascetic* values which contradict this account, instead of modifying the account, he *condemns* the 'monkish virtues'.
7 In the same broadcast, Winch says: '. . . the idea that these beliefs are universally valid is a view *about* the nature of these beliefs . . .' (Italics mine.) The contrast is, of course, with the *content* of the beliefs. The universalist claims are, according to Winch's view at least at that time, no part of the content of the belief!
8 It would however be disastrously wrong to conclude from this that what the members of the tribe do believe, does not have the implications in question at all, and must be interpreted as meaning something quite different, something more innocuous. The world is full of beliefs with unacceptable implications which are ignored for the

time being, till the moment comes when either the implication becomes attractive or, when its unacceptability can be invoked against the initial belief.
9 'Do not the criteria appealed to in the criticism of existing institutions equally have a history? And in whose society do they have that history?' Thus Winch, in 'Understanding a Primitive Society', op. cit. The answer he offers to these rhetorical questions is that it *must* be inside the society itself: '. . . outside that context we could not begin to grasp what was problematical.'
10 I have argued the case against the Principle of Universal Sympathy in anthropological interpretation, at greater length in 'Concepts and Society', *Transactions of the Fifth World Congress of Sociology*, Washington, 1962, 153–83; also above, pp. 18–46.
11 I hope it is not necessary to guard against the misunderstanding that what is being claimed is some version of a 'racialist' superiority of the societies in which the scientific–industrial form of life emerged. The form of life depends on the social organisation and ethos of the societies in which it occurs, and is manifestly independent of the 'genetic' composition of the populations involved.
12 In their comments on this article when it was first published: see P. Cohen, 'The Very Idea of a Social Science' and J. W. N. Watkins, 'Anthropomorphism in Social Science' in I. Lakatos and A. Musgrave, eds, *Problems in the Philosophy of Science*, Amsterdam, 1968, pp. 407–26.
13 Cf. J. W. N. Watkins, 'Ideal Types and Historical Explanation', *British Journal for the Philosophy of Science*, 3, 1952–3, 22–43.

5
THE ENTRY OF THE
PHILOSOPHERS

In general one might suppose philosophy to be a revolutionary subject, and sociology a conservative one. Philosophy questions basic assumptions, thereby rocking the boat. Sociology seeks the social roots of what, logically, may seem absurd. It shows that social structure has its reasons of which the mind knows nothing. It thus tends to stabilize the boat.

If this is the normal relationship between the two subjects, it was curiously and totally inverted in postwar Britain. Philosophy was fashionable during the earlier part of the postwar period, a time of national tiredness and complacency. It reflected this mood in an exaggerated and indeed caricatured form. The dominant fashionable school taught that we live, conceptually, in the best of all possible worlds, or as near to this condition as makes no difference, and that its own task was to defend the conceptual status quo and bring back to his senses anyone misguided enough to wish to change it. A minor aspect of this mood was a contempt for sociology. Its very name was a joke.

Yet ironically, at the very heart of the doctrine of the complacent philosophers, there had been *a* sociology. They might scoff at the name, but they used the thing. Their key premise may be an untenable one, but it was, unambiguously, one which concerns sociology. It ran: the cognitive, intellectual and other practices ('types of discourse') of a society can be validated, and can *only* be validated, by their place in a society and its culture (a 'form of life').

This view is absurd, and *very* little elementary reflection can show it to be such. (In ways to be shown, this reflection was evaded.) This view faces a simple dilemma: either *all* 'forms of life', all cultures and sub-cultures, with all the practices embedded in them, are valid, or only *some* of them are.

Take the first alternative. It leads to a complete and indiscriminate relativism: it will make witchcraft, in its context, as good as medicine, trial by oracle as good as trial by evidence, and so on. Whether or not such a view is acceptable emotionally, it is not acceptable logically. The modern world, and most others for that matter, simply does not contain neat isolable cultural units, inside each of which the internal norms could be sovereign. It contains a jumble of overlapping cultural units, internally divided concerning their own norms. They cannot face their choices by appealing to local norms, for there is a plurality of such norms and no one knows how to delimit that which is 'local'.

The other alternative is to be selective, to say that some practices are valid and some are not. There is nothing inherently wrong with such a view. (To my mind, it corresponds precisely to the truth of the matter.) But it comes into headlong conflict with another essential principle of the philosophy of complacency. If there is to be selection, and if the selection is not to be random and arbitrary, there must be *principles* of selection. These must then sit in judgment on the various practices, whether or not they are parts of 'forms of life'. But at the very heart of the complacent philosophy was the view that the actual employment and context of expressions (which in effect includes cognitive practices) is sovereign, and that to judge it in terms of extraneous and independent criteria is the cardinal sin.

Thus either alternative is disastrous, and there is no further one. How could so simple yet so conclusive a refutation be ignored? The answer is interesting. *Formally*, the philosophers of complacency embraced the first, the relativist alternative. *Formally*, their major premise was that all forms of life rightly confer legitimacy on the cognitive and other practices contained in them. But in practice, this universal licence was not used for all and sundry. In fact, it was only applied selectively, indeed with amazing and notorious narrowness. It was applied to the one form of life of which the philosophers themselves were members. Other forms were simply forgotten. This was a relativism with one term only. (If examples from the outside were considered at all, they were invented, pseudo-anthropological ones, customs of fictitious tribes invented ad hoc and abandoned as soon as some minor point was made.)

Thus the notorious narrowness of philosophy and the complacency of the wider society of the time were intimately connected. It was not merely that the philosophy expressed the mood and provided a pseudo-logical justification of it. It also depended on the wider mood for its own viability. Without the wider complacency, which excluded any sense of social alternatives, the philosophy could not work: the curious combination of formal relativism with de facto blindness to all alternatives would not have been feasible.

The general climate changed about 1960. A sense of malaise replaced the complacency. The problems of the time could hardly be contemplated without a sense of social alternatives. Thus a philosophy which combines a complacent relativism with de facto blindness to alternatives no longer suited the wider mood. At the same time and against the same background, sociology came to enjoy its present vogue. It came in because the sense of malaise seemed to call for change. Its prestige ranking rose as that of philosophy fell.

It would be pleasing to be able to report that at this point the philosophers abandoned the previous doctrine and also apologized to the sociologists for their contempt. Nothing of the kind. The doctrine merely became more ecletic, syncretic and watered-down, the élan and confidence went out of its propaganda, it became a relatively hole-and-corner affair, and there we shall leave it. But what is interesting is a minority of thinkers within this movement who, both before and after the sociological vogue, noticed the important connexion between their own views and sociology, and came to offer advice to the social scientists. They were not modest men. They came to teach, not to learn. Sometimes they did not even bother to learn the basic mores of the land they wished to enter as missionaries bringing methodological salvation. What they came to teach is not true, but it is interesting. Two important local examples are Professors Peter Winch and Alasdair MacIntyre.

Members of this trend have one central aim and one central idea. Their aim was the attainment or preservation of a humanist sociology, the retention of the human image of man. Is this threatened? The scientific ambition of many sociologists seems to threaten it. Science explains phenomena by subsuming them under laws. If sociology is to be scientific in this sense, it will do the same. For one thing, these laws will then deprive their subjects of their freedom. For another, these laws, being general, will only refer to some features of the situations they cover, features selected for their causal or other importance, and thus ignore the full richness and idiosyncrasy of individual cases. Take one example, the sociology of religion. If laws exist to be discovered in this field, they will, if they are to be worthy of the name, have to cover at least more than one religion each. But religions differ in doctrine. Hence the laws will have to be in terms of traits *shared* by religions (e.g. type of organization or ethos), and treat the variegated *content* of faith as irrelevant.

In brief, scientific sociology might explain men and societies not in terms of their own concepts and beliefs, but in terms of other concepts imposed by the sociologist from outside. The 'internal concepts' might be shown to be irrelevant or illusory. The thinkers under consideration are anxious above all to deny this possibility. On the whole they accept that anthropomorphism is out in natural science (though not all of them, and not unambiguously), but they wish to save *the anthropomorphic image of man himself*.

This is not an unworthy or a self-evidently absurd aspiration. Moreover, their central idea, which they took over from the fashionable complacent philosophy, was admirably suited to provide a premise for a would-be proof of such a conclusion. This idea concerns the intimate connexion of concepts and institutions. The complacent philosophy saw concepts *as* institutions (not quite in these words). It claimed to validate concepts by showing their institutional role in a society.

Now this idea was to be used in the reverse direction: institutions *are* concepts, or at any rate involve concepts in an essential manner. Social behaviour—e.g., the acts of a judge, teacher or merchant—can only be identified as verdicts, as instruction, or as trade, not in terms of some recurring patterns of physical movement, but in terms of the *meanings* they have for the participants. The meanings, the concepts, make them what they are. This is an old idea; now it was to be used with new vigour to establish the desired conclusion.

If the meanings make the acts into what they are, it seems to follow that any 'external' method, which ignores or denies those meanings, and replaces them by a new set of its own, must be mistaken. The comparative or generalizing method, which in the interest of achieving generalizations empties the conduct it deals with of its locally idiosyncratic content, its 'meaning', must be in error. A fortiori, behaviourism or causal explanation is out. Either social life is exempt from causation (Winch), or social causation is of a special kind, without generality, and internal to the ideas of the participants (MacIntyre).

A promising field for this doctrine would seem to be social anthropology. The anthropologist used to go out into a strange society and his first task was to learn its culture and language. Thus he would seem to fit the philosopher's recipe, of explanation by means of 'inner' concepts.

It is thus that Professor Winch eagerly uses the social anthropologist as the paradigm of the social scientist. But he is anxious to set the anthropologist right should he ever be tempted to suppose, in his account of tribal concepts, that

> the European is right and the [tribesman] wrong. This addition
> I regard as illegitimate and my reasons for so thinking take us
> to the heart of the matter.

The reasons are general in kind, not tied to any special example—so, by symmetry, they must apply to the concepts of all tribal societies, and are intended so to apply by Winch. His reasons are not some milksop *Wertfreiheit*: he is not urging that the anthropologist abstain from judgment, but that he should endorse the local concepts. The 'heart of the matter' to which he refers us is: 'Reality is not what gives language sense . . . the distinction between the real and the unreal and the concept of agreement with reality themselves belong to our language.' In other words, there is no independent and pre-eminent reality, but only a multiplicity of realities, each based on distinctions *within* given languages, and all languages are equal. Professor E. E. Evans-Pritchard is ticked off for being even tempted to suppose that his own language might be superior in its manner of drawing the real/unreal distinction to the language of the tribe he was studying. Thus Winch wishes to save our concepts, and those of all peoples, not merely from being irrelevant, but also from ever being systematically, collectively mistaken.

In fact, the anthropologist's practice does not fit Winch's account at all. The anthropologist must, it is true, learn what the local concepts are. But he must also give an account of how they work. To do this is not to endorse them. On the contrary, it generally requires that the concepts be treated with the utmost reserve and suspicion, and often involves the discovery that these concepts involve much falsehood. For instance, an anthropologist who shows how witchcraft beliefs 'function' and systematically escape falsification, must first of all know that they *are* frequently falsified. The account of how they evade the recognition of falsification presupposes that they are falsified. The commonest precept in the training of the anthropological field-workers is the rule that local concepts, 'stereotypes', must never be taken at face value.

The defender of Universal Endorsement will reply that what was falsified was not the local concept, but a mistaken translation of it into our language. This is just what Winch does say: 'Oracular revelations are not treated as hypotheses and, *since their sense derives from the way they are treated in their context* they therefore *are not* hypotheses.' (First set of italics mine.) One could hardly find a sentence illustrating more neatly just how the Context and Use (alias Treatment) theory of meaning leads inevitably to universal endorsement, of oracles, witches and all, as Winch openly wants it to. Sense, and hence the criteria of validity, are conferred by local use and context. Hence no concept with a local use and context can ever be wrong. (Individual application could be, but not the concept as such.)

Alas, this will not do. It would exclude, quite a priori, the systematic use of absurdity or ambiguity for social ends. Does this never occur, in our society or in others? Equally, it would exclude all those who, in the name of extra-social and trans-ethnic norms, would reform the local concepts and the uses to which they are put. Are we to ignore the men of the Reformation or of the Enlightenment? They were not unaware of the fact that the concepts of the unreformed church or of the *ancien régime* had their uses and context. It was those uses that they complained of. The issue is not whether they were right or wrong but that we cannot ignore them. The point is that Universal Endorsement becomes hopelessly self-contradictory when applied to such cases and averts its eyes. It cannot all at once endorse both the unreformed church and the Reformers, the *ancien régime* and the *philosophes*. Yet plainly they were parts of one and the same society.

MacIntyre's main or specially elaborated mistake concerns the nature of social causation (the quotations come from 'A Mistake about Causality in the Social Sciences', in *Philosophy, Politics & Society II*, Blackwell, 1963):

> Weber . . . presents us with . . . action as the conclusion of a practical syllogism . . . this *logical* relationship between belief and action . . . And because the achievement was this, the use of Mill's methods is *entirely* out of place; we do not need to juggle with causal alternatives. India and China did not strengthen and could not have weakened his case about Europe. For it is not a question of whether there is a purely contingent relationship between isolable phenomena. *And so constant conjunction is neither here nor there.* (Italics mine.)

This, if true, would be a great discovery indeed. A relationship (stretching over centuries, from early Calvinist divines to Benjamin Franklin!) which was generally believed to be causal (if it held at all), is now shown to be *logical*, to be independent of any comparative checks, of the normal scientific inquiry into whether a constant conjunction in fact obtains. It would seem to follow that statistical verification of such constant (or partial) conjunction therefore has no place in sociology. MacIntyre notices this implication, or has his attention drawn to it, and finds a new role for statistics:

> If I explain your action as a conclusion from your premises, I must be able to identify both actions and premises as yours. What the statistical material shows is that enough of the same people were Protestants and engaged in the relevant kinds of activity. Thus statistical inquiry has as great a role in sociology on this view as it ever had. But its correlations are put to uses which are not quite what classical sociology conceived them to be.

This passage is curiously, and one wonders whether deliberately, ambiguous. If it means that one must check statistically whether the *same* people both had certain beliefs *and* acted in certain ways, then what it says is quite correct. But then it does not warrant a correction of 'classical sociology' and, above all, it is in blatant contradiction with the earlier assertion that 'constant conjunction is neither here nor there'. What the statistics would in this case verify is precisely whether, or to what extent, there was *constant conjunction*. So one must assume instead that what is being said is that statistics establish whether that logical and indissoluble *whole* of belief-and-action, which needs no evidence of 'constant conjunction', is also regularly joined to its owners.

There is something truly surrealist about this suggestion that sociologists do, or could, or should chase naked owners of hitherto ownerless acts, and reunite them by means of statistics. Occasionally psephologists, archaeologists, and criminologists do deal with ownerless acts—votes without voters, tools without users, crimes without criminals—but in the overwhelming majority of cases we only encounter acts in the company of the actors. A world in which this were not so, in which statistics were required to reunite free-floating actions with their owners, would be a Psychedelic Happening indeed. First, this thinker overstresses the context-bound nature of acts; later he is willing to give us acts free not only of context but of agents! In the attempt to escape the consequences of one absurdity—a priori, 'logical', uncheckable connexions—a further and diametrically opposite, absurdity is committed.

This doctrine of privileged access to social causation, free from normal comparative checks on whether constant conjunction occurs, relying simply on the 'logical' apprehension of meaning, self-sufficient and self-validating—is but a special and as it were dynamic variant of Winch's principle of self-authenticating meaning. For one author, belief in witchcraft makes witches real; for the other, beliefs which entail certain actions make real, if not the actions, at any rate the nexus between the beliefs and the actions.

As if to underscore the Idealist nature of these arguments, MacIntyre says that an agent's action 'is identified fundamentally as what it is by the description under which he deems it to fall', and it 'must fall under some description which is socially recognizable as the description of an action'. To clinch it all, 'to identify the limits of social action in a given period, is to identify the stock of descriptions current in that age'! Our descriptions delimit social reality.

What is curious is that such a view should wish to claim to be 'Marxist'. (Like Winch's position, it is in fact a kind of philosophic variant of Christian Science. Christian Science seeks to exile pain from our world by excluding it from the 'stock of available descriptions'.) Marxism in fact has a theory, or rather a schema, of social change. Formulated in this kind of language, it runs roughly as follows: periodically, a time-lag occurs between the requirements of the basic productive activities of a society and its social super-structure, articulated in terms of the currently available 'stock of descriptions'. Such a disparity can only be set right by violent social convulsions, in which the reality breaks through that 'stock'.

This schema may not fit all cases of social change, but it probably fits some. But in any case, whether or not it fits any, it is quite impermissible to exclude it a priori! The bland manner in which MacIntyre introduces what is in effect an extreme Idealist theory of society and social change underscores something for which there is independent evidence anyway—namely that this kind of Carnaby Street Marxism is a form of Idealism. These exegeses of Marx, based on juvenilia of which he came to be ashamed in maturity, would leave one utterly puzzled why Marxism ever came to describe itself as a form of materialism, or why that remark about standing Hegel on his feet ever came to be made. For MacIntyre, there can be no possible reason for supposing that Hegel was ever the wrong way up.

Both Winch and MacIntyre are Idealist in the simple and crucial sense that (*a*) they offer us guarantees that the stuff of human and social life is made of thoughts, and (*b*) they offer us painless and uncheckable avenues towards alleged knowledge. The only thing which is new about this Idealism, which gives it an appearance of freshness, camouflages it and helps protect it from obvious criticisms, is that it uses the newish idiom of semantic philosophy.

There are, of course, interesting differences between the two positions. Winch would, as described, entirely close the eyes of the social sciences to phenomena of radical collective self-reform. MacIntyre, on the other hand, is in no way blind to these. He clearly thinks he is taking part in one of them. But where Winch's rather static Idealism would make sociology ignore these events, MacIntyre's dynamic version forces him to offer intellectualist accounts of them. The causes must come from within the 'stock'. He does in fact discuss two examples, the emergence of capitalism and of Stalinism. The merits of the specific explanations as such do not matter: the first is only intended to be a restatement of the Weberian thesis, and the second happens to be wildly fanciful. What does matter is that in his new view of causation, the accounts must always be 'internal', intellectualist: whereas in fact, while *some* such accounts may be true, there is no way of guaranteeing a priori that such accounts *always* apply.

The point is simple. MacIntyre wishes to reinterpret the nature of causation for the social sciences, to show that it is not regular succession *à la* Hume but the inner logical connectedness of the 'practical syllogism', the meaningful link between socially available descriptions and conduct. But is this diagnosis to cover *all* connexions in the life of a society, or only *some*? Either alternative is disastrous. The former one would imply that we live in a Realm of Meaning, into which no blind and extraneous necessity intrudes: an Idealist view, and absurd. But if only *some* connexions are of the 'internal' kind, then we can hardly tell a priori *which ones* and the methodological recommendations no longer follow. (The fact that an activity is accompanied by verbalization can hardly be sufficient evidence that it is a 'practical syllogism' in action.) We shall have to check by normal methods.

On the other hand, there is also evidence for another possible interpretation. Marx is carefully excluded from the list of those guilty of the mechanical mistake; yet he is also credited with the perception that certain things (democracy) cannot be realized in pre-industrial conditions. This certainly sounds as if there were brute, Hume–Mill causal obstacles in the way of pre-industrial democracy. (It can hardly be poverty of the 'stock of descriptions'. That would have been easy to remedy.) What particularly puzzles me on this interpretation is that pre-industrial early Calvinists, in the Weberian example, are granted entry into a Realm of Meaning, where the Practical Syllogism is king, whilst semi-industrialized Russians in the twentieth century must struggle, Laocoön-wise, with tentacles stretching from the Realm of Necessity (which may yet be self-invented?).

There is no way out of this jungle of muddles. What they basically illustrate is the difficulty of fusing, as MacIntyre tries, the guru whom he shares with Winch (i.e., Wittgenstein), with the guru whom Winch does not share (i.e., Marx). Wittgenstein taught that we are already in a Realm of Meaning, Marx taught that we may only enter it fully after some tribulations. Is it for now or only for the future? Are we there, or not yet? What *has* happened to the Realm of Necessity? Reading MacIntyre, one gets no idea of how this contradiction could be resolved. Perhaps it is one of those fruitful internal contradictions in the 'stock' which, on his view, provide the motive power for further development. One can only watch with interest to see whither it will propel him next.

Of course it matters little whether this form of Idealism is or is not acceptable as Marxism. I have no desire whatever to enter the internal disputes of Marxist theologians. What does matter is that it is totally unacceptable as sociology. Some may find all this reasoning too elusive and abstruse to seem either true or false. Hence it may be worth stating certain simple important and crucial facts, which are systematically denied by the views under discussion.

Understanding the concepts of a society is indeed important. But no amount of such understanding can ever give anyone a priori knowledge of causal connexions, and give a dispensation from the ordinary comparative checks establishing 'constant conjunction'.

The 'stock of descriptions' is both too narrow and too broad for social explanations. It is too narrow, in as far as it would ignore the intrusion of unconceptualized forces into social life. It is too broad in so far as most or all societies possess reserves of substitute and rival descriptions for the same acts and their members know how to invoke these according to convenience. No amount of logical insight can ever tell us which (if any) of the invoked 'descriptions' was really operative.

Institutions are indeed 'made' by the concepts of the participants. But, however embedded a concept may be in one or a set of institutions, this never proves the concept or the theories or assumptions built into it, to be true. Institutions may embody falsehoods, protect them, and be sustained by them. This then does not turn them into truths.

Human and social life consists of the interplay of 'conceptual' or 'intelligible' factors on one hand, and brute blind forces, extraneous to the ideas and illusions of a culture, on the other. There is *no* way of telling a priori which kind of factor is crucial at any one point, and no way of guaranteeing a priori (or at all) that we live in an untainted realm of meaning. We do not. A methodology which 'proves' anything of the kind, which hands out free certificates of citizenship of such a realm, is a fairy tale.

6

TIME AND THEORY IN
SOCIAL ANTHROPOLOGY

Philosophers have recently discussed whether an event may be caused by another later than itself. I shall discuss issues connected with a less obvious question—namely, whether events may be explained by *earlier* events. What makes this particularly interesting is that it has arisen, in a lively way, not from a marginal, doubtful and above all *ex officio* paradoxical pursuit such as psychical research, nor in formal philosophy, but from the day to day work of a respectable empirical discipline, social anthropology.

I propose to discuss a central theme—perhaps the central theme— of a recent book by Mr E. R. Leach, entitled *Political Systems of Highland Burma*, with the subtitle *A Study of Kachin Social Structure*, published in 1954 with a foreword by Professor Raymond Firth. This book was, rightly as far as I am qualified to judge, acclaimed by social anthropologists as one of the best and most important mono- graphs to appear since the war. Its author is a well-known and respected professional social anthropologist, who has received his training from men who are acknowledged leaders in that field; briefly he is himself not merely an initiated but an important member of the tribe of social anthropologists. I mention these facts to indicate that an examination of his thought will present a picture, not indeed necessarily of just what anthropologists think, but of the general manner in which they are liable to think and of the problems they face.

The theme which I shall discuss is certain considerations Leach puts forward concerning the relationship between the anthropolo- gist's thought and the reality he is investigating. This, quite plainly, is a philosophical theme. The dissection of what Leach has to say on this matter is of interest to philosophers in that it will show the very old epistemological argument re-appearing in a new and concrete setting, and re-appearing so to speak spontaneously. Leach is acquainted with philosophy and the bibliography of his work on Burmese hill tribes contains, oddly enough, the names of Vaihinger, Bertrand Russell and Wittgenstein; but it seems to me on internal evidence that the epistemological doctrine under discussion was suggested spontaneously in the course of grappling with his ethnographic material, and by his interpretation of anthropological theory —not by philosophers.

This dissection might, however, be of interest also to anthropologists, showing how very general considerations, which in the past have arisen from analysing the relation between thought and things as such, have entered anthropological theory in the misleading guise of something specially intimately connected with anthropological material.

Before proceeding any further it is necessary to tell the philosophical reader certain things about the intellectual milieu in which anthropologists operate. Anthropologists distinguish between ethnography and anthropological theory. Very roughly ethnography is supposed to mean the brute facts about a society, whereas theory consists of some kind of conclusions drawn from these facts, conclusions which need not be obvious. Indeed it is preferred if they are not obvious. An anthropologist naturally has a greater sense of achievement if he succeeds in showing that something which seems to perform one role in fact also or primarily performs another, or that something which seems to perform no role at all or one that only makes sense in the idiom of the society concerned (but not objectively), does perform an intelligible role after all. More merit attaches to showing that a feud really contributes to the coherence of the group, or that the religious ritual has important economic consequences, etc., than to saying that the overtly or apparently economic really is such, or that the apparently pointless ritual really has no point at all. This natural and legitimate preference for discovering the new rather than the obvious may of course degenerate into a pursuit of paradox, or an exaggeration of the way in which various human activities are interrelated. But still, anthropology is, more perhaps than other sciences, the study of how things are more and other than they seem.

Anthropologists tend to think of themselves as distinguished from non-anthropologists by their ability to draw such conclusions and to draw them correctly, rather than by being people who know, preferably by direct contact, some very odd facts about odd peoples, which is the way the general public tends to think of them. I shall not here go into the quite difficult question of the logical nature of those conclusions. A typical anthropological study is a kind of inverted sermon. Whilst a sermon begins with a text and proceeds to illustrate it, an anthropological study begins with empirical material and proceeds to extract from it some interesting proposition.

There are analogies between the Functionalist anthropologist and the linguistic philosopher. The latter, having abjured the doctrines leading to translation, reduction, of actually made statements to simpler models, seeks instead their meaning in their use (function?) in the actual situations in which they occur. The anthropologist, debarred by his calling from discounting primitive religion, magic, etc., simply as error, mistaken technology, etc., again seeks their 'meaning' in their function (use?) in their social context. Ironically enough, at the very time when philosophers, in analysing and classifying types of 'meaning', are turning to the actual context and activity for a clue, we shall see one whose professional concern is with just those activities and contexts turn to philosophy and what is perhaps a slightly dated theory of meaning (parallelism, mirroring) for aid.

Functionalism, in the broad sense in which it can be said that most British social anthropologists are Functionalists, consists essentially of seeking explanations in the interrelations of various features of a society with each other, in their reciprocal usefulness, as opposed to seeking them in their genesis. In practice this approach is combined with an insistence on thorough and intimate field work, on not taking either information or explanation offered by members of a society at its face value but on the contrary checking both by close observation or even participation. One should add that in practice, especially of late, this approach is also combined with careful collection of evidence about genesis when such evidence is available; but when this is done it is not clear in view of the anthropologists' general outlook just what the relevance of this information is to be, as Leach points out.

Naturally, Functionalism can be formulated both as a regulative and as a constitutive principle, as a method or as a doctrine. Its merits in the first form are as great as its defects in the second are obvious. (This verdict is perhaps analogous to Kant's critique of teleology: and indeed, teleology is a kind of cosmic Functionalism.) But anthropologists do not necessarily or *ex cathedra* distinguish between the two aspects: they may even deliberately abstain from doing so for teaching purposes. The preoccupation with the truth that everything is, to some extent, functional, has obscured the even more important truth that some things are *far* more so than others. If Functionalism is to be taken seriously as a doctrine rather than as a method, one can only say that it fluctuates between two extreme formulations. At one end of the scale there is the doctrine that societies are perfect organisms or mechanisms, whose every custom, institution, etc., is ideally adjusted. At the other end of the scale there is the doctrine that customs, institutions, etc., all have many complicated and indirect consequences, and that in any society that has managed to survive these effects cannot be altogether bad. The first interpretation is grotesque, and the second is trivially true and probably an understatement. The truth must lie somewhere in between, but Functionalism as a doctrine is semi-vacuous in that it fails to say just where. Or, to put this another way, Functionalism implies that the features of a society must be what they are, given that its other features are what *they* are. Now, quite apart from the fact that only structural and not cultural facets of a society are supposed to be so uniquely determined, the question arises—how many of the variables must be given before the others can be uniquely inferred? Can the whole animal be re-constructed from one bone, or must all bones but one be given before the last can be deduced?[1]

Anthropological custom—one might say ritual—is to spend about two years acquiring intimate knowledge concerning a society and then to 'write up' the material that has been gathered. If the published material is to earn the label 'anthropology' rather than be relegated to 'mere ethnography', it must as indicated contain 'theoretical conclusions'. Now it may strike philosophers as odd that conclusions should be expected from single instances. The final justification of this procedure cannot be attempted here, but it is worth while making certain observations about it. The practice raises few logical problems when the theoretical conclusions are negative; as, for instance, a general theory of promiscuity amongst primitives is refuted by the demonstration of marriage and family rules amongst people who by all other criteria fall amongst the most primitive societies extant. The habit of drawing conclusions from a single field study may have been stimulated by the fact that early studies were sometimes most interesting in as far as they constituted such demolitions of general theories. Another point is that two years in the field and *n* years writing up the material is a long time, during which the anthropologist has much time to think; he cannot humanly be expected to restrain his theoretical ingenuity and inventiveness simply in deference to a textbook methodology that warns against premature generalisation. The gathering of empirical material tends to take longer in the social sciences than it does in the natural ones, and the customary ratio between the quantity of fact and theory must adapt itself to this, if only for such purely pragmatic reasons.

Furthermore, it may be that though *a* society is in one sense a single instance, in another it is a large class of events, and that the anthropologist's theory has this large class as its field rather than all of them seen collectively as 'one society'. Other possibilities are that the theory just is a frankly rash extrapolation intended to serve as a guide to other studies and expecting to be knocked down by their findings; or on the contrary the theory is not even expected to hold outside the bounds of the society whose facts it explains. This may be true without even leading one to some doctrine that anthropological understanding is a case of *verstehen* of a unique object.

The book under discussion is a case in point. Its author presents a quantity of ethnographic material which, however, he does not consider important as such, if only because, according to him, most of it had been published before. Through it, however, and above all through difficulties encountered when describing and explaining it, he comes to certain conclusions which he considers of importance for the development of the subject, and it is these conclusions which interest me. I shall let Leach state these conclusions in his own words, though I am here editing them by selection, re-ordering and occasional italicising:

> The social anthropologist . . . endeavours to employ a terminology which is completely unambiguous. He therefore adopts . . . a language of special terms which have no meanings at all other than that with which the scientist endows them. Such expressions as exogamy . . . etc. . . . used by anthropologists . . . mean just what the anthropologist says they mean, neither more nor less. *Consequently* structural systems as described by anthropologists are always static systems (p. 103).
>
> Is it then possible to describe at all, by means of ordinary sociological categories, societies which are not assumed to be in stable equilibrium? (p. 4).
>
> The structures which the anthropologist describes are models which exist only as logical constructions in his own mind. What is more difficult is to relate such abstractions to the data of empirical field work. . . . (For) Real societies exist in time and space. The . . . situation does not build up into a fixed environment, but into a constantly changing environment. Every real society is a process in time (p. 5).
>
> When an anthropologist attempts to describe a social system he *necessarily* describes only a model of the social reality. This model represents in effect the anthropologist's hypothesis about 'how the social system works'. The different parts of the model system *therefore necessarily* form a coherent whole—it is a system in equilibrium. . . . on the contrary the reality situation is in most cases full of inconsistencies . . . (p. 8).
>
> In practical field work situations the anthropologist must always treat the material of observation as if it were part of an overall equilibrium, otherwise description becomes almost impossible. All I am asking is that the fictional nature of this equilibrium be frankly recognised (p. 285).

The italics are mine throughout. Where Leach italicised something I have left his italics out, but I do not think this alters his meaning significantly at any of these points.

Further examples could be given, but I do not think it necessary. I have picked out those passages which illustrate Leach's central argument without referring to the ethnographic material, which is far too complicated to be re-stated here.

A philosopher reading the above quotations will rapidly recognise the argument—indeed he will recognise it as an old friend, stated here with admirable pungency and brevity. Leach is, in effect, saying: concepts have determinate meaning, and being thus determinate must therefore be static. But reality is not static. Therefore concepts cannot correspond to reality. He seems to feel that concepts describing change would themselves have to be changing concepts. A much earlier philosopher might have put his point thus: you cannot enter the *same* society twice; nay, you cannot even do it once. Leach goes on to conclude therefore, concepts do not refer to reality directly, but only through an intermediary, a schizophrenic broker (to borrow Professor Ryle's expression used in another context) who has the ability to look both ways. As changing and disorderly reality cannot be the objects of determinate and neat concepts directly, it can be their object only indirectly through a Third Man. This latter assistant Leach calls a *model*.

The first comment one can make on Leach's argument is that it is valid. If Leach and perhaps other anthropologists wish to speak in this way, they may. But they should consider the consequences. For one thing, not merely will saying things like 'Kachin society is patrilineal' be a case of referring to 'models'; but so will saying 'It is a nice day today'—especially in England—or 'I am sitting at my desk'—why, I fidgeted whilst I typed it, an instance of change unreflected in the concept 'sitting'! All these will also be cases of referring 'merely' to 'models in one's mind'. *All* references to reality will be mediated by models. Models will be an inescapable iron curtain between all our words and the things they refer to. We have all been busy constructing such models of reality all our lives, rather as Monsieur Jourdain has been speaking prose. The second consequence they will have to face is that they risk being misled into thinking that there are entities called models over and above meaningful words on the one hand and things and events on the other, for Leach does not mean actual physical models such as an engineer might build. He uses 'models' in a sense such that every time a precise concept refers to changing reality, there is, necessarily, a 'model'. Moreover, all concepts must have some precision and all reality undergoes some change. . . .

It seems in fact that what Leach has done is to apply to social anthropology the general argument which from the premiss that words must have determinate meanings in order to mean anything concludes that they are therefore a kind of static thing, and then noticing that reality is not static, finally concludes that words can either not refer to reality at all or only through some further inter-mediary.

To say this about Leach, however, is not to explain his argument sufficiently. Leach, like reality, is more complicated. As I wish to discuss Leach and not a model of Leach—an ambition which I do not think the very nature of knowledge will frustrate—I must add certain complicating touches to the above sketch. These complicating touches will have the interest of showing how the purely philosophical argument becomes enmeshed in considerations which are specifically connected with anthropological concepts and not merely concepts in general, and with the social organisation of Burmese hill tribes rather than with objects of knowledge in general.

It is not wholly clear to me after reading the book whether the argument is meant to follow from something about concepts in general, or about certain current anthropological concepts in parti-cular. Secondly, it is not clear whether the difficulty which Leach is solving arises when *any* reality is related to concepts, or whether it arises only when unstable, changing things are so related. I think that in connexion with both these issues both the general and the more specific interpretation is possible, and perhaps Leach himself is not altogether clear as to which one he is putting forward. Some of the quotations given above support the 'general' interpretation. For instance:

> . . . expressions . . . mean just what the anthropologist says they
> mean. . . . Consequently . . . systems as described by
> anthropologists are always static systems. (But) Every real
> society is a process in time.

In order to see the 'specific' interpretation of Leach's argument, one must look at least briefly at his theory of meaning and sym-bolism, his theory of ritual and his theory of social change, all these being closely related. I shall not go into his theory of meaning in detail, partly because it would take too long and partly because an excellent analysis of it already exists.[2]

Roughly speaking, Leach believes that language, systems of pro-positions, describe reality in virtue of reflecting it in some fairly literal sense, in other words he believes in what might be called the parallelism theory of meaning. This is what we need know of his philosophy. As a matter of anthropology, he believes that ritual reflects the society in which it occurs in a similar way. Furthermore, he seems to equate 'social structure' with ideas in people's minds as to how their society *should* be ideally organised, with how power should be distributed within it. We thus get four entities which are parallel or 'reflect each other', or, in the last case, are actually identical: verbal description of a society by an anthropologist, ritual in that society, the ideal of that society as envisaged by its members, and finally the structure of that society itself. Leach must take a very 'dispositional' view of 'ideas' for this last identity to hold, and there is indeed independent evidence that he does take such a view. This equation in Leach's terminology is facilitated by the partial overlaps in the *normal* meanings of the members of the following series: 'Ideal', 'correct behaviour', 'expected behaviour', 'social structure'. Readers who might boggle at the equation of 'ideal' and 'structure' may see its justification in this context.

Now the relevant part of Leach's theory of social change, though not necessarily of *all* social change, is that it occurs when two contradictory ideals are present in the minds of various members of one society or even the same members, and actual reality then fluctuates between the two ideals. The part of Leach's theory of social change amongst Burmese hill tribes that I have given may seem, when stated thus in isolation, to be tautologous; for contradictory ideals which at the same time *are* the social structure can only explain changes in that structure in a circular way. In fact, Leach explains the fluctuations in terms of the detailed *operation* of the two structures (which I cannot reproduce), not merely by saying that there are two. This fluctuation of the social structure, however, does not require a similar fluctuation in ritual, despite the fact that ritual was said to mirror both social structure and ideals; because, although ritual is in Leach's view a kind of language which describes society and can even convey negative assertions and deny that a given kind of organisation obtains, *it is a sufficiently vague language to incorporate both of two contradictory ideals.* This is the point in Leach's anthropology proper that it was necessary to reach for the purposes of the present argument.[3]

This point can be cited in support of what I called the 'specific' rather than the 'general' interpretation of Leach. It seems to show that it is not simply the fact that anthropological concepts are concepts that prevent them from faithfully reflecting reality, but the fact that they are precise. It shows this because Leach is now seen to think that ritual can, thanks to its vagueness, mirror even an 'inconsistent' and hence fluctuating social structure. One might at this stage remark, rather unkindly, that if lack of vagueness is the only thing standing between some at least amongst anthropological concepts and reality, there should be nothing to worry about. Take a concept such as 'equilibrium', or the concept of 'solidarity', which according to anthropologists is generated by ritual. In discussing this notion Leach mentions an instance where ritual occurs with allegedly this consequence but where subsequent events force one to say that the solidarity is dissipated immediately after the celebrations that had the function of promoting it. Come to think of it, we are most of us

acquainted with this kind of thing from our own experience. . . .
Leach seems nevertheless inclined to retain the notion of solidarity
for explanatory purposes even for such cases. *If* 'solidarity' is really
to be an explanatory concept for ritual despite the fact that the ritual
and immediate accompanying emotion may be the only manifestation
of it, then we should have to draw attention to the fact that Durkheim, who popularised it, was a compatriot of Molière's medico. But
it is only fair to add that many anthropological concepts, notably
those connected with kinship, are not at all imprecise; and furthermore that others, such as 'witchcraft', may rightly be vague, and that
the attempts of some anthropologists to make them more precise
may well be misguided, springing from a failure to appreciate that
these concepts should have an 'open texture'.

But whether Leach would settle on the general or the specific interpretation of his thesis, the over-all point holds. If he settled on the
general one, the philosophical comments indicated are called for; if
on the other hand he is to be interpreted in the 'specific' way, his
arguments are still open to the same philosophic criticism, but one
could say that he is by misleading means getting at something which
is true, namely, that Functionalist *theory* does have some difficulty in
incorporating social change. One might go on to say that this theory
is absorbed into the concepts occurring in it, though I am not sure to
what extent this is so and the extent to which it is so probably varies
from concept to concept. It is true that when equilibrium theory or
Functionalist theory comes to be used in its extreme form—when no
feature of a society is allowed to be without function and, for instance,
it is said that there are no cultural survivals—then Leach's thesis that
change is something incompatible with the concepts employed becomes true. I have heard Functionalist theory used in this way.
Within such a scheme substantial social changes other than exo-
genous ones are indeed hard to conceive. Anyone who had taken this
kind of outlook seriously would, I think, naturally find himself thinking along lines such as Leach's when faced with similar material.

One way, however, of showing the error of the solution presented
by Leach is to point out that it leads to a regress; if precise concepts
cannot reflect shifting reality, why should the model that is intended
to mediate between them be able to do so? Might not a further
mediator be required, and so on? Leach seems aware of this difficulty
and worried by it. As, however, the 'model' in his sense is a myth-
ological entity, it is hard for us or Leach to decide what it can or
cannot reflect.

Leach has, incidentally, an ingenious device for getting round the
difficulty of how models succeed in reflecting changing societies,
arrived at by combining his theory of social change and his theory of
meaning. He advises anthropologists to cope with fluctuating societies

by specifying the contradictory ideals that are operating—which can be done through 'static' models employing 'static' concepts—thereby simultaneously indicating the mechanism of change *and* describing a changing society by means of two unchanging models, thus achieving indirectly what to his mind is (almost or totally?) impossible to do directly, namely to describe change. As, however, the difficulty may be unreal, the ingenuity of the device for getting round it may be wasted.

Another way of bringing home the fallacy of the central argument might be to show that however much we maltreat concepts to make them reflect more faithfully a chaotic and untidy reality, we shall never have much reason to think that they then reflect reality more faithfully. If we invent rapidly changing concepts to deal with changing societies, or contradictory concepts to cope with societies in conflict, we may find ourselves with an unmanageable language, but we shall still not be able to be sure that the concepts change or internally conflict in just the way that the society is changing or conflicting. Or alternatively if we devise concepts as vague as according to Leach the 'concepts' of ritual actually are, what will happen to us if society suddenly confutes us by going all orderly and neat? The answer is of course that no such simple parallelism between concepts and things such as Leach seems to expect is required in the first place, nor does it exist between ritual and social structure, and that consequently no devices are required to solve alleged difficulties arising when the parallelism ceases to hold. The concept of 'change', for instance, does not itself change yet it can 'reflect' reality as much as the concept 'stability'; neither of the two is any vaguer than the other. It would be mistaken to think that the concept 'stability' is itself stable, or indeed unstable, except in the sense that it has a determined and unchanging meaning, and *that* it has to no greater or lesser degree than the concept of 'change'. Both have an equally good prospect of describing things denoted by them. As far as these formal considerations go, a changing or unstable society is no whit less knowable than an utterly static one.

Of course there are certain factors which do make it easier to study, describe and understand stable societies than unstable ones. There are the practical advantages of stable societies; they enable one to settle down, to gather material over a wider time span, to sort out the typical from the deviant—all of which may be impossible in a society in turmoil. The second point is that 'society' *means* a *fairly* stable pattern of personal relationships, though not nearly as closely and exclusively as functionalism suggests. But these considerations do not justify the conclusion that change or disorder are undescribable. Even *indescribable* disorders are occasionally described.

Leach in effect sees *other* Functionalists as holding a kind of Platonism. Only the static is properly knowable, it is merely approximated by the empirically real, and moreover the static is superior not merely for purposes of cognition but also morally and from the viewpoint of social health. Leach's own variant to all this is a kind of Hegelianism: reality changes because it is in conflict, the conflict is a conflict of embodied ideas, and the change and conflict *are* knowable by means of concepts that are themselves in conflict in a parallel way.

Now whilst Leach's central argument seems to me mistaken and unnecessary, the conclusions he draws from it seem to me true. He is attacking a position which should indeed be re-considered, but he is doing it in a misleading way. The correct conclusion is that anthropologists should pay more attention to change and hence to historical evidence which alone provides information over larger time-spans, than at least one of the official theories of what they are doing suggests. The reasons why this conclusion seems to me valid are different from the ones given by Leach. In order to make them clear I shall try to consider and speculate why, as Leach points out, some British social anthropologists tended to be anti-historical or a-historical and what this amounts to. In their hostility to historical explanations anthropologists sometimes seem to an outsider to get near to what may be a kind of Russellian paradox. They insist that anthropology differs from 'mere' ethnography by also having theory; on investigation of this theory, called Functionalism, it turns out to be in large part the doctrine that anthropology should be nothing but ethnography. Or rather—*good* ethnography. For Functionalism amounts largely to the recommendation to study societies as they are and 'function' rather than speculate about how they came to be. Anthropologists seem to me to exaggerate the sharpness and genuineness of the distinction between brute ethnographic facts and 'explanations' which are not historical.

In as far as anthropologists have been anti-historical they may have such an attitude for a number of separate reasons:

Firstly there is the brute fact that illiterate societies have no records, and that in consequence past social organisation is hard or impossible to reconstruct. The anthropologists' attitude is 'Whereof we have no evidence, thereof we must be silent'. This is impeccable, except that the only way evidence may come to light is by speaking first and thus noticing such evidence as might after all exist; without speaking first in violation of the above principle, possible evidence is not likely ever to be noticed. In any case, this objection to the historical approach to anthropology is not theoretically very interesting, even if correct. This objection has no deeper roots, logically speaking, than an objection to mapping the craters on the other side of the moon; we know that there are some but we are by practical difficulties prevented from ascertaining just where. It is worth adding that this attitude of anthropologists sprang from a healthy reaction against unverified and possibly unverifiable speculations about the development of societies when energy and time could much more profitably be devoted to a study of actually observable societies as they are at present.

Secondly there is a philosophically much more interesting resistance to taking notice of the past, a resistance whose logic may not be wholly clear to all who are affected by it. This resistance is curiously analogous to the familiar one in physics against 'action at a distance'. Just as one is intuitively repelled by any causation between bodies that is not a case of 'push', so one is repelled by the idea, which *seems* implicit in 'historical explanation', that what goes on here and now, what men living now are doing, requires for its understanding the specification of events or situations long past. It is even more repellent than action at a distance; for in some sense it is true to say that 'the past does not exist' and the present does. How could, one might say darkly, the unreal and non-existent shackle the real and existing? When anthropologists say, as sometimes they do, that 'there are no survivals', meaning that present goings-on must be explained in terms of their present role and not genetically, what they say seems equivalent to saying that the past has no effects, or no significant ones. (They may be prepared to explain what is merely 'cultural' genetically, *ipso facto* implying that it is a mere historical accident, whilst refusing such explanations for 'structural' facts. Roughly speaking, the fact that we express respect by taking off our hats is cultural, but the fact that certain groups receive expressions of respect is structural.) But if the past has no effects, what has? Is not the past the *only* thing that could have effects? The argument is in a sense valid—only present forces can *operate* at present. In other senses it is invalid—and the most important of these is that the past may be and often is a necessary source of evidence about what forces are operating at present. Roughly: the dynamics of a situation could never be worked out from a snapshot alone.

'The explanation of the present must be sought in the present.' This argument is never stated as openly as this but it does support, and is in turn supported by 'Functionalist' theory which maintains that a society is a 'system in equilibrium with mutually determining parts', with the crucial implication that explanation must be sought in the interrelation of those parts rather than in anything else. If this doctrine were stated openly its difficulties would promptly appear, if for no other reason than that the interdict on the past on such grounds would strike on everything except the literal, immediate and shifting present—a basis too tenuous for even the most 'functionalist' and equilibrium-minded anthropologist. There is a wealth of philosophical perplexities here, probably related to Zeno's. For 'The past can never be a cause' and 'The past is the only thing that can be a cause' both have some appeal. Or in other words anything truly *past* is too infinitely distant, separated by the chasm of the unreality of the past, to affect the present, even if it is only past by a second; a miss is as good as an epoch. At the same time the present is too thinly insubstantial, too devoid of weight, to *cause*. Anyway, can one think of a series of self-causing instants? Moreover, no instant has any extension, and however many of them we add together we get no continuum; zero multiplied by any number is still zero. Thus the apparent vistas of time are illusory; there is but one eternal instant. This is not the place to pursue these puzzles, but it is worth while indicating them as a kind of last backcloth to the more concrete discussions about change and the past in the anthropological context.

A similar dispute occurs within psycho-analytic theory, between the view that the events of infancy are literally of aetiological importance and the view that only the psyche 'as it is now functioning' matters. Analogously, some anthropologists are tempted to say that 'remembered history (alone) matters'. I have heard this kind of view expounded by an anthropologist and attributed with grateful recognition to Malinowski. But Malinowski is dead. How long can a dead Functionalist be influential without a pragmatic contradiction?

The reason why the extremist argument operates, as I suspect it does, at the back of anthropologists' minds, is that it is mixed up with other considerations, some of them very cogent, and is a kind of limiting, metaphysical variant of them. These various considerations overlap and tend not to be distinguished, but I shall attempt to sort them out.

One of them is hostility to what one may call the fallacy of origins. Suppose a historical series of situations ABBBBB, or even a series of ABCBCBCBC; a person is the victim of this fallacy if he believes that to discover and indicate the occurrence of the initial situation A is all that is required, and all that could be provided, for the explanation of the present situation (B or BCB . . .). There are indeed occasions in daily life and in historiography when this type of explanation is held sufficient. If I come into my room after an absence and find a strange object on the floor, the fact that the cat brought it in is sufficient. But the real reason why this specification of the initial episode in the history of the object on the floor of my room is sufficient is that the principle underlying its subsequent staying there is so obvious that no one would dream of bothering to make it explicit: barring earthquakes, hurricanes, etc., inanimate objects of certain weight do not move away from their positions on level floors. The situation may be analogous, sometimes, in historiography, though here the anthropologist rightly has his doubts, for the life of nations is not a level floor and institutions, culture traits, etc., are not inanimate objects. With some anthropologists, a distrust of historical explanations is combined with a distrust of (some at least) historians, who are suspected of using as obvious or trivial principles of explanation principles which may be either not trivial or not clear or not true. Historians are particularly suspect of 'ethnocentricity', of facile projection on to others of temporarily, geographically or socially local motivations, outlooks, assumptions, etc. Anthropologists consider their own initiation or *rite de passage*, field work in an alien society, to be an effective cure for such projections, though perhaps some of them then tend to project the assumptions of the culture they studied.

Slightly different and more sophisticated than the fallacy of origins is what I am tempted to call the sociological versions of the genetic fallacy. One tends to use this expression in connexion with beliefs, to designate the mistaken attitude of someone who thinks that the history of the acceptance or holding of a belief is sufficient evidence for the assessment of its truth and merit. The sociological version of this is the assumption that the specification of the series leading to the present explains the present. This is a little superior to the fallacy of origins in that the whole series and not merely a privileged episode in it is required, but it is still insufficient in that a sequence is not an explanation; one wants the generalisations connecting the items in it or the glue between the links. Anthropologists certainly do. Hitherto, they tended to concern themselves with the glue between links of a chain of the form BBBBB—in other words with the mechanics of the self-maintenance of stable systems, as Leach points out. Leach himself is in the more specific parts of his book preoccupied with the mechanics of a series of the form BCBCBCBC. But anthropological theory has been so much preoccupied with societies which seemed to be of the BBBB kind that he thinks that those which are not are epistemologically intractable; and his worry is aggravated by the realisation that to some extent all societies are *not*-BBBB.

Ironically, anthropologists had initially come to be preoccupied with stable societies mainly because they were interested in primitive ones not *qua* stable, but *qua* evidence for genetic explanations. Nowadays, genetic explanations are out of favour; 'Structural' explanations are the thing. It would take too long, and be too difficult, to attempt to analyse that notion here.

The appeal of genetic explanations is curiously powerful. It is extremely hard to convince people not acquainted with anthropology that in studying the such-and-such people, one is *not* preoccupied with 'where they came from'. The genetic approach, for instance, probably also underlies many epistemological fallacies, operating through the assumption that specific *source* must be found for any item of knowledge. One is tempted to speculate about the genetic outlook itself being a survival from the social forms in which to place a man genealogically was to place him in other ways too, or from those cosmogonies which are content to explain everything by specifying the initial episode.

The objection to explanation by origins could be formulated so as to bring out an interesting analogy between physical cosmology and social studies, by asserting as a principle that *there are no privileged moments*;[4] that a symmetry operates such that no time–place position requires more or less explanation. Though the universe is not the same all over, the same fundamental laws operate all over. The principle is explicitly denied by many religions—a difference which is probably a crucial and defining difference between the two kinds of thought-systems. In a science such as physical cosmology which must make such extensive use of extrapolation, this principle is constantly in use. The interesting thing about the social sciences, in which the ratio of extrapolation to independent confirmation is quite different, is that the assumption operates though it is held to be false. There are privileged moments in human affairs if there are, as is presumably the case, 'decisive moments of history', *i.e.* single episodes with vast effects, where the episodes themselves were quite unpredictable—not because of an inherent indeterminism but because, as with the fall of a penny, too many factors too minute to be considered came into play, or because they entered the system from outside. Who could foresee the shape of Cleopatra's nose? The occurrence of Cleopatra's Noses isn't denied, but they simply elude explanation in the social sciences as such. In the natural sciences, *e.g.* in biological genetics, Cleopatra's Noses such as mutations can be dealt with statistically; but that again is impossible in the social sciences for our runs and populations are not large enough, and our focus of interest too specific.

Explanations by origins violate the principle of no privileged moments by implying that the origin alone explains, and explains sufficiently. Functionalist anthropologists when rightly rejecting this have gone too far and insisted that origins never explain at all. Also, when rightly insisting that stability as well as change requires explanation, they have tended to equate theories of society with theories of the maintenance of stability—so much so that the paradigm of explanation of a social feature is held to be an explication of how it contributes to the maintenance of the *status quo*.

The late Professor Radcliffe-Brown said that the trouble with conjectural history (speculations about the development of illiterate peoples) was not that it was history, but that it was conjectural. The real situation seems to me to be that the trouble with it is neither that it is history, nor that it is conjectural, but that, *by themselves*, past events are no explanation. One might say: the trouble with hen-and-egg questions is not that we don't know but that we don't care. It would not advance our understanding of hens or eggs. But 'functional' hypotheses can *also* be conjectural; the real contrast is not really between conjectures about the past and tested truths about the present, but between sociological hypotheses tested in the present *and* the past, and genetic accounts that pretend to greater logical force than they can possess, or to being the only possible explanation. That a genetic reconstruction is purely speculative is an aggravation of the offence, but not its essence.

Thus distrust of history has some validity but calls for some cautions. For one thing, though historical facts alone do not constitute explanations, they are evidence for explanations of another kind, and moreover this other kind finds as rich a field in the past as in the present. The importance of documentation for purposes of reconstructing the past may be exaggerated, and the line between 'conjectural' and 'genuine' history drawn too sharply, for even when documents are available they are not evidence without interpretation, and other things may throw light on past social structures. Moreover, no virtue should be made of other people's necessity—the documented past should not be ignored where documents are available, on the grounds that there are none on the Trobriand islands.

The physiological analogy springs to the minds of anthropologists easily; indeed, the investigation of the functioning of an organ is quite independent of the biological history of the species. But the physiologist can ignore phylogenesis only because the life-cycles of succeeding generations really are *cycles*, they really do not differ sufficiently. He cannot ignore the life history of the single organism, even when considering, for instance, the heart, whose rhythmic motion might *prima facie* also be held to constitute a mechanism whose understanding does not require considerations of the past. The physiologist does consider temporal processes over a relatively small span, and ignores those of a large span because he can rely on them to be wholly repetitive, with differences insignificant for his purposes. The anthropologist cannot *rely* on anything of the kind, whatever the span may be. The special attention given to stable societies without records and the kind of theory this tended to produce have made the physiological analogy seem more plausible than it is, and have, rightly or wrongly, led to anthropological theories appearing to carry the analogy between societies and organisms further than is justified. Even the human body has the functionless appendix. Anthropologists should be willing to concede that some societies may sometimes have appendices too, even if they are rightly incensed against the magpie theory of culture which makes societies consist of nothing but appendices. By 'Magpie theory of culture' I mean the doctrine or method which implies that a society can be explained by specifying when and whence each item in its make-up came, as historians of ideas sometimes seem to think that they have accounted for a climate of opinion by locating the books and authors in which its constituents first appeared.

It is instructive to compare the paradigm of explanation as conceived by the historian, and by the anthropologist. A historian is, I imagine, overjoyed to discover a contemporary or later institution in a more rudimentary form at an earlier date. To have a fairly continuous series of such forms beginning with something that is almost zero, so to speak, is to have a good account of 'the development' of the institution and hence an explanation of it. The anthropologist seldom gets an opportunity for achieving something of this kind, but if he did he would not be satisfied with it. His instinctive reaction is, I think, to reflect that 'in its rudimentary form' the institution probably played quite a different role from what it does in its later, 'fully-developed' stage, and that the tie-up of the two stages, apart from being quite possibly based on nominal or superficial similarities does not explain the function and functioning of the institution at either of the two times. He may add that the historian is tacitly employing a premiss that is both nebulous and questionable, namely that it is enough for a precedent to exist for it to be repeated and improved upon, which is what tracing of developments amounts to. This will not do, for paradoxically there are both more precedents than repetitions, and more activities than precedents. The anthropologist may feel, with some justification, that the historian takes for granted and lucid just that which is most problematic—the glue between segments of a temporal sequence, above all between similar segments, between stages of stable society.

The historian may reply, also with some justification, that the Functionalist anthropologist anxious to explain the present by the present has, to take the extreme example, no way of including what may be called explanations by *trauma*. The documented histories of literate peoples provide examples of exceptional and dramatic events which, as we say, 'left their mark'. There is no reason for supposing that none such occurred in the past of peoples whose histories cannot be reliably reconstructed. But the marks such events have left cannot be adequately accounted for without reference to those events. Now the point which is brought home so strikingly by these traumatic events in fact applies equally to all events, traumatic or not, which are, at any remove, amongst the efficient causes of present situations.

In this opposition, it seems to me clear that the historian may err through inadequate interest in the nexus between succeeding events, or willingness to accept superficial accounts of it, an error not likely to be committed by the anthropologist; *his* interest in the 'social structure' is in effect an interest in what kind of events resulting from the interplay of which factors do and can follow each other in a given social environment. But having formulated the problem more correctly, he may err through neglecting the past as a storehouse of evidence about it. Leach seems to me to be right in pointing to this error, but wrong in diagnosing it. This error does not depend on the fact that societies change whilst concepts do not. It would continue to be an error even if no society did change, though it would not then do much practical harm, and even although in fact concepts do not change, not being the kind of thing that either changes or does not. (A concept that has changed is not the same concept. There is a sense in which 'concepts change', but it is not relevant here.)

It must be stressed that many anthropologists do not in fact disregard the past when they have relevant evidence; nor does Leach say that they do. He merely says that when they do consider it, this does not fit their concepts, and they do not know what to do with it. Even at the level of meta-theory, of assessing their own activities the situation is not wholly clear cut, for one very distinguished British social anthropologist, Professor Evans-Pritchard, recently classed anthropology with history. But it is not yet clear how such a slogan would fit into the main tradition of British anthropologists' way of looking at their subject.

Anthropologists' rejection of explanation by origins reminds one of Professor Popper's critique of historism (not -icism). At the same time, however, their attitude to stable unchanging societies is different. They are not hostile to them, nor do they exaggerate the extent to which 'tribalism' is free from moral and social doubt, status-insecurity, etc. Direct contact with tribes has refuted not merely Hobbes, but equally the 'safe, cosy social womb' theory. Past idylls, even when rejected, are suspect things. If the foetus could speak, the doctrine of birth trauma might have to be revised, and what Adam's views were on the garden of Eden is not well established.

These then are the considerations which may lead some anthropologists to reject history, and I hope to indicate that either they lack cogency or when properly understood do not imply a disregard for history. Thus Leach's final conclusion and recommendation are right, but he need not have undertaken his excursus into Idealism in order to demonstrate it. His book may also give one an exaggerated impression of the extent to which contemporary anthropologists are in need of this lesson.

One of the main objections to failing to consider historical evidence is that concepts with which social anthropologists operate are, most of them, what philosophers call 'dispositional' ones. A statement concerning, for instance, the real functions of a chief or of a ritual in a given society simply cannot be verified without taking into consideration what would happen in situations other than the one which holds at present, and one important source of evidence about such alternative situations is the past. Professor Ginsberg has said that the concept of 'social class' denotes not a real group but a *potential* one. One should notice that this is true of very many sociological concepts.

Another consideration is that in studying the pattern of cause and effect in a given society, anthropologists are not so much interested in the initial conditions of a sequence, as in the generalisation specifying the relation between the condition and the consequent states of affairs. This is so, and should be so; though in order to use this as a satisfactory analysis of anthropological explanation, one would have to go further and take into account the fact that the generalisation itself is something that needs explaining, as in other sciences though in a manner which may be peculiar. For one thing, the generalisation itself may describe a regular connexion which is a state of affairs characteristic of a society, and this fact itself be the consequent in a more general sequence; but in order to know this we must also know the antecedent, and thus *historical* evidence becomes absolutely necessary.

I do not wish to give the impression that I criticised Leach's argument as an example of ordinary error. If it is erroneous, it is so in a way in which interesting philosophical doctrines are. On the contrary, it is perhaps the most lucid statement of a certain kind of Idealism that I know, and teachers of philosophy could profitably use a selection of his statements as a means of explaining to their students what such Idealism is about. They certainly could do no better than use Leach's book if they wish to illustrate how philosophical problems can spontaneously grow out of first-order work in an actual science. Moreover, the criticised argument is used to point a moral which is in fact a good one; and philosophical error analogous to his own is as present, if not as clearly stated, in the views he criticises as in his own.

NOTES

1 Cf. Ronald Fletcher, 'Functionalism as a Social Theory', *Sociological Review*, n.s. 4, July 1956, 31–46.
2 Cf. a forthcoming article by Mr Paul Stirling.
3 The doctrine that ritual and belief systems mirror the social organisation in which they occur has wide currency amongst social anthropologists. It is, in fact, a very suggestive and illuminating idea, helpful in formulating questions for research and in organising material. As a formally maintained doctrine it has logical defects of which anthropologists may not be sufficiently aware. Mainly: the idea of 'reflection' or 'mirroring' presupposes, as a minimum requirement, that there be a one-one correspondence between the two mutually reflecting systems. But neither system—neither social organisation, nor a system of ritual or belief—consists of easily separable, identifiable, countable 'parts'. The principles of individuation of such parts are largely arbitrary. It follows that any anthropologist who wishes can always, as far as this condition goes, with some ingenuity or ruthlessness interpret *any* material so that it fits the 'reflection' thesis.
4 Cf. C. Lévi-Strauss, *Les Structures Elémentaires de la Parenté*, Paris, 1949, p. 27.

7
SOCIOLOGY AND
SOCIAL ANTHROPOLOGY

The distinction between sociology and social anthropology is itself a
social rather than a logical one. In other words, the distinction can
best be understood not by looking at some neat dividing line in the
subject matter of the disciplines or in their method, but in the concrete, and hence untidy, factors which operated in various times and
places to cause people to class themselves as 'sociologists' and as
'social anthropologists'. This is highlighted by the fact that this distinction, and similar distinctions, are drawn differently in different
countries. If the facts or logic of the case imposed the distinction, one
should expect it to be drawn similarly in most places. To say this is
not to claim that there is no logical content at all to the distinction;
merely that, as so often, logical, pragmatic, opportunist and accidental factors all contribute to the drawing of a distinction between
two groups of people.

What are the logical or substantive elements in the differentiation?
What are the various watersheds along which the frontier is or has
been located? I shall list a few obvious ones.

The first distinction which springs to mind is the contrast Ad-
vanced/Primitive. This is certainly the first rule of thumb by means
of which one distinguishes the concerns of sociologists from those of
anthropologists. Nevertheless, it gives rise to formidable difficulties,
both theoretical and practical, if it were to be treated as an inter-
nationally recognised frontier. The practical difficulty is this: anthropologists do not cease to be anthropologists, in their own estimation
or that of others, when they study, for instance, middle-class kinship
in London and Chicago. At a pinch, villages in Western Ireland,
Wales or Italy, or even the working classes of industrial cities, could
be classed as a kind of honorary savage. But middle-class professional
families?

The theoretical objection can be formulated, in simplest terms, as
follows: the classification of societies into advanced and primitive, or
more elaborate versions of such a classification, presupposes at the
very least a tacit acceptance of an evolutionist view of human
societies. What happens if such a schema is rejected? Any workable

definition of the subject must surely refrain from prejudging the truth or falsity of theories *within* the subject. Are not anthropologists (or, for that matter, sociologists) entitled to reject evolutionism?

Of course, one might attempt to make the delimitation concrete and specific, and consequently free from attachment to any evolutionist doctrine of 'stages' of unilineal development. One might draw the line between large and small societies, or between complex and simple. But the small societies which concern the anthropologists are sometimes disconcertingly complex, and at least one reasonably interesting theory of modern society ('Mass Society') makes it out to be simple, at least to the extent of being composed of similar elements. Moreover, anthropologists do not lose interest in a community when it is incorporated, politically or otherwise, in a world-wide social network.

Could it be claimed that anthropologists are concerned with societies as totalities, whereas sociological researchers isolate various *aspects* of society? There are various factors which point in this way. Anthropologists are able to concern themselves with a whole society when that society is small, and they are *obliged* to do so when that society is previously relatively unknown, so that the characterisation of any one aspect of it requires at least the sketching in of the rest of that society. Sociological researchers *cannot* do this in large complex societies, and *need not* do so in as far as some general knowledge of society can be taken for granted. Moreover, anthropologists have recently been less inclined to do comparative work, and hence had less need to isolate 'aspects' for comparison, whereas sociologists, when theorising at all, have had to do this. Despite all this, one could nevertheless not draw a definitive boundary here. A typical anthropological thesis is also concerned with specific aspects of a society; and sociologists sometimes attempt to see a society globally, and the most all-embracing and global of theorists have counted as 'sociologists'.

Perhaps one should attempt to differentiate the two disciplines in terms of their attitude to time? For many people outside sociology and for a few within it, the paradigm of a sociological theory is still an account of 'stages'; whereas what characterises many anthropologists is the preference for the synchronic method. But although I shall have a good deal more to say about this crucial question of time, clearly no such simple frontier can be drawn here either. It would condemn sociologists who are evolutionists, or anti-evolutionists, to the wrong side of the frontier, and it would ignore the quite effective efforts of anthropologists to deal with change over time.

One might at times be tempted to see the distinction not in the kind of theory employed, but in the attitude to theory as such or in terms of its very presence or absence: one might be led to this by the manner of speaking adopted by some anthropologists, who distinguish between ethnography and sociology and mean by the latter the general, theoretical conclusions drawn from field observation. But again, this will not do. Heaven knows, there are untheoretical sociologists too.

Or, again, one might be tempted to seek the distinction in the type of method employed. Anthropology suggests above all field work, participation, intensive pursuit of the social reality under the social appearance and a careful mapping of both, a pursuit of latent functions. Sociology suggests extensive rather than intensive research, general observation, comparison. But it is hardly necessary to repeat that, once again, this cannot give us an acceptable boundary.

One might say that a different contrast underlies the two disciplines. Sociology is born above all from preoccupation with social change within Europe, from an attempt to understand how the European present and future arose from the European past. Anthropology, on the other hand, was born of the contact between Europeans and others, and the question is not 'how did we emerge from our ancestors', but rather 'how did they get left behind or diverge from our path?'

Anthropology was born of the interest in the contrast between western and savage man. Sociology was born of the contrast between the present and the past of western man. This highlights the somewhat paradoxical fact that anthropology began by being *more*, not less, past-oriented than sociology. Present academic social structure bears witness to this: in university curricula, anthropologists are still often linked with archaeologists. Anthropologists were differentiable from sociologists even before the days in which this differentiation was conceived in terms of the cult of field work: but in the early days, the differentiation was in terms of a concern with the distant past as opposed to a closer past (in both a literal and a geographical sense). Of course, when the concern with primitive societies as surrogate time-machines was replaced by concern with them as exemplars of social structure as such, officially this preoccupation disappeared: but it is still there, somewhere in the background. Since the Second World War, of course, both these two contrasted contrasts were replaced by one all-embracing one, that between modern industrial society on the one hand, and *both* 'feudal' and 'pre-industrial' and 'oriental' civilisation, *and* tribal societies, on the other. This strikingly illustrates one of my main points—perhaps an obvious one—that the contrast with which we are concerned is not merely not a neat one, but also a highly unstable one: it fluctuates in time and place, according to background intellectual doctrine, and according to general social preoccupations.

There used to be a joke to the effect that whereas in Oxford, dons were preoccupied only with what past thinkers had taught, in Cambridge they were preoccupied with the teaching of Cambridge dons in the recent three decades. The truth actually is that whereas in Cambridge they are preoccupied with the teaching of Cambridge thinkers in the past three decades, in Oxford they are preoccupied with the teaching of Oxford dons in the past two years. Some similar dialectic exists perhaps between sociology and anthropology. The distance of the horizons, the range of concern, the centre of intellectual gravity has shifted, expanded, shrunk and varied, and though this question of the temporal horizon is crucial, no simple characterisation of it will do justice to the facts. Nor is there anything regrettable in the changes which have occurred.

It is not, then, in some neat distinction of subject or method, or even in a less than neat conjunction of such distinctions, that we must seek the boundary, but in the actual social structure, ethos and history of the two disciplines, and this moreover will vary from country to country. From actual observation, I can only speak concerning Britain or a part of it. In Britain, it is or was relatively easy to distinguish an anthropologist from a sociologist, though possibly the differences between one kind of a sociologist and another are even greater than those which separate both of them from anthropologists. But just *this* is the crucial distinction: the valid joke in Britain is that the two disciplines mirror the type of society with which, in the popular imagination, they are associated. Anthropologists study tribal societies and they are a tribe; sociologists study anomic modern societies, and they are notoriously and excessively anomic. Anthropologists have a coherent and cohesive tradition and a great deal of similarity in training and outlook. Sociologists come in all shapes and sizes, and some are so far removed from each other that they do not even engage in any sustained dialogue, or sometimes any dialogue at all.

If, then, no neat boundary separates the two subjects, one should nevertheless be able to distinguish and characterise the two cultures, the sociological and anthropological: but the characterisation will have no universal validity, either in time or in space. The only characterisation I can offer is based on observation of the two disciplines in Britain in the recent past. Sociologists are still in a heroic age: no consensus, no central authority, and the populace affiliates itself to heroic figures who, each of them, can carve their own intellectual principality. By contrast, anthropologists enjoy a consensus and a moral community which knows how to impose its norms on its members. They have a fairly stable internal segmentation.

What are those norms? The 'structural–functional' method, and a certain shared attitude to time. I shall say more of these, and I shall not dwell on the familiar matter of homogeneous recruitments, initiation by field work and so forth, with which one would have to be concerned if one wished to explain the precise social mechanism by which those norms are imposed and maintained, by means of which they are internalised, by means of which each individual anthropologist acquires a deep inner investment in the traditional approach which ensures that he is sufficiently like his fellows to communicate with them easily and to produce comparable and hence reasonably cumulative work.

First of all: *time*.

Modern anthropology springs from Malinowski and is characterised by a synchronic attitude towards the interpretation of society. Simplifying: earlier anthropology was distinguished by a greater concern with the past, and a preoccupation with a more distant past, whereas modern anthropology is characterised by a disregard of the past.

Now I happen to be fully aware that this is a gross simplification, and moreover one which is by now vehemently repudiated by many anthropologists, including some who have earned the right to speak with authority about their own subject. Nevertheless, the simplification contains an important truth, and it seems to me that the qualifications and repudiations which have been made are the *wrong kind* of qualification and repudiation. I know that one distinguished anthropologist has defined his subject as a kind of history,[1] and that another one has carefully demonstrated how patiently and attentively anthropologists do look at the past of the societies which they interpret.[2] Notwithstanding all this, and for reasons which will be stated, I think that the synchronic approach is the correct starting point for understanding what is really happening in the discipline.

The first point which it is necessary to make is that the manifest' and latent reasons given for the synchronic approach are not identical. By manifest reasons I mean those which were actually given in so many words; by latent reasons I mean those underlying reasons which are, first of all, valid (in my view), and which also through their cogency and validity had the effective consequence of making anthropological research so very fruitful, effective and cumulative, and which consequently sustained the application of the method. I trust that it is as legitimate to apply distinction between latent and manifest function *to* anthropologists, as it is legitimate for them to apply it to the peoples they investigate. But it is worth stressing that my notion of the 'latent', in this context, is doubly loaded: it suggests both logical validity, *and* social effectiveness. The two of course do not necessarily or generally go together, but in this case, providentially, they did.[3]

To begin with, a brief sketch of the manifest reasoning underlying the synchronic approach. First, there was the inaccessibility of the past in an illiterate society without records. The consequence of this state of affairs, it was asserted, was that reconstructions of tribal history were mere speculative reconstructions, which it was impossible to check and which consequently had little or no scientific validity. The trouble with this is that, whilst partially true, it is only partially true, and no one really knows just how big the two parts are, and in any case there is no reason to assume that the past is equally accessible or inaccessible in all places. Can one really say that there is no element of validity at all in the attempts by archaeologists to reconstruct past social structure by the method of their craft, or in the attempts to reconstruct history from systematically collected oral traditions? And if there is at least some validity, some possibility of valid results, who is to say that in some places, at least with greater ingenuity or greater luck, or with respect to some particular problems, the results should not be very fruitful? It is always dangerous to claim that something cannot be done. Especially if it is manifest that *some* of it *can* be done.

Coupled with the rejection of the past on the grounds of lack of records and the undesirability of uncheckable speculation, there was also a more interesting reason. This is a theory of social causation, and is perhaps best expressed in the slogan associated with Malinowski—'there are no survivals'. One can easily grasp the underlying idea. When people do things, they have motives for doing them—*now*. The motives as well as the action are in the present. Human actions are not inert objects, which can be left behind by the past like artefacts (though the magpie anthropologists who had assimilated customs to artefacts might have thought so); they have to be caused or willed anew each time they occur. Hence their explanation must be sought in the circumstances, inclinations and so forth which brought them into being at the time they were done, and not somewhere in the past. Is that not obvious?

One is at this point reminded of the metaphysical doctrine that the world is recreated anew each instant (say by the Deity), because manifestly the past has not the power to create the present. For one thing, the past is now quite inert: for another it no longer exists. How could it contain a hidden mystic power to generate and control the present? We cannot maintain ourselves in being, it is fortunate accident that we persist: the miraculous gift of existence is granted us anew every instant that passes. And so it is. The metaphysical intuition which generates this doctrine can also be applied specifically to human societies and institutions, and I do believe that it is one of the factors underlying the synchronic predilection.

But the trouble here again is that we are dealing with something which is only partially true. But in the case of the 'lack of evidence' argument, we are dealing with something which was 'partially true', and indeed also 'partially untrue', in a very straightforward sense. The inertness and ineffectiveness of the past, on the other hand, is true and untrue in a much more complicated manner, being true in some senses and not true at others. We are here not in a situation where we can say 'It is true to such and such a degree, because there is evidence at this point but no evidence at another, and evidence concerning this problem but not that'. The sorting out of the true and the untrue elements requires some more complicated distinctions. Here again, we see that the thesis—in this case, the thesis of the impotence of the past—cannot be wholly true. Any social process consists of a series of events in which people react one day to what somebody else may have done the previous day, and so on. Of course, in one sense the past may be claimed to be wholly dead: I can only react today to something someone else did or said yesterday, if that action or utterance of his of yesterday had left some kind of mark in the present, literally present, situation. But it *has* left a mark: that literally present situation would be different if what had happened yesterday had been other than it was. Deny this and you end up with a quite absurd position, a series of wholly discrete and discontinuous incidents, quite independent in their content and structure of each other.

But if this extreme position is not intended, what is meant? Is there a kind of sociological 'specious present', within which interaction is permitted? If so, how long is it? A few days, a season, a year, a generation? From the viewpoint of the metaphysical intuition which underlies the argument, the intuition that only the present can operate in the present, a miss is as good as a mile: if the events of yesterday are relevant, then the invocation of events of any past period, however distant, are in principle permissible . . .

There is another way of highlighting the fact that the idea underlying the slogan 'there are no survivors' cannot be pushed to the limit, that it must be allowed to have some exceptions—and, of course, once this is allowed, the question arises concerning how many exceptions are to be allowed and how important they are. Take an example which, it is said, was discussed in Malinowski's seminar: those peculiarly pointless buttons which are found at the end of the sleeve on male coats in our society. *Prima facie*, these are of course splendid candidates for the status of being a 'survival': one assumes that, in the sartorial past, they performed some function, but they really do nothing whatsoever now. Yet, at the same time, it is not at all difficult to find some kind of synchronic, functionalist, Malinowskian explanation of their presence. They are, for instance, part of that sartorial elaboration which, through its very pointlessness, manages to sift out in our society those who have the resources and leisure for attending to their clothes from those whose poverty or occupation prevents them from doing this. In a society in which low status accrues to those who can not attend to pointless sartorial niceties, the buttons on one's sleeve do make a contribution, albeit a humble one, to the maintenance and expression of social stratification.

So far so good: an explanation of this kind is plausible, and some explanation along those lines may well be true. But the 'functionalist' explanation really only applies to a certain aspect of the pheno-menon: to its formal aspect, so to speak, the fact *some* pointless sartorial elaboration is necessary, an elaboration which requires time and/or money and which thus helps to segregate the possessors of either from those who are deprived of them. Such an explanation might be quite powerful in the sense of being pretty specific, in narrowing down the 'functional requirement' very specifically: the explanation might for instance deduce from independent evidence about our society just the precise amount of pointlessness that is re-quired. It might show that our society is just sufficiently egalitarian, mobile and utilitarian not to permit great excesses in pointlessness, whilst at the same time requiring a kind of minimal modicum of it. It might then be shown that things rather like buttons on sleeves fit the requirement precisely.

But this kind of explanation, useful though it may be in the hands of a skilled practitioner, does not explain why it is *just buttons* and not something else, containing exactly the same amount of pointless-ness, which is employed. Why *ausgerechnet* buttons on sleeves? Obviously there is an infinity of possible adornments, which would satisfy the requirements. Why just buttons? Why just at the bottom of the sleeve?

Here surely the functionalist anthropologist will be driven to say something like this: the structure of society or a social situation is explained synchronically, but the culture, the precise symbols that happen to be employed and so on, can be determined historically, by the past. A certain degree of elaborate sartorial pointlessness is re-quired by this social situation, but the symbols or tools employed for it are determined by the accident of the past.

But this concession, which I think is inevitable, again operates as the thin edge of a wedge. If some cultural content is allowed to be determined by the past, where is one to draw the line? If some cul-tural content is determined in that way, why not a lot of it, as indeed is likely to be the case? And if a lot of it is so determined, is it really plausible to say that at no time do the accidents of cultural *content* have a crucial influence on the structural *form* of the society? The distinction between structure and culture is an enormously im-portant one, and highly valuable in field work and in analysis: but it is not a sharp one, and it would be a daring anthropologist who would maintain that 'culture' is always causally powerless.

So once again, for different reasons, one finds that the powerlessness of the past in the strong and exceptionless sense cannot be maintained, and if qualifications and modifications are introduced, it is not clear how much is left of the original thesis.

There is another consideration, curiously seldom noticed: there is a certain contradiction between the synchronic method and functionalism—notwithstanding the fact that so many anthropologists embraced both, and indeed considered them to be mutually reinforcing. In some ways, no doubt they are. But in one way, they are in contradiction. Functionalism in a way amounts to this: when interpreting an institution, look for the ways in which it contributes to social stability. Functionalism as a *method* consists of the requirement that one should seek these contributions to stability; functionalism as a *doctrine* consists of the view that all existing institutions do make such a contribution.

But all this presupposes that we know the society in question to be *stable*. This means, of course, that we suppose it to have been the same in the past as it is in the present and, indeed, that we expect it to continue in the same condition in the future. But how on earth can one say, almost in the same breath, that one does not know anything about the past of an illiterate tribal society (there being no records), *and* that one knows it to have been the *same* in the past as it is in the present? How indeed. One can say it in the same breath, provided one does not say it in the same words. The presumptuous doctrine claiming knowledge of past stability was not put in these words, but was tacitly incapsulated in the very notion of 'function', meaning, roughly, contribution to *stability*, whereas the more modest principle of disclaimer of speculative reconstructions of the past was asserted, bravely, in so many words. This deception was not, of course, deliberate: it just happened.

What I am saying is that the reasons for the timeless approach, in as far as overtly formulated, were inadequate, imprecisely formulated (and then false on a strong interpretation and inadequate on a weak one), and in some respects downright self-contradictory. Yet underneath, there were other, cogent, valid and important reasons. What were these? They are connected with what seems to me a very valid perception concerning social causation: a kind of sociological rejection of action at a distance.

The trouble with traditional evolutionism was that it had an inbuilt tendency towards a vicious kind of abstraction. I am not saying that this vicious tendency always and necessarily had to manifest itself: but it was a strong tendency, strong enough to vitiate much if not most of the work of evolutionists. It amounted to a tendency to seek causal connections at too high a level.

Evolutionism was concerned with the Great Path. Consequently, and this is an important point, it tended to take stability for granted. It was the great *change* which had to be explained, and hence stability seemed a kind of inertia, requiring no special explanation. Consequently, it is mainly interested in seeing and explaining how one Big Stage causes the next one. But does causation really occur at this level of abstraction?

The answer is—Yes, it does; but before we look at the causation at *this* high level of social abstraction, we must first of all look at the more atomic level of social interaction. Consider an imaginary and very, very stable society, leaving aside the question whether really stable societies exist. An evolutionist with a grand vision might pass this society by, for it is of no interest to him since the time it was generated by the preceding 'stage' or until the time when it begins to generate the next 'stage'. But can such a neglect be justified? This stable society is not, after all, in any kind of social rigor mortis. Bend over the ant-heap, look at it carefully and in detail, and obviously its members must be quite active—perhaps even very, very active. A persisting society, even or especially a stable one, consists of people doing the many things required to keep themselves alive, to reproduce themselves, to maintain order amongst themselves, to ward off the various shocks which an external social or political environment invariably gives to any society—all these things have to be *done*. Is there not a problem here of how this is managed?

Malinowskian anthropologists set about answering precisely this kind of question. They found themselves small-scale, technologically primitive societies, assumed them to be stable (on the somewhat self-contradictory grounds that they did not know their past and consequently could not assert them to be *un*stable), and proceeded to do immensely valuable work in so doing. The explanations they put forward had to be in 'structural–functional' terms, for their terms of reference precluded (rightly) the invocation of something external to the present society altogether, such as its past condition. The explanations then must be 'structural', in as far as they must be about the relationship of the parts of the society to each other. (There is nothing else in terms of which it could be.) They must also be 'functional', for the problem is 'how does the society maintain itself in a condition of stability', and the answer must be in terms of how each individual institution or custom etc. contributes to this effect, and how it in turn is kept in place by the other institutions, etc. Not only are explanations in terms of the past excluded, but the method itself also automatically excludes explanations in terms of unique events, such as the occurrence of an idea or of an outstanding personality, for such a *deus ex machina* explanation would not be a real explanation of stability unless a mechanism was specified which caused its reproduction regularly, and of course if such a mechanism *is* specified, the crucial event ceases to be unique. (It is then acceptable to the method, of course.)

The point towards which I am working is that the 'structural' method, which I am not defining very precisely, but which implies a good look at the self-maintenance properties of organisations (and ignoring supposedly unique events, treating everything anonymously instead), is profoundly implied by the 'timeless' approach, but—and this is enormously important—it does not imply it in turn. In other words, the historic service performed by the shock of timelessness introduced by Malinowski was to make people into structuralists: when they became structuralists, they could then cease to be timeless.[4]

Once the habit of looking at molecular causal connections, so to speak, within a society has become second nature for the social investigator, it can easily be reapplied to *unstable* situations as much as to stable ones, to situations obtaining in *the past* as much as in the present. It in no way requires a rejection either of change and development, or of concern with the past. It had been injected, forcefully, into anthropology as part of a timeless attitude: once it is securely present, it has no need whatever of that timelessness.

Causation does of course occur at both molecular and molar levels (or perhaps one should say *many* levels). Institutions, customs, activities interact and produce the stability, *or* change, of the society, as the case may be, and also in another sense total states of a society produce the subsequent states: but the nexus existing between total states cannot be fully explained without the prior specification of the molecular interactions of which it consists, and whose existence it presupposes.[5]

This shows that those anthropologists who want to save anthropology from the charge of timelessness are somewhat misguided. No doubt they are quite right in their facts, and anthropologists have never neglected the past where evidence was relevant. But this throws out the baby with the bath water. Timelessness was most valuable in throwing out evolutionist pseudo-history: and it is all to the good that it never threw out genuine history as well. But the elimination of evolutionism was a great achievement, and the defence against a minor and not very important charge obscures that achievement. Since the shock of the timeless approach, and thanks to it, concern with molecular causation, and an unwillingness to take stability (*or* change) for granted, have become second nature with anthropological thinking; and this too is an enormous achievement. Why obscure it by being worried with a minor and inaccurate charge?

To sum up the argument: anthropologists are most interestingly distinguishable by their attitude to time. The extreme formulation of that attitude is invalid and yet was, through its very extremity,

valuable: for though mistaken in itself, it brought with it the habitua-
tion, indeed the profound internalisation, of the 'structural–functional' method.

If one believes this method to be most valuable, as I do, it is perhaps desirable to define it, and the crucial notion of 'structure', in
greater detail than has been done so far—for, so far, it has really been
made equivalent in this argument with something like 'attention to
molecular causation'. Hence such a more detailed account must be
the next step in the argument.

What is a functional system, or at any rate a stable functional
system, 'in equilibrium'? It is a system of interacting parts such that
a stable order is maintained, this in turn being defined so that any
change going beyond specified limits will be prevented by mechanisms
within the system. This definition already highlights the fact that the
notion of a functional system is rather elliptical, and becomes determinate only if the limits which must not be transgressed are clearly
specified. The limits cannot be *too* narrow, for some change characterises any system made up of living beings—if only the change
consisting of a turnover in personnel due to the passage of generations. The limits cannot be too broad, of course, without making the
attribution of functionality tautological.

As indicated, such a system may but need not be teleological. Indeed, whether or not it is may sometimes be just a matter of phras-
eology. For example, many children believe the world itself to be a
functional system, in which cats were created to keep down mice, and
dock leaves were created to keep in check the pain caused by stinging
nettles. Now this belief can be formulated in a causal manner, by
simply saying that the whole system is kept within certain limits
through the effect of the behaviour of cats on mice, and of dock
leaves on the pain generated by stinging nettles. Alternatively, it can
of course be formulated (and generally is) in a purposive manner, in
terms of what cats or dock leaves 'are for'. The content of the two
assertions need not differ, though of course it can differ in as far as
the attribution of purpose also contains the idea that there is some
mind responsible for the creation of the whole system, a mind for
which the purpose in question was a decisive consideration.[6]

Now the idea of a self-maintaining order is an interesting one and
deserves some further elaboration. An order is 'self-maintaining' not
only relatively to the permitted limits of change, as indicated, but
also, and in somewhat different sense, it is relative to the amount of
permitted external impact, i.e., the amount of external impact which
it can, as it were, assimilate or digest or react against. A snail, for
instance, is presumably a reasonably self-maintaining organism, but
when crossing a road it cannot resist the external impact of a steam-
roller. Most systems, excluding the universe as a whole, must count

with some external impact, and the attribution of self-maintenance must, once again, contain the specification of just how much external impact can be accommodated. A good deal follows from this point. For instance, it might be argued in defence of the applicability of the 'functional method' in modern circumstances, that the functional interpretations developed concerning traditional society must be tested by the adaptability of traditional institutions in modern circumstances.[7]

I doubt whether this particular defence is generally acceptable. The kind of steam-roller effect which the modern world has must be well beyond the range with which traditional institutions can, in general, cope, or can indeed be expected to.

Another consideration is of course—how much external impact can it tolerate, and how much internal potential for disruption does it possess? A perfect example of a functional equilibrium is a *vacuum*. One may reflect that the most elegant solution for the Creator would have been to create *absolutely nothing*, thus saving Leibniz his question as to why there was anything rather than nothing. Why indeed? There is something inelegant about creating something, and then needing other things to balance it, with the corollary that creating this rather than that opens the Creator to the inescapable charge of arbitrariness and partiality. It really would have been much more elegant to leave the whole thing entirely vacant, for ever and ever, no nettles and no mice.

This is something which does of course occur to the child if it becomes sceptical. Had not the Deity created mice, It need not have troubled Itself with the creation of cats. If only the Deity had not created stinging nettles, It need not have bothered with dock leaves. The world may be functional, but it is cumbersomely so. It contains one thing to counteract another, when it would have been much simpler to have neither one nor the other.

The functionalist anthropologist may not be tempted to play the part of a Leibnizian philosopher and ask why there is anything at all: he may well be content to find out how one thing sustains another and so on in a circle, and leave unasked the questions of why the society exists at all. This only highlights the no doubt trite observation that institutions and activities are not functional in themselves, but only in relation to each other. Perhaps we do not need to justify the circle as a whole, but we do need to establish that there is a circle. And to give an account of the method, we must specify the general nature of the relationship by means of which one institution sustains another. The activities of the one 'cause' the activities of another, or keep them within the appropriate limits. But just *how*?

The very best model for a functional system in equilibrium is an absolute vacuum, which after all has no potential disturbances either

inside or outside. The next best approximation is some rigid im-
mobile homogeneous body which, excluding inner corrosion, is
strong enough to resist external impact up to a certain level of
vehemence. But neither of these resembles a social system, which
after all consists of disjointed moving parts. A good model for a
social system in equilibrium is perhaps one of those situations in
chess in which neither player has any choice and the whole situation
is repetitive. *This* is a social system 'in equilibrium': it is not at the
mercy of the will of the participants, but perpetuates itself *whatever*
they do, within the limits which are open to them.

One might say this of extreme functionalism: it takes the stalemate
in chess as the paradigm of a society.

But the chess situation differs from a social equilibrium in one very
important respect: and the highlighting of this particular feature is
the main merit of using the chess situation. In chess, the rules which
limit the movements of the players are supplied and given *from the
outside*. What corresponds to this given element in the social situation?

A social system is like the game of chess in which the activities of
the players generate and sustain not merely the situation in which
they find themselves, *but also the rules of the game itself*. Nothing in
the very nature and constitution of things prescribes the playing of
this or that game, the rules of which would then lead to stalemate
situations (in the case of stable societies) or progressive situations (in
the case of developing ones). Or rather: very nearly nothing. *Nature*
does impose certain limits. This provides part of the answer: compatibility, rules by which some things are required, are *in part* stated
by nature. No complex of institutions which precludes the nourish-
ment and physical reproduction, for instance, of a given population,
can be self-maintaining. Certain rules of compatibility and incom-
patibility are thus supplied by the physical basis of human existence.
But only some: for if one thing is obvious, it is that the natural
environment plus the need or desire to survive do not uniquely determine social structure. It is simply not the case that given the same
physical environment, and the same size of population, only one
social structure is possible. What else, then, narrows down the range
of possibilities?

In the case of the vacuum or a homogeneous inert mass, the question of 'compatibility' hardly arises. But in a complex made up of
parts, what is it that makes one part compatible with another, or
what makes one part 'sustain' another? In this context, we think
too much in a spatial metaphor: we think of a jigsaw puzzle, where
compatibility is easily understood. But institutions are not shapes
occupying space, whose compatibility or mutual support are easily
understood. They are activities, and above all, repeated activities. It

is important to stress here that for these things, the notion of compatibility is far from self-evident.

We tend to take social causation for granted. But it is in fact a rather puzzling phenomenon. There is here no push or pull. Somebody does something in one place, and *in consequence* somebody else does something else in another place. A man fires a shot and six runners set off on a track. A man raises a signal and an engine driver starts a train. What is the link?

When a man passes food to another and thus enables him to survive, or pushes him to his death, or even when he impels him to do something by a threat, there is a kind of intelligible physical causation present. But nothing of this kind is present in the examples cited. The physical world is perfectly conceivable in which the man fires the starting gun and the runners choose not to run. The connection has at any rate no immediate physical basis. If, then, nature did not supply the connecting rules, who or what did?

One is tempted to say, as the first attempt at a reply, that the *concepts* of the social order in question dictate the connection, or its conventions, or something of that kind. But that won't quite do: what dictates and sustains those concepts or conventions? Anyway, they are not always effective. We are, when facing a social system, facing something very odd indeed: a system whose parts interact by means of connections which *it itself generates.* (I am not here concerned with the question of how we discover social causal connections. I believe we discover them in the same way in which we discover any others, though we may be guided in our search by insight, by *verstehen.* I am concerned with what a social or cultural connection *is,* as opposed to a natural one, rather than how we discover or establish it.) How is the connection maintained?

The first and less puzzling sense in which institutions can be connected with each other, or the society of which they are a part, and have effects which contribute towards the 'explanation' of that society (be it stable or not), is the one arising when a given institution has, for instance, the consequence of safeguarding the food supply in a simple physical sense. Here a 'rule of the game' is supplied by nature, to the effect that a society does not persist unless its members are fed, and a 'move' is made, in the form of the working of an institution or complex of institutions which helps satisfy the need in question. But, as indicated, the rules are not always so supplied by nature. What happens in the other cases?

First, consider what may be called the Idealist solution. It would run something as follows: the concepts of the society themselves acquire a force as great as the rules supplied by nature herself: as great, or almost as great, as the rules demanding the supply of food, the conditions of procreation and so forth. It is the concepts of the society itself which supply some of the 'rules of the game', analogous to the rules of chess in our previous example. When we say that a society is a stable functional system in which the various institutions sustain each other and check each other (or, for that matter, if we say that it is an unstable system leading through the interaction of its parts to a changing end result), the *nexus* between one institution, activity, etc., and its social effect, is provided by the *ideas* of the society itself. Just as nature, a set of data supplied from the outside, decrees that the consequence of the availability of food is the possibility or reality of survival, so culture, the set of ideas of the society itself, decrees for instance that the consequence of one situation (e.g., a certain transgression has been committed) is a certain consequence (e.g., a certain punishment is applied according to certain rules to certain people connected directly or indirectly with the transgression). It is a set of connections like these, dependent on the *ideas* or *concepts* of the society, which leads to the additional interplay of cause and effect (over and above that supplied by nature), and the play of all the complementary chains produced in this effect leads to a stable end result (or an unstable one, as the case may be).

There is an obvious and immediate problem here: the concepts which, as it were, provide the glue between one activity and its social consequences, which determine that *this* should cause *that*, socially speaking, are themselves in a very important and real sense institutions of the society in question. They in turn must be sustained and, for the matter, checked, protected from developing cancerous growth. This makes the system complex, but that is not necessarily an objection: societies *are* complex. There is one well-known short-cut available here, which happily and rightly has, on the whole, dropped out of anthropology: to claim that one sustaining mechanism is sufficient to explain all the concepts which abound in a given society, namely the mechanism of education. The argument is that, particularly in the case of primitive societies, men are so flawlessly indoctrinated, 'conditioned' into the concepts of that society that no one can conceivably think or act outside them. In fact, primitive societies are not such perfect specimens of a retrojected 'Brave New World'.

Eliminating this short-cut, we are left with a picture of causal connections in a society, either based on a nexus supplied by nature, or supplied by culture in the form of a concept of the society, these concepts then being in turn sustained in various ways, so that the social system as a whole is a by-product of natural *and* cultural connections, where the reliability of the cultural connections themselves is a by-product of the system.

But, in this unqualified form, this picture is part of what I've called the Idealist approach and, when left unqualified, incorrect. Basically, it exaggerates two things: first, the power of concepts to guide the behaviour of men and, secondly, the length to which societies can indulge their free fantasy in living by this or that concept. The whole picture, as sketched in so far, would suggest that there is no limit to the kind of connections between activities which a society can impose in virtue of having, or creating, the appropriate concept. For instance, to take a relatively extreme example, a society such as Erewhon could exist, in which people were punished for illness but treated medically for criminal acts, and other societies could exist in which connections were not merely inverted versions, of what we are familiar with, but, in our eyes, totally arbitrary. There would, on this version of the theory, be no restrictive rules on what kind of concepts can exist.

I do not believe that the conceptual and social worlds are so limitlessly flexible. But what then is the alternative to the rejected, idealist picture? The alternative can, appropriately, be called the Materialist account. It would run something as follows: social causation remains very close to physical causation. Examples of physical causation are the nourishing effects of food, or the debilitating effects of undernourishment. When one social event is causally connected with another, what is happening is in principle similar to these examples. There are also things which cannot be physically defined, being conceptual artefacts, so to speak, of the society in question: some of these things might be called 'ideology' or 'culture' or something like that. These things are effected by physical causes but do not significantly react back. The real linkages in a social system, whose sustained interaction leads to stability or change in a society, are between things susceptible to causal connections, such as those summed up as hunger, fear, etc.

The materialist approach amounts to saying this: that which corresponds in sociology to the externally given rules of chess in the stalemate situation, are rules supplied by the physical environment of man (including, of course, those governing his own physiology, etc.). The most important and influential version of sociological materialism is somewhat less extreme than this, in as far as it seems to be saying something like this: the by-product of the interaction of man and environment, and man and man, is the production of certain tools. These, then, form part of the system and have effects of their own, and it is indeed the effects of type of tools which are the crucial factor in understanding and determining the shape of social systems.

How does the so-called structural–functional method stand with respect to the two extremes on the spectrum, from the idealist to the materialist answer, concerning the stuff and nature of social connections? It is, I believe, much closer to the materialist end than to the idealist one, without for all that being in the very least identical with it.

How could one characterise this method? I would like to sum up once again the formal framework within which, on my account, it must be fitted: a social system is an aggregate of parts; its 'parts' are human activities, etc., which interact with each other to produce a certain result; and the *manner* of their connection, the nexus by which they interact, is itself either one further institution of the society in question, or something supplied by the natural environment. We have here a structure in which *some* of the bricks are supplied by nature, but many are, as it were, themselves supplied by the structure and help to hold other parts of it in place.

It is worth noting that the (in my view rightly) fashionable concept of *structure* combines the valid aspects of the underlying intuitions of both materialism and idealism. The sensible aspect of the intuition of materialism I take to be this: our explanatory models should be built up in an orderly and systematic and economical way, in such a way that the properties of the model as a whole should as much as possible follow from the properties of its parts and their arrangement, and that these more primary properties, as it were, should be limited in number, clearly defined and, as far as possible, 'intelligible'. (Rigid materialism, of course, may well have been wrong in trying to work with a very restricted set of such properties, reducing them in as far as possible to the impenetrability of extended matter.)

Idealism, on the other hand, sets out from the perception that in social, semantic, psychological and other systems the *context* provided by the system as a whole is essential: the essence of the part is its role in the system. To take the simplest example, from the theory of meaning: a name is not just a relationship between a sound and a thing. The 'meaning' of a sound, which makes it a name, derives from the fact that it is part of a system in which other names exist, or at least are possible, and have a given role, and that this (not necessarily delimited) system of names relates to a whole set of things, isolated from the continuum in which they occur in accordance with certain principles, and so forth. In other words, one cannot even perceive that something has a name without first of all understanding the system within which it exists and is named.

The notion of 'structure' as used by anthropologists incorporates both these insights. The models are built up with care and with a minimum of invocation of explanatory notions or alleged connections which are not deducible from fairly elementary and manifestly powerful human tendencies. At the same time, the whole orientation of 'structural explanations' drives the investigator towards 'placing' any given activity in the context of the system of which it is a part, which gives it its 'meaning', and towards trying to make that large system explicit.

The same point can probably also be made concerning the ideas underlying Information Theory, cybernetics, etc. The 'Idealist' insight is powerfully present: the models invoked presuppose, fundamentally, that the meaning of a message is its place within a system of alternatives and the rules or pattern of that system. There is no 'echo' theory of meaning here. On the other hand, of course, the fact that this approach leads to the building of concrete physical models highlights its 'materialist' connections—the system is material and its properties depend on the properties of its parts, and there is no suggestion that the system is itself somehow outside the world. In as far as these systems are 'idealistic', they could be described as a kind of mechanised idealism.

Under the impact of explicit and implicit procedural rules, modern anthropologists have developed a distinctive and easily recognisable style of reconstructing the social systems of the societies with which they are concerned. There are certain things an anthropologist will tend *not* to do. He will not rely on allegations of strange motives, a strange concept, or on inertia. Finding a strange custom, he will not invoke the alleged fact that the locals believe something or other (from which belief the custom is meant to follow): he has far too strong a sense of the fragility of belief, and also of the fact that the belief itself needs to be sustained, notably by the very custom which is justified in its name, and cannot constitute an independent and adequate explanation. Similarly, he will not suppose that the locals have been fashioned into possessing some strange and specific motives from which the set custom follows: the same kind of tacit reasoning excludes explanations of this kind. Least of all would he suppose that the custom can be explained by the supposition that it was once established in a specific situation and has since persisted by sheer inertia. (This kind of account, which of course is often built into the local legends themselves, he will contemptuously dismiss as 'just-so' stories when used by old-fashioned anthropologists.)

These things he will refrain from doing. But there are also certain things he positively will do. One is what I would like to call Power Accounting, or a Power Balance-Sheet. I believe that a Power Balance-Sheet is implicitly present in every good anthropological account of a given society. This consists of showing how the persistence of a given political or economic, etc., system is the result of the interplay of given forces in the given environment, observing the negative rules mentioned above—i.e., without placing too much explanatory strain on the assumption of an automatic persistence of strange beliefs, etc. The assumption is that people are very roughly similar all over the place, and are not perfectly socialised, i.e., are not total slaves of either the overt or the tacit norms of their society. Men will go off any kind of social rails. A Power Balance-Sheet shows how the system maintains itself even on the assumption of a reasonable amount of deviance (and, incidentally, a reasonable amount of external disturbance as well).

The negative rules cited above do indeed contain an assumption which can be summed up as the very rough generalisation that people are much the same everywhere. Of course, in fact they are not: but it is a sound methodological rule, built into this method, to minimise the invocation of individual differences. To minimise is not necessarily to exclude altogether: but the requirement to try to find an explanation within the Balance-Sheet first of all is an *excellent* requirement.

The requirement that eccentric beliefs or aims should not too easily be invoked by way of explanation is not the same as their exclusion altogether. The method consists really of placing the onus of proof heavily on the side of the demonstration that strange beliefs, etc., are really present, operative, and sustained by other social factors. If this is indeed established, as it sometimes may be, *then* the further invocation of the eccentricity is permissible.[8]

The structural–functional method, as I am describing it, was not really internalised in the soul of the anthropologist by means of the official summaries of it which exist, but by the real education of the anthropologist: field work, and the subsequent systematic discussion of field work results in seminars by his peers and seniors. It is in these two crucial anthropological activities that the set of rules which I am trying to make explicit was forged and sustained. The method, and its deep internalisation and persistent effectiveness, was the causal, rather than the logical, consequence of the cult of field work.

The ideas of Malinowski, taken in isolation and coldly, may not be particularly original and hence, in that sense, not particularly important. But his position in the history of the social sciences is perhaps, in one respect, rather like that of Lenin in the history of political thought: it is impossible, or at any rate pointless, to investigate his ideas without at the same time being concerned with the institutions which were engendered by them. The importance of Malinowski lies perhaps in his fusion of a certain set of ideas into a kind of whole *and*, above all, in setting up the institutions, the traditions and the ethos which perpetuated the *application* of those ideas in cumulative and profitable research.

Two interesting theories of knowledge were associated with the cult of field work: knowledge by total immersion, and cognition by trauma. I have some sympathy for the former, the Baptist theory of knowledge, so to speak, but am rather sceptical about the second, at any rate when it is generalised. Many people have experienced the trauma of alien mores, without thereby gaining social understanding. Does the trauma work only if it is anticipated? And, in that case, is it genuinely traumatic?

The situation here is parallel to what I claim holds concerning the modern anthropologists' attitude to time: a mistaken doctrine of the self-sufficiency of the social instant served as premise, and overt stimulus, for a perfectly valid attitude towards social explanation. Similarly, an attitude to field work, justified by arguments which were not always cogent, and an attitude which itself may be exaggerated, led to the internalisation of what seems to me a valid type of social explanation. Of course, field work is an excellent thing, partly because it is interesting and enjoyable and partly because it brings in material which otherwise would not be available and which is generally of a far higher quality than that supplied by non-anthropologists. But the analytic method which is internalised by means of the cult of field work and its subsequent discussion by peers has merit quite independently of whether it was indeed preceded by, and internalised by means of, field work; and it can in fact also be applied to non-field-work material.

An additional note about the Power Accounting: the field work habit not only forces the anthropologist to account for the persisting situation (or the situation believed to persist) in terms of the operating forces, but it also forces him to make a kind of survey of all the forces operating in the society and show how they spend themselves. He must ask: why does *this* sub-group not break out, what constrains an individual in this position, etc., etc. This is implicit in the habit of spending a lengthy time in a fairly small community, taking a sociological census, and so on. This imposes a further check of facile and excessively abstract, context-less explanations. What is there must be included in the Power Balance-Sheet, just as the final result at the end of the Balance-Sheet must follow from what is documented in a recognised field work manner.

We can now see how this method differs from what I've called the Materialist and the Idealist accounts of how a social system is built up, and how it is rather closer to the materialist approach than the other. It might be called a 'multiform materialism', to differentiate it from the materialism which carried the doctrine, or the suggestion, that one material base implies one type of 'superstructure'—in other words, a doctrine of a one–one relation. The 'structural–functional method' certainly is not materialist in the sense of carrying any suggestion of such a one–one correlation. It differs from the materialist approach in being quite willing, if the evidence warrants it, to allow explanation in terms of institutions which are social, cultural artefacts, which are not simply dictated by the interplay between nature and an imaginary pre-social man. But it is close to the Materialist approach in placing a heavy onus of proof on any such claim, and thereby placing a healthy restraint on sociological fantasy. All this is, of course, closely connected with the cult of field work, which itself curbs fantasy.[9] One might object at this point: is this, then, all that the 'structural–functional' method amounts to?—an abstention from various kinds of facile explanations, a requirement that the accounting of social forces be thorough, and that the resultant situation be worked out, and effectively be compatible with the forces which are operating, and documented as such; and a cautious but not rigid approach in allowing cultural artefacts to play a part similar to the forces and requirements of nature? Is this really *all* there is to it?

This is indeed, I suspect, a good deal of what it does amount to: but I reject the implication that that isn't a great deal. It may not seem a great deal when cosily and briefly summed up in this manner. But its systematic implementation and application in the study and account of societies *is* a great achievement: indeed, the achievements of social anthropologists bear witness to this. The great achievement of Malinowskian social anthropology was perhaps the establishment and perpetuation of those social institutions *within* the anthropological community which led to the persistent, compulsive, thorough, cumulative applications of these relatively simple rules. Anthropologists were of course also aided by the general characteristics of the societies with which they were concerned: the communities in question were often small, and hence the kind of 'accounting' described could indeed be attempted on the basis of, say, two years of field work. The communities were indeed 'simple' in the sense that, relatively speaking, they wore their social hearts on their sleeves: not in the sense that what their members said corresponded to the reality of the situation, but that the reality of the situation itself could not be hidden in quite so many clouds of ambiguity as it is in complex 'developed' societies. All these advantages are often denied to the sociologist. But, given that the anthropologist did frequently have these advantages, nevertheless modern anthropology must be credited with having found the tools for exploiting them brilliantly.

The merits of the method have not changed or diminished (though there is no further need to tie them either to an attitude of timelessness or to a cult of field work). On the contrary, it seems to me that progress in sociology is conditional to a large extent on applying a similar attitude to large, complex and rapidly changing societies.

What has changed is not the merit of the method, but the external environment which once so greatly favoured the implementation of the method. Roughly speaking, tribes are getting rarer, and the colonial system has (almost wholly) disappeared.

What are the implications of this? In the beginning, I stressed that the differentiation between sociology and anthropology, and hence the relationship between them, was itself as much a social as a logical matter. It follows that the future fate of the method I have attempted to analyse must itself be seen in social terms, i.e. in terms of its fate as operating in effective contemporary conditions, as much as in abstract logical terms.

The connection between modern social anthropology and the colonial system is obvious and has been commented on.[10] Firstly and most obviously, the colonial system made field-work-based anthropology possible by making residence in tribal societies safe, by making the tribal societies relatively accessible (but not so accessible as to destroy them rapidly) and, often, by providing a certain protection for tribal institutions. Colonial administrations were not the same in all places, but in sufficiently numerous colonies they were willing to maintain traditional structures, from one motive or another, provided practices too deeply repugnant to the European moral sense were not indulged and sometimes even without such a proviso. Colonial administrations sometimes had their own version of functionalism, unaided by anthropologists. Some anthropologists are liable to overrate the originality of the functionalist doctrine of the meaningfulness and usefulness of even surprising tribal institutions in their particular social contexts.[11] It would have been surprising if this idea had been novel, for after all it had been the stock-in-trade of conservative political theory for quite some time. The ideas of Burke could be applied to tribal societies as much as to European ones—indeed, in view of the fact that tribal societies were assumed not to have been disrupted by a few centuries of rapid change, they might be supposed to be *more* applicable. What was true of England might, after all, apply equally well to northern Nigeria. Far from it being the case that anthropologists obligingly supplied the colonial administration with an ideology for using the tribes against the newly emergent, disrupted and hence revolutionary classes, it might well be that the anthropologist had brought back his functionalism in part *from* the district officer, who had picked it up from a conservative political background. Be that as it may: the anthropologist's employment of functionalism was considerably superior to the use made of it by conservatives, for conservatives had invoked it as an omnibus *carte blanche* justification of any unspecified archaisms in their own society, whereas anthropologists had used it in a concrete and specific manner to work out what I've called the Power Balance-Sheet of the communities they were studying.

The colonial system aided the field anthropologist not merely by providing him with security and transport. The anthropologist may not have been the intellectual lackey of colonialism, but he was in various very important ways ideologically inoffensive and hence there was no reason not to tolerate him. The anthropologist's aim was to find out how a tribal society worked, to draw the Power Balance-Sheet of the community he was studying, to describe how it *really* worked. For at least two reasons, whatever he found or claimed to have found out was unlikely to be ideologically offensive to the new ultimate power holders, the colonial administration. For one thing, he was naturally, at any rate in the earlier years, concerned with finding out how the tribal society had worked prior to the colonial interference, and hence he tended to abstract from the goings on of the administration, imagining things in their state of sociological purity. If, in all good faith, you abstract from the administrator, you naturally are not likely to say things about the administrator which will annoy him. Secondly, the administration had no ideology of its own about how the tribe 'really functioned', and hence could hardly be upset by any findings on this topic (especially if, as indicated, the findings were liable to abstract from the activities of the administration itself).

There were other factors still. A colonial administration tended to be a genuine bureaucracy: that is to say, its functioning tended to follow set rules, and a member of it, however junior, who observed these rules was reasonably safe. Even if he was not safe, the possession of his post was not something so enormously superior to the professional openings available to him at home as to make him desperately keen at all costs to maintain it. This is not to say that intrigues or conflicts were absent in its ranks (though, on the other hand, the opportunities for intrigue amongst territorially dispersed district officers must be less than amongst bureaucrats in a ministry, with adjoining offices); but, nevertheless, the individual member of the bureaucracy was not involved in a crucial struggle to maintain his position, he was not precarious in the face of those he administered, and he did not need to involve them one way or the other in his intrigues, such as they were.

The situation is different in the post-colonial period. Take an independent ex-colonial country with a multi-party system (they do exist, contrary to popular belief): though the country probably subscribes in a nominal manner to the doctrine of civil service impartiality, in fact the civil servant, or the local administrator, is almost certainly involved in a very serious political struggle, in which the career stakes from his own viewpoint are very great indeed. He is unlikely to welcome an independent observer and busybody who amongst other things provides locals opposed to himself with the possibility, or the illusion, of a new channel of information and communication with the capital.

Or consider one of the more typical one-party states. The same facts operate, in as far as there may be conflict within the one political system, and the anthropologist, being outside the local system of sanctions and authority, provides a disturbing break in the authority structure. Moreover, both his existence, his views and, finally, the report he publishes may be in conflict with what is ideologically required to be true.

It is not so much that under the colonial system the anthropologist had on his side the prestige of belonging to the dominant race, whereas now he does not: he still often does, by virtue of his contacts and his familiarity with the modern world, possess a privileged position amongst the local population. It is rather that the privileged position he now occupies tends, in the political setting, to act against him, whereas in the past it acted on his behalf. It is for this reason that the post-colonial world is not particularly favourable to anthropological research.

But these practical difficulties might be overcome by a skilful and determined field worker. Or, at least, they might be overcome in favourable circumstances. It is not the practical difficulties which constitute the biggest and most significant change in the working conditions of the anthropologist. The really important change is taking place in the nature of his subject matter, in the societies he is studying.

To begin with, a point by way of introduction: it is generally assumed that the forces of the modern world destroy small intimate communities, and substitute large structures. In one sense, this is not true. A colonial occupation, or a modernisation drive by a newly independent country, does not always rapidly destroy, for instance, the kinship structure or family organisation of a given people. An anthropologist can arrive, decades after the effective incorporation of the local community in a wider political system, and find these molecular social patterns, so to speak, relatively undisturbed. It is the *larger* units, the political achievements on a grander scale, which tend to disappear most rapidly, be it because they are rivals of the new institutions or because their functional prerequisites are more precarious. There are of course exceptions to this: the emirates of northern Nigeria, or the kingdom of Buganda spring to mind. But by and large, it is the large-scale groupings and institutions of the traditional world which disappear most easily (and where they do not, to what extent is there a real social continuity, as opposed to a merely nominal one, in the institution surviving from the traditional world into the modern one?).

Perhaps this generalisation will not survive careful scrutiny. But suppose it does; what follows? Are the modern political and other large-scale institutions which replace 'tribal states', where these existed, as amenable to anthropological enquiry as were those traditional ones which they replaced? In other words: is the district officer, or the secretary of the local branch of the political party, as amenable to anthropological interpretation as the chief or the cult priest?

The answer must be: *ultimately*, yes. 'Ultimately', it *must* be so if I am right in my contention that socio-anthropological method, 'structural–functional' interpretation is simply the paradigm of correct sociological method in any context. If this is so, then in the long run it must of course be applicable. It simply embodies the recognition that social life has at its base the repetition of certain activities, and that these cycles of activity, as well as changes in the pattern of the cycles, must be causally explained, and that the system of sanctions or incentives which canalise the concrete doings of individuals into grooves compatible with these cycles must themselves be explained without facile invocation either of nature or of conscious intention and belief, and so forth.

But, in the short run, the world of the district officer and of the secretary of the political party does differ very significantly from that of the chief and of the cult priest. The point is this: the technological limitations of 'primitive' society were a considerable help in narrowing the range within which one could seek the causal mechanisms which maintained the social structure. What are the sanctions, the multiple swords of Damocles, hanging over any society? Above all, starvation, anarchy, external aggression. A sociological account must explain how, outside the Garden of Eden, both life and order are maintained by a society in an indifferent or hostile environment. The means of production and of coercion available to primitive society are, by definition, very limited. This considerably simplifies the search for explanations. This also, in my view, gives a very special interest to those larger groupings and institutions and political structures which are sometimes evolved in primitive society: the achievement is so much greater, its mechanisms so much more interesting. A skyscraper built of mud is more interesting than one built of concrete.

Modern society differs from this in that it can allow itself a kind of sociological fantasy. Where productive and administrative techniques are so very powerful, the society can, from accident or ideological predilection, build up structures which are not the simplest or optimal means of attaining certain effects. There is here a clear analogy with the notion of 'functionalism' in architecture. Where technology is limited, one can see how the materials 'dictate' a given style of building. Where technology is as powerful as it now is, it is only the architect's preference for simplicity, in other words a particular aesthetic doctrine, which keeps him within 'functional' solutions. He can easily allow himself non-functional solutions, if his taste or that of his clients happens to require it. It is in this sense, amongst others, that functional interpretations are not immediately and easily applicable to modern societies. They have far too much technological and administrative leeway.

It is significant that anthropologists think of 'functionalism' as essentially a descriptive doctrine, whereas architects think of it as a normative or prescriptive one. 'Functionalism' seems descriptive in sociology and prescriptive in architectural aesthetics. The reason is of course that modern building materials allow architects ample scope *not* to be functional, so that if they proceed 'functionally' it is from preference and not from necessity. The same may yet happen to societies. Not quite yet, perhaps: one still hears, for instance, that industrial society has certain kinds of functional preconditions which are not compatible, for instance, with strict Muslim religious observances, or that the functioning of secular Israel is not easily squared with strict religious Jewish observance. But the time may come when the progress of automation will make the strictest industrial discipline compatible with the greatest Muslim religious rigorism, and when a massive electronic automated *shabes-goi* will make an industrial theocracy feasible. In other words, it is possible that fully industrial society will exceed in ritual and doctrinal fantasy anything achieved by 'primitive' society.

The present relevance of this point may very well be challenged, and I would not wish to be dogmatic about the extent to which it is now significant. It might be challenged as follows: the administrative power of modern societies should not be overrated. Consider those numerous and striking failures to mobilise populations in accordance with the wishes of the administration. Just because the central power possesses means of coercion, bribery, propaganda, information and communication, etc., that does not mean that these provide it with effective and adequate levers for organising the society according to its wishes. The actual life of societies is outlined within limits set not by deliberate plan, by what I called sociological fantasy, but by social reality. Is it not just for this reason that sociologists are now so fashionable, so very much in demand as advisers on the implementation of social reform and development?

There is clearly a good deal of truth in this counterassertion. The reply to it in turn consists of two points. First, and not very interesting, is that this is a matter of degree. The fact that the power of deliberate manipulation is not limitless, and in certain cases totally absent, despite the presence of modern administrative and technological means, does not mean that it is non-existent, and that it can be ignored in those many cases and areas where it has radically transformed the situation. Secondly, and more interestingly, there is this consideration: there is now a rather different relationship between the nominal and the real social structure of any given society. There is a sense in which, in traditional societies, the nominal political or religious structures were also parts of the real structure: however distinct from the real structures and however illusory or divergent from them in content, nevertheless the nominal structure usually had an important part to play. Its illusions or ambiguities were 'functional', in contributing something to the real functioning of the society which they were in and described. The society could not allow itself the luxury of what I called sociological fantasy.

This is not so in modern societies. The real functioning may still be subject to very real limitations (though less so than in the past), and these are inadequately explored. But it is too easy to build up nominal hierarchies of authority on ideological precepts, social theories and so forth. It is very easy, the limits are so wide as to be hardly discernible, and there is very little presumption of 'functionality'. It is for these reasons that modern nominal structures are so very much less interesting than the old ones: it is not just romanticism which makes some anthropologists more interested in the old structures of a tribe than in a ministry or a district office. The former may be sociologically more significant: it may reveal the limits of what can be done, organisationally, with certain limited means. If assumed to persist over time, there is a strong presumption of functionality.

This brings one to the problem of typicality. The following objection is sometimes raised against anthropological method: an anthropologist will pick his village and investigate it intensively, and then present his findings as the structure of *the* Ruritanian village, without having any real basis for his explicit or implicit contention that the village he chose is typical of Ruritanian villages in general. There is a twofold answer to this: first, typicality is not at issue. Of course, an anthropologist should not make claims of typicality where he has no evidence to support such a claim, but a single Ruritanian village is of interest irrespective of whether it is typical or not. Given the limited resources available to Ruritanian villages, any one village constitutes important evidence of what can be done, given those resources. Secondly, the limitation of resources itself constitutes some evidence of typicality, even where there is no survey of the traits of Ruritanian villages in general. If one knows the general ecological conditions obtaining in Ruritania, and the institutional and conceptual devices available in Ruritanian culture and language generally, one automatically has *some* evidence of the limits of possible structures to be found in Ruritanian villages. (This evidence may be misinterpreted, and should of course, whenever possible, be supplemented by a genuine survey: but all the same, it does constitute some evidence.)

Both these arguments are of course very much weakened for a modern context. Where the presumption of functionality is weaker, good evidence of typicality matters more. There is much less of a presumption of a kind of limiting achievement within given means, and there is also much less of a presumption that one can know the limits of the cultural tools available: there is too much instability, change and heterogeneity in the modern world. For these reasons, knowledge of typicality becomes very much more important, and investigation of community in isolation correspondingly less valuable.

Typicality in space brings one back to the question of typicality in time, and the question of the presumption of stability as a tacit premise of 'functional' interpretations. In my earlier account of what underlay this assumption, I concentrated on the *logical* considerations: on the assumption of stability as a camouflaged form of the insistence on a realistic assessment of causal connections, which, once appreciated as such, can indeed be dissociated from that assumption of stability which had introduced it, and equally applied to unstable situations. (The latent function of a-historism, I claimed, was a realistic, structural approach to social conditions. Once this latent function becomes manifest, the old manifest rationale can be dropped.) But this (to my mind) admirable premise was not the only consideration present. There was also an empirical matter. Primitive societies were assumed to be stable in as far as they lacked the technical means for being *un*stable. They were assumed to lack the means to get anywhere from their present conditions, and a similar argument could be extended backwards: no special means were available in the recent generation to make the present condition an exceptional and temporary one but, on the contrary, it could be assumed to be somehow 'normal' for the society in question. Now this argument is something of a *non sequitur*: for although technological power generates rapid change, not all rapid change is generated by technological power. As no one put forward this argument *explicitly* (as far as I know), no one can be specifically charged with it, though I believe it was tacitly operative in helping to make the stability assumption acceptable. But there is, once again, an element of truth in it, despite its unacceptability as a generalisation. The element is this: stability can be assumed as a first approximation where there is no evidence to the contrary in primitive societies, whereas the strongest possible presumption against it exists in modern contexts. In modern contexts, positive evidence for stability would be required before one could really assume that recent generations were in a condition similar to the present one.

When this is true, the realistic assessment of causal connections, which on my argument is at the heart of sound anthropological and sociological method, cannot begin by simply looking for the way in which current practices contribute to their own perpetuation, because this perpetuation cannot be presumed to hold, and the method cannot proceed without positively trying to ascertain what the past situation was. To resume the earlier formulation, typicality cannot be assumed either over time or over space. Take this in conjunction with the fact that social structures are not the limiting exploitations of given means, for the means of the modern world are as yet unexploited, together with the fact that the divorce between nominal and real structures is sharper and different in kind from that which obtained in traditional societies, and you can see that the anthropologist working in modern conditions lives in a world very different from that which formed his method and traditions a decade or so ago.

SUMMARY OF ARGUMENT

One of the crucial things about social anthropology is its method.

This method, when reduced to its bare bones, may sound obvious. Nevertheless, obvious though it may be, few men who investigate societies or theories about them have succeeded in not sinning against it. The distinctive and important thing about social anthropology is the creation of a tradition which sustains the effective application of this (theoretically obvious) method, and which minimises the danger of sinning against it. It is a tradition which itself contains institutional checks enforcing the 'right approach'.

The method consists in the first place of seeking causal connections between various institutions and activities. (Only in appearance is it teleological.) Obvious though this may seem, the effective implementation of this requirement distinguishes social anthropology from many styles of enquiry which only seek causal connections in an ineffectual and unrealistic manner. Furthermore, the method requires that the causal connections themselves should be explained: leaving aside those connections which are imposed by nature, there is nothing inherent in the nature of things which requires that one activity should have the modification of another one as its effect. If it does have such an effect, this is itself a social fact. It in turn requires support from other activities or institutions. Anthropological method requires that this circle be, as far as possible, closed. *This* is the essence of functionalism. Functionalism is not really a doctrine about what societies are like: it is rather an obligation placed upon anthropological enquiry. It contains excellent recipes for avoiding facile ways of achieving this end.

This method and its application was engendered and sustained by various factors within the anthropological tradition and in the wider world in which it operated. Some of these factors were doctrinal and, it so happens, mistaken, but the abandonment of these mistaken ideological props does not require the abandonment of the method itself. (Examples: the doctrine of social stability, built into 'functionalism', or the doctrine of the irrelevance of the past.) Others were customs of the anthropological community itself, such as the institutionalisation of field work. This is a good but not a necessary thing, and can again if necessary be abandoned without the abandonment of the method itself. Others still were social conditions of the wider world, notably those prevailing under the 'colonial system', and these are in any case disappearing. Thus many of both the doctrinal and socio-environmental props of the method are disappearing. These are general features of the modern world which make the application of the method more difficult.

Thus the application of the method to new situations and in new conditions is more difficult than it was in the past. It is, however, eminently desirable.

NOTES

1 Cf. E. E. Evans-Pritchard, *Essays in Social Anthropology*, London, 1962, Essays 2 and 3.
2 Cf. I. Schapera, 'Should Anthropologists be Historians?', *Journal of the Royal Anthropological Institute*, **92**, July 1962, 143–56.
3 Latent functions were not discovered by anthropological functionalists. Long before, they were familiar to philosophers as the Cunning of Reason.
4 This shows how mistaken it is to attack 'functionalism' along the lines adopted by Kingsley Davis, who argues ('The Myth of Functional Analysis as a Special Method in Sociology and Anthropology', *American Sociological Review*, **24**, December 1959, 757–72) that 'functional' explanations do not differ from any other kind of explanation in sociology and that consequently functionalism is a myth. Functional explanations may indeed not differ from other causal explanations: but the whole point is that the doctrine and method against which functionalists were reacting was, in a very important way, vacuous in its supposedly causal explanations. Functionalism thus differed from *inadequate* causal explanations.
5 This point in no way prejudges the order in which various connections are noted or established. One may perceive a molar connection without having fully worked out or understood a molecular one, and of course vice versa.
6 It is interesting to note that primitive societies tend to have their own evolutionism and their own functionalism. They interpret the world purposively, but they also explain its causal arrangements in terms of antecedent events, whose effects somehow continue to pervade the world.
7 This was argued to me in conversation by Dr Ioan Lewis.
8 It is sometimes claimed that the anthropologist, as such, has no opinion about the validity of, e.g., witchcraft beliefs. (This claim is to be distinguished from the stronger, and even more mistaken, view that local concepts are never mistaken.) This seems to me incorrect. In fact, the anthropologist knows full well that witches do not exist, and that *consequently* he is obliged to explain how witchcraft beliefs are sustained. *True* beliefs do not require to be explained nearly as much—though they too need a social explanation. There are social explanations of true beliefs just as there are of false beliefs, but when beliefs fly in the face of evidence the social mechanism presumably needs to be that much stronger. But it is precisely the anthropologist's awareness of the false elements in local belief, that helps him select the areas requiring special explanation.
9 There is a puzzle about the Materialist approach which I do not quite know how materialists themselves face. Their position treats the social, cultural, conceptual artefacts as a kind of epiphenomenon. But if some class of human activities is mainly or largely epiphenomenal, why should it exist at all? What need is there to have an excrescence which echoes, but does not in turn have significant effects? Is it just a kind of causal accident, it just so happens that society generates it, without it being in any way essential to the system? I suspect Materialism is ambivalent and inconsistent at this point: it both treats the 'superstructure' as epiphenomenal, and yet also as pretty essential to the maintenance of the system—which suggests that it does have crucial effects after all. Anyway, if it is epiphenomenal, is its *specific* content irrelevant? Could a society of one kind have *any* kind of cultural superstructure? And, if not, can the superstructure be epiphenomenal? And there are distinctions to be drawn: what is epiphenomenal—the fact that there is a superstructure at all, or the specific cultural content it has? And, if the latter, to what degree of specificity is it determined by the substructure?
10 Cf., for instance, Peter Worsley, *The Trumpet Shall Sound*, London, 1957, p. 260.
11 Cf. Dr Ian Hogbin, 'Malinowski's Theory of Needs in R. Firth, ed., *Man and Culture*, London, 1957, pp. 245–64; see esp. p. 248.

8
ON MALINOWSKI

Social Anthropologists are defined not by the fact that they study tribes but that they are a tribe, just as sociologists are distinguishable by the anomie they display as much as by the one they investigate. The structure of the anthropological tribe is like that of many academic groups, in the main (disregarding complications arising from the influence of the late Professor Radcliffe-Brown) unilineal and segmentary. At the apex of each clan stands the common ancestor, descent from whom delimits membership. In the volume under review,[1] members of the brilliant clan claiming descent from Malinowski, in the main the currently cathedral generation, give accounts and assessments of their ancestor and in so doing naturally and inevitably also give an account of the clan itself and its development. Even if not all segments are represented, there could seldom have been so impressive a list of informants so neatly lined up (each mapping one of the many aspects of Malinowski's work) nor could one wish for a clan more worthy of investigation. It deserves investigation because, over and above the merits of its ideas, it is closer than many academic traditions to achieving enough cohesion for communication and cumulativeness and yet not so much as to thwart progress—unlike some of the either undirected, or on the other hand *gleichgeschaltet* populations around it on the departmental map.

A curious thing is that the Malinowski clan as self-portrayed in this volume is the only documented case I know of the occurrence of the Freudian version of the social contract. A number of the contributors more or less frankly confess their ambivalence and comment on its roots in the fact that in criticizing, they are striking at their intellectual father, and note that in such circumstances a blow must be hard and determined if it is to be made at all. So, a common ambivalence, a shared paternity and a shared guilt appear to be the social bond . . .

In a sense, of course, the very existence of this book is a paradox. One of the key ideas of the Malinowskian approach was the irrelevance of the past as such: '. . . the past is significant *in-so-far* as it lives in the present' (quoted on page 243, italics mine). This being so, and Malinowski being dead—does only the remembered and not the real Malinowski matter?—and what if the two diverge? Much of him is in fact very much alive, whether remembered correctly or not. The paradox is accentuated by those who (rightly) stress that the *rejection* of the past must itself be seen *in its historical context* (as a means of combating facile and superficial explanations of present institutions as 'survivals'). So the historical context seems necessary for at least one explanation. At least two of the informants explicitly see Malinowski's ideas themselves as he would have us see those of tribesmen. Professor M. Fortes says (p. 164): 'Functional theory as developed by him is an impressive attempt to provide what he would have called a "charter" . . . for the kind of field research . . . of which he was the unrivalled master.' Mr Leach says something similar on p. 124: 'Functionalism in Malinowski's hands became something very like a religious creed.'

Alive though he is in present practices, it is not always the same Malinowski who is remembered. Informants sometimes contradict each other—as informants will—and one of them is engaged in forging some dubious but very suggestive genealogical links to justify a present alignment. Professor Parsons tells us (p. 67) that 'Essentially Malinowski's social psychology turns out to be a modification of the instinct theory of McDougall'. He had (p. 70) '. . . without full understanding, decided that Freud's theory was culture-bound and could not explain Trobriand facts [and] dropped it and never made serious use of it . . .' Per contra, Professor Fortes tells us (p. 168) 'Thus, psycho-analysis fitted Malinowski's general approach. It also fitted his conception of human nature.' 'Malinowski's debt to psychoanalysis is obvious in much of his work . . . but nowhere so markedly as in his description of Trobriand family structure . . .'

Or: Professor Raymond Firth tells us (p. 14) 'Malinowski had not seemed to be particularly conscious of himself as a Pole in any politically nationalist sense.' On page 13, he quotes a letter of Malinowski's written in 1914 in which he says 'We had the best treatment in Austria and as a confederation of fairly autonomous peoples, A. was one of the most passible [*sic*] states . . . This is my *confession de foi*.' On the other hand, Miss Lucy Mair (p. 232) says 'Malinowski's own experience, as a Pole under Austrian rule, of the situation of ethnic minorities in Europe, was never far from his mind . . . In Europe this consisted essentially in the suppression of overt modes of behaviour . . .' And, on page 235, 'Again in part because of his own experience as one of a subject people in a European empire, he was deeply sympathetic to African discontents . . .'

The informant who seems to be forging a link is Mr Leach. Rightly discerning an important analogy between Malinowski's approach in anthropology and William James' in philosophy, he goes on from this to claim that Malinowski was 'grounded' in James just as the authors of the book themselves were grounded in Malinowski. Leach's motive in forging this link appears to be a desire to align anthropology with what he considers to be a successful current movement in philosophy and to argue that current anthropology is superior to Malinowski's as linguistic philosophy is superior, in Leach's estimate, to Pragmatism.

Now the forging of the link is itself harmless enough: what is more serious is that having done so, Leach accepts the legends of the movement (linguistic philosophy) to which he is connecting himself: 'Down to the end of the nineteenth century most philosophies . . . were based on Aristotelian logic, which assumes that all Truth is of one kind and that the validity of statements about God can be tested by the same criteria that might apply to statements about the sun' (p. 122). Conjectural history about a documented subject like philosophy is not merely un-anthropological, it is also rash. Mr Leach must learn to distrust informants in Cambridge as he would in Burma or Ceylon. What *is* true is that only of late has the idea of the diversification of logic been pushed to the point (beyond Pragmatism) where there can no longer be any general criteria and hence no criteria at all, so that any conceptual change becomes unintelligible. This is indeed analogous to an extreme form of Functionalism which also treats certain phenomena (such as ritual statements) as sui generis and context-bound and thus makes both comparison and social change unintelligible (for similar reasons).

The one contributor who claims to have gone radically beyond Malinowski is Professor Parsons, who finds him defective on the subject of the relationship between the individual and the social system. Parsons provides us with the following premisses: Malinowski was not definitely first-rate as a theoretician of social systems. Those very defects in his treatment which prevented him from being definitely first-rate were however avoided by 'Parsons, Bales *et al.* (1955)'. Modesty has apparently prevented Parsons from completing the syllogism.

A contributor who attempts to defend Malinowski precisely at the point at which Parsons thinks Malinowski failed to advance far enough is Professor Piddington. Piddington attempts to defend, as few would wish to do nowadays, the use of explanations in terms of 'Basic Needs'. The difficulties inherent in the notion he thinks can be overcome by making use of the *Cultural* Standard of Living (as opposed to a merely material one) and by realizing that basic needs are generic, only acquiring their specificity in a social context. But these devices, reminiscent of the neo-Marxist attempt to prove that workers are still at the starvation edge because this edge is relative, seem to me to make the whole argument circular: if social factors decide the standard which must be attained, that standard is no longer basic, no longer the independent variable, and if the needs are merely generic, to indicate them is to classify rather than to explain. What is true is that a society must survive to exist, and to do so its members must eat, procreate and avoid death by exposure and illness. It does not follow that the nature of the society or of its members' aims can be explained by starting from this consideration.

Professor Piddington also attempts to save Malinowski from the critics of his a-historism by invoking the time-span involved, wishing to allow 'cultural lag' for shortish time-spans. But this won't do either. In one sense, there are indeed *no* historic survivals: what is done, is done now and *ipso facto* has a motive now. In another sense, there are cultural survivals: causal chains, including repetitive circular ones, can and do continue to operate over *long* as well as short periods. Thus Piddington's compromise is both too weak and too strong. It is better to say that the a-historism was a confused doctrine but an excellent charter for good investigations which do not take continuity for granted—and leave it at that.

Whilst disagreeing with Piddington's attempts to save basic needs, Parsons' claim to have advanced the subject by more elaborate and differentiated conceptual schemes seems to me mistaken. The key notions of those schemes are not themselves original or difficult, and their baroque elaboration has not, so far, either illuminated the past nor inspired, or even 'chartered', new and fruitful researches.

One theme which appears a number of times in the volume is that of the ethical and practical implications of Malinowskian anthropology. For it makes a powerful impact in a number of ways—through its relativism, its functional and hence implicitly conservative interpretation of institutions, and its functional and hence implicitly tongue-in-cheek interpretation of social doctrines, ideologies, myths. In connection with the conservatism, Mr Ian Hogbin remarks (p. 248) '. . . in 1922 Malinowski published a paper . . . which the general public must have found revolutionary. He put forward a theory of culture as an integrated whole and stressed that if any part was tampered with a general collapse might follow.' A conjectural reconstruction of the general public's reaction? I should be surprised if the general public found quite such novelty in an idea that has long been a commonplace of conservative political theory. What *is* novel about Malinowskian anthropology is not the idea, but its detailed and thorough application. Conservative political theorists have on the whole contented themselves (and still do) with just *asserting* it, possibly embellishing it with an illustration or two. (Sometimes they add the doctrine of the impossibility of social *understanding* as well

as of social tinkering, thereby obviating even the possibility of pur-
suing the idea further.) The important thing about Malinowski is not
the assertion *that* it is so, but the fact that the assertion was a charter
for detailed investigation of *how* it manages to be so. The assertion
is partly false but the investigations are fruitful, and will in due
course show the extent to which the idea holds—and fails to hold.
For this reason I think that Functionalist social anthropology is not
really, appearances notwithstanding, conservative in its ultimate
effects, and is unlike and superior to the woolly functionalism of conservative political theory.

Another fairly novel feature of Malinowskian functionalism was
its fusion with a-historism, an unusual combination. The European
conservatives who speak of wisdom of institutions generally also
speak of the wisdom of a tradition and a past. But the Malinowskian
combination is not so surprising if one reflects that many of the
Evolutionists against whom he was re-acting were also rationalists
(for which they get little credit nowadays, a current stereotype lumping them together with 'historicism'). His a-historism was the obverse
of their evolutionary approach, his functionalism the denial of their
rationalistic interpretations.

Another idea with profound ethico-political implications is the
social view of myth and ideology. Both Professor Firth (pp. 12 and
13) and Professor Nadel (p. 205) quote similar and rather moving
expressions on Malinowski's part, one written in 1931 and one in
1936, both tending to the view that traditional religion is a necessary
barrier to social disaster; of the two passages the latter is, not sur-
prisingly, more openly committed to the pragmatic need for even
untrue religion as a necessary condition of civilization. The passage
written earlier is still agnostic about this need. Nadel very aptly comments that such pragmatism is close to the cynicism of Plato's 'noble
lie'. I agree: and it is apposite here to point out that, on the ethical
level, my objection to the post-pragmatist developments favoured by
Mr Leach, the linguistic functionalism which in the name of the
diversity of logic sees *all* types of statements as legitimate in their own
realm and all realms legitimate, is that it obscures the fact that this *is*
cynicism, much as at the level of theory it makes nonsense of intellectual progress.

The volume in fact deals with all aspects of social anthropology
and in analysing and assessing his contribution it also portrays the
developments that have taken place since. Having picked out some
themes for comment, mainly those which have provoked disagreement and neglecting those many where I agree or am incompetent to
disagree, it is necessary to correct the possible misunderstanding that
the book as a whole is being criticized. On the contrary—this book
is to be whole-heartedly commended, not only to those interested in

anthropology but also to anyone interested in seeing thought in action, a living tradition laid bare. There could hardly be a greater compliment to Malinowski and the tradition he has initiated than the fact that a *Festschrift* of this kind, instead of being uneven, disjointed and academically formal, should be so exciting (I read the book almost at one sitting) informative and complementary without being repetitive. It is complementary even—or especially—in its disagreements, and in its unresolved problems, such as the delimitations of structure, function and culture, where the definitions are both divergent and unsatisfactory (though I doubt whether this matters for practical research purposes); and it gives one so dynamic a picture of the subject of social anthropology that one can practically see it moving before one's eyes. It is of course far more than a portrait of a clan, it is a convincing account of a science in action, an account which succeeds in explaining its past but also inspiring admiration, confidence and interest in its future.

NOTE

1 *Man and Culture*, An Evaluation of the Work of Malinowski, edited by Raymond Firth. Contributions by J. R. Firth, Raymond Firth (two), M. Fortes, H. I. Hogbin, P. Kaberry, E. R. Leach, L. Mair, S. F. Nadel, T. Parsons, R. Piddington, A. I. Richards, I. Schapera. London, Routledge & Kegan Paul, 1957.

9

ON EVANS-PRITCHARD

The views of the most admired of living social anthropologists on the problems involved in comparing one society with another cannot but be of interest to circles far wider than the anthropological one. So it is with the first essay on the Comparative Method, in *The Position of Women in Primitive Societies and Other Essays in Social Anthropology*. Apart from being full of substance and elegantly presented, it is also a somewhat sad, but not despairing or dispirited, record of a quest:

> *Myself when young did eagerly frequent,*
> *Doctor and saint, and heard great argument . . .*

Evans-Pritchard now seems resigned evermore to come out by the same door as in he went: the quest for sociological generalisations, to be attained by means of the comparative method, seems unavailing. With irony he observes that, indeed, it was much easier to formulate generalisations during the pre-history of anthropology, when the paucity of well-documented facts gave each generalisation a somewhat longer life-span than it can hope for now. Yet, rightly in my view, he does not think either that we should desist. Even if this holy grail is never found, the search will have profited us in other ways.

Superficially, some of Evans-Pritchard's argument seems conducted in terms of a mistaken opposition—as the followers of Professor Popper will be quick to point out—between the merely 'illustrative' method, in which 'examples are cited in support of some thesis deductively arrived at' (p. 14), and sound method, in which 'proper understanding of the ethnographic facts must come before any really scientific analysis' (p. 34). Is not the proper antithesis between on the one hand testing hypotheses (arrived at deductively or in any other way) against the hardest cases, and on the other hand merely seeking confirmative illustration? Yet elsewhere this is recognised: 'Clearly, little advance can be made unless each new piece of research is done in relation to hypotheses . . .' (p. 31). No mention

here of the priority of proper ethnography over science. Yet, interestingly, I believe he is by implication too modest, in this last
remark, about the achievements of that tradition of social anthropology to which he has contributed so much. In fact, it *is* possible for
a social anthropologist to do useful work without setting out to test
any 'hypothesis'. The reason is that socio-anthropological method, as
effectively developed, practiced and transmitted by Evans-Pritchard
and his colleagues, already contains in itself, implicitly, a set of
questions and even hypotheses (often negative) which, if a researcher
does his job at all competently, lead to results which are not merely
fairly reliable, but above all usable for further and comparative work.
It is the development and systematic application of a loose set of
standard questions, a high level of thoroughness in answering them,
and the deeply engrained avoidance of facile accounts and explanations (e.g. psychologistic ones, which are still common currency
amongst non-anthropologists), which constitutes an important part
of the achievement of social anthropology.

Evans-Pritchard records a view he recently held, jointly with some
other anthropologists, to the effect that 'intensive comparative investigation on a limited scale [is] most likely to lead to initial results
of value'. It is unclear from his formulation whether he still holds this
view, though he reports that with respect to the Nilotic peoples, it has
not proved productive. But there is a kind of pragmatic contradiction
between this view and a complaint he voices two pages later (p. 31),
that a later specialist in witchcraft, Kluckhohn, ignored Evans-
Pritchard's own study of the Azande when investigating the Navaho.
My own guess is that the idea underlying the complaint is sounder
than the one underlying the commendation of 'limited scale': it is
true that, when a group of people shares a historical or geographical
background, differences which nevertheless exist call for special
explanation, and help to highlight explanatory factors; but the interesting comparisons seem to be those which take analogous phenomena without regard to distance, as for instance between the Azande
and the Navaho.

It would be a pity if Evans-Pritchard's modesty and partial dis-
couragement concerning the attainability of sociological generalisations, were allowed to give comfort to those complacent souls who,
only a very few years back, were invoking this argument against the
recognition of sociology. For one thing, *he* is entitled to say this: he
did 'frequent doctor and saint, and heard great argument', and contributed much to it, and if he now feels tempted by a limited scepticism, he has earned the right to it. Some of those who spoke loudest
about the failure of sociological generalisations did so without serious
acquaintance with attempts to reach them, and with the support of
arguments which were not merely deductive, but also hopelessly

muddled. (One instance only: I remember hearing a professor of politics argue in all seriousness that because the most ambitious sociological theory, Marxism, was false, therefore sociology as such was impossible . . .)

But there is more to this than the difference between the argument from knowledge and the argument from impertinence. There is an immeasurable difference between the kind of real knowledge of human societies, found for instance in Evans-Pritchard's work, and the type of facile 'social thought' which is still in some places considered academically respectable (if only because social thought is held to be a kind of intellectual slumming, which, not being serious anyway, ought at least to be entertaining and hence, above all, not intellectually strenuous). Consider the so-called 'history of ideas': this name can, of course, cover a real inquiry. But when concerned with 'social' ideas, which generally are not difficult—after all, they must be ideas accessible to whole populations, or large segments of them—it is often a kind of worthless crypto-sociology, presupposing and hence insinuating, without however seriously defending, the view that human societies are formed by ideas, that these are invented in books and arrive in some kind of intelligible sequence, etc. As these views aren't seriously held, but only presupposed for the sake of the facility of the 'research' and the presentation they imply, they should really be called the postprandial-Hegelian style. The postprandial-Hegelian genre is still far too common and far too widely tolerated: anyone seeking for contrast, an example of what genuine social understanding really can be like, could hardly do better than start with Evans-Pritchard's work.

The second essay in the volume, which gives it its title, seems to me in various ways the least typical of the author's work and the least satisfactory. From a publisher's viewpoint it is no doubt preferable to use *The Position of Women* in the title, rather than say *The Comparative Method* or, worse still, the *Imagery in Ngok Dinka Cattle-Names*, but otherwise there seems to me to be little reason for singling out this essay—other than, perhaps, the fact that ironically it illustrates some of these very dangers against which the first essay warns with so much knowledge and insight.

This essay contains a number of generalisations about women in primitive and in modern society, generalisations which at best seem to me in need of expansion or qualification—and, moreover, I have some difficulty in recognising that modern society ('our own', according to the title of the lecture, delivered in 1955) which is introduced for purposes of contrast. May one suspect that the ordeal of having to entertain Bedford College for Women (as it then was) for an hour, led the author into a genre he would not otherwise have adopted?

One of the generalisations is this one: '. . . among those things that first strike a visitor to a primitive people is that there are no unmarried adult women.' If this means, as it seems to, *any* primitive people, and if 'unmarried adult woman' means what it says (as opposed to 'woman who has never been married'), then I'd say, inspired in the first place by my own observation, that this is one of those hapless generalisations which must go to the wall. When what Evans-Pritchard says conflicts with my own observation, then (I say this with no irony whatever) my first reaction is to suppose that something must be wrong with my own observation (there often is). But I am encouraged to take a more resolute stand by the fact that, for instance, a distinguished observer of a society related to the one I studied, Professor Jacques Berque, noted the same thing and also observed that, contrary to common belief, the 'unmarried adult woman' is *not* a rarity. And more than this: how *could* she be a rarity, in any society in which divorce is easy and common (a condition which, in turn, is not infrequently satisfied)? At the very least, there must be solitary women corresponding to 'frictional unemployment', as it were—in the interregna between husbands. But it is difficult to believe that the mechanisms for reallocating them work so perfectly as not to leave any of them permanently in the frictional state. (This is just one of the things social anthropology teaches: do not overrate the invariable effectiveness of social mechanisms. When something is claimed to work each and every time—'*no-one* breaks the taboo', '*everyone* performs the ritual', etc., the chances are you are faced with a stereotype, and not a reality, of behaviour.) What is somewhat closer to the truth is that in such a society, isolated existence being impracticable or very difficult, the adult husbandless woman must return to her previous social group: no solitary careers, and in particular feminine ones, are available. But that is already a different generalisation.

Continuing to speak about primitive-woman-in-general, Evans-Pritchard goes on to say that 'she does not envy her menfolk what we describe as their privileges' (p. 45); she does not see herself as a member of an 'underprivileged class as against a class of men with whom they seek to gain social equality' (p. 52), she does not feel 'that her status as such should be changed' (p. 51). Is this merely a corollary of the contention that in primitive societies, the idea of fundamental social reform is generally absent? (Always???) But as a generalisation about primitive *women* it may again be doubted.

I once had a fascinating conversation with a village tart in a tribal society, which made me comment in my notes that I had met a suffragette: she explained her choice of calling precisely in terms of desire for equality, for only in this profession could she talk with men sensibly and as an equal, instead of being constrained to behave in a 'feminine' manner. I thought no more about it, supposing that the case might have been untypical (though the woman in question was most unlikely to have come in touch with modern egalitarian or feminist propaganda), until I heard papers given by other anthropologists concerned with societies with strong 'agnatic' values, who had systematically considered the place of women in these, and who pointed out that in such contexts, a woman who dislikes the ascription of what is locally considered feminine, does have a way out—into 'shameful' occupations such as prostitution, folk-medicine, magic etc., or combinations of these—which do however carry the reward of enabling her to assume male characteristics. Thus this desire—and, far more significantly, the framework for its articulation and partial satisfaction—does sometimes exist.

The remaining twelve essays are on relatively specialised topics, which is not to say that they will not interest the layman, provided he has a modicum of interest in the diversity of human societies. The curious may go to the essay on Zande cannibalism, or on obscenity. In connection with the latter, it is interesting to compare Evans-Pritchard's theory of verbal licence with the more recent theory of Dr Edmund Leach concerning behavioural licence in carnivals, etc. (in 'Time and False Noses'). This essay, first published as early as 1929, is also of interest in showing the author's early, and becomingly cautious, flirtation with psycho-analysis. He 'deemed [it] wise to draw attention to this [i.e. Freud's] broad and comprehensive theory of culture, in order that our explanation of obscenity on ceremonial occasions should not stand alone . . .' (p. 96). He comes close to noting that this theory explains *anything*, but still seemed to think it an advantage that his own theory should not 'stand alone'. But when he comes across an article in *Imago* which claims that primitive man gets over his inertia and repugnance for labour by sexualising his task, and treating them as 'an equivalent of, and substitute for, sexual functioning', a sense of reality takes over. 'I must confess to a doubt as to the precise meaning attached by writers of this school to much of their terminology' (p. 100).

Of these remaining essays, about four and a half deal with the Azande. Of these, leaving aside the *frissons* one can obtain from the survey of the evidence of cannibalism amongst them, I found the one on the Zande state the most interesting. It is with regret (and the hope that he is mistaken) that one reads Evans-Pritchard's conclusion here that further research in this field will not yield new results. Field research is, indeed, unlikely to provide further data about a condition which is now in the fairly distant past. But is this not an area where a more determined effort to illuminate the material by comparison, could well have been useful? The Azande are not the only originally migrant people, with a mobile economy, who have conquered extensive areas, settled, and incorporated large alien populations in a new political system. A fair amount must be known about this type of pattern, from anthropologists and others. Evans-Pritchard complains of Kluckhohn's failure to use his work on the Azande in dealing with Navaho witchcraft: could one not complain that, for instance, Professor J. Barnes on the 'snowball state' is not invoked in this essay?

And one further carping complaint: one must of course be grateful that these essays are available at all, and the volume certainly illustrates, as the preface claims it was intended to, the wide range, territorially and topic-wise, of an anthropologist's interests; but would it not have been possible to make a more determined attempt to make the Zande material less dispersed? Apart from those already published elsewhere, at least two further ones, contemporaneous with or subsequent to the latest ones of this book, failed to get in. The diaspora of Zande essays bears comparison with that of the Zande royal clan.

Finally, I'd like to quote the account of the education of Zande princes, which, without spelling out the conclusion, makes the comparative point that Zande court training achieved the same ends, by the same means, as a good public school (p. 127):

> Sons of princes had shorter and less intimate home life than sons of commoners. . . . They only saw their father when he entered the outer court, and it was only occasionally that they saw their mothers . . . they . . . had to endure what a commoner's son did not suffer. . . their older brothers made them fag for them and gave them a hiding if they did not carry out their duties promptly and properly. This education undoubtedly inculcated self-reliance and shaped their characters. . . . Cunning and ruthless . . . natural dignity of bearing, unostentatious pride, courteous manners, cordiality, composure, reserve, intelligence, prudence. . . . Pride and reserve. . . . polished manners, simplicity of adornment, . . . poise, and an air of authority . . . even of [those] who lacked office. One could pick them out among commoners at a glance.

10

ON STRUCTURALISM

A spectre is haunting the intellectual scene—structuralism, or better, *le structuralisme*. It is important, it is fashionable, but what the devil is it? Is it indeed a new revelation, a key, a break-through to untold intellectual wealth, or on the contrary, have we all been structuralists ever, speaking structuralism as we speak prose? Is it just the latest Left Bank fashion, filling a gap left by the exhaustion of Existentialism? Or is there an element of truth in each of these suspicions?

For my own part, I should bet my money on the last of these suppositions. *Le structuralisme* is a cluster of attitudes, ideas, styles and people, ranging from portentous café doubletalk to some of the most exciting and promising developments in contemporary thought. No-one to my knowledge, has yet codified those ideas with definitive and satisfying lucidity. Mr Lane's effort in this direction (*Structuralism. A Reader*), both through his introduction and his collection of articles, is gallant and genuinely useful. He does not finish the job—which would be too much to expect of anyone as yet—but, in the meantime, he is genuinely useful to all of us who seek to clear our minds on this matter.

What, one may begin by asking, is the relationship of contemporary *structuralisme* to old, common-or-garden preoccupation with *structure*, which may be held to be virtually co-extensive with science itself? One of Mr Lane's contributors, Maurice Godelier, invokes as his motto a striking remark of Karl Marx's: 'Science would be superfluous if there were no difference between the appearance of things and their essence.' Indeed. And, one might add, science would be impossible if there were no underlying structure behind the appearance of things. The illustrious Mr Locke, distinguishing between secondary and primary qualities, was in effect concerned with separating structure from mere appearance. In social studies the old distinction between structure and culture is an echo of the same Lockian insight: structure is concerned with primary social qualities (i.e. organisation), and culture with secondary ones, whose perception and whose very existence is more closely tied to the conceptual equipment of the

observer than it is to the independent nature of the objects themselves.

MANIFESTLY SQUARE

In consequence, may one say that Locke and Radcliffe-Brown were,
in the contemporary sense, structuralists? It seems implausible. Is
this merely because Locke and Radcliffe-Brown were both manifestly
square, and not with-it thinkers, and *structuralisme* is only too much
part of the scene? As the poet says, the world is too much with it. Is
it just fashion—is contemporary structuralisme simply the dressing
up of old ideas in current terminology—or is there more to it? I
believe that there is a more genuine differentiation.

Mr Lane, in his very useful Introduction, lists three characteristic
theses of *le structuralisme*. It is not quite clear whether these are
meant to be the defining doctrines of modern structuralism, for he
introduces them as the theoretical assumptions that, according to
critics, are 'important and untested' and hence 'are attacked'. Hence
it is possible that Mr Lane is here identifying not the essence of
Structuralism, but merely its most exposed and interesting flank. But
I think not: these seem to me selected for attack because they are
central, rather than simply because they are questionable.

They are, roughly:

1. All social behaviour resembles codes.
2. Man has an innate structuring capacity which limits the possibility of codes and hence of behaviour.
3. Binary oppositions are crucial, or ultimate and exclusive, in the
   internal economy of these codes.

This list of Mr Lane's seems to me a most creditable attempt on his
part to identify the central tenets of Structuralism. Personally I
should be tempted to add some other characteristics, though admittedly these have an intimate connection with some of those listed by
Lane. Those additions would further highlight the way in which
Structuralism differs from good old-fashioned interest in underlying structure.

4. Structuralism has a special concern with what might be called
   (in no pejorative sense) the Appearance Sciences.
5. When dealing with their objects, it seeks structure where the
   ancients saw merely 'meaning' or appearance, and it seeks meaning where the ancients sought or suspected merely inert
   structure.

THE HUMAN VOICE

This perhaps requires some elucidation. The old structure/culture distinction, or primary/secondary qualities distinction, saw science as concerned basically with the former element, with structure, because it was concerned with what is objective, universal, so to speak hard, and has explanatory power; by contrast, culture, or the warm qualities of sense, were consigned to the poet, to description, to documentation perhaps—but not to the hard area of explanation. Modern structuralism on the other hand seems inspired by the idea that it is Appearance, that which is 'lived' by the participants, which has a structure of its own, and conversely, that the hidden latent structures which are unearthed by inquiry, speak in a human voice, are articulated in terms derived from the powers of the human mind.

The natural home for this kind of Structuralism is of course the human sciences, or what I have called the Appearance sciences—those concerned with phenomena of whose very essence it is that they 'mean' something to participants. But language, myths or kin relations for instance, are *made* as well as perceived by our minds.

For a tree or a planet or a particle, it is quite incidental that it is perceived by men. The perception is a source of information about it, but it hardly figures in the explanatory theory covering it. On the other hand, it is essential and not accidental that a phoneme, a kin term, a legend, exists for someone. *Modern* structuralism seeks structure in the appearance itself, and in as far as it looks for an underlying substrate, expects it to speak in something resembling a human voice. This, as far as I can see, is the difference between Structuralism and the old, common pursuit of underlying structure. This, if I understand it correctly, is also Lévi-Strauss' account of the difference between neolithic and modern science.

MYTHS AND LEGENDS

What is novel and valuable in this approach, I suspect, is that it sensitises people to the question concerning how these meaningful worlds are, in the Chomskian phrase, *generated*: instead of, as was the old way, naively taking these worlds for granted and then painfully seeking to identify casual sequences within them, this insight leads one to try and identify the principles which alone can generate this or that given world *at all*. The insight—that this needs to be done —is in itself not new, perhaps, but what may be new is its persistent, concrete and rigorous implementation, at least among the best of those who may be called Structuralists. At their worst, on the other hand they seem merely to be men who have found a new style and jargon for rearranging old materials portentously, without genuine illumination. Like one of the critics cited by Mr Lane, I am most doubtful about the value of the language of 'binary oppositions'. On one interpretation, the thesis of the universal presence of binary opposition may be a simple tautology, in as far as all distinctions can be reduced to a reiteration of binary distinctions; but otherwise, it is probably false.

Moreover, some of these 'binary oppositions' do not genuinely explain or generate anything; they are just a kind of floral arrangement. In phonetics, it may well work: perhaps it can be shown how all the phonetic distinctions we use and recognise can be generated by the application of a set of binary oppositions, which then genuinely explains the structure of our phonetic world, of the range of discriminations of which we are capable in making and identifying noises credited with meaning. But myths are different. The telling of a story, such as a legend, presupposes the prior existence of a world of meanings in which the story is articulated. Hence the analysis of the myth cannot explain the generation of that world. Does it, then, by taking us to the very limits of that world, by conspicuously exhibiting its polarities, which are the oppositions which are highlighted in the story—does it so to speak teach us the limits of that world? Are myths and legends the conceptual equivalents of beating the bounds?

PRETTY PATTERNS

Those who have indulged in structuralist accounts of myths and legends have not faced or answered this question clearly enough. Until it is answered, structuralist analyses will be open to the suspicion that they are just the pursuit of pretty and fanciful patterns, in a language which is suggestive but which, like the various Hegelian and Freudian languages, is over-adaptable and hopelessly loose. They talk as if their pretty patterns explained the worlds in which they occur, when in fact they presuppose them, and explain nothing. Something of the same danger arises for the structuralist. His bedrock concepts, far from explaining or generating a world, may be drawn from the same stock as many others in the world they are meant to explain, and presuppose that world.

11
IDEAL LANGUAGE AND
KINSHIP STRUCTURE

This paper is inter-disciplinary. Its disadvantage is that the author is not sufficiently conversant with the disciplines it is *inter*. He may, however, like Lord Wavell, claim that at least the thread that binds them is his own.

The paper is of philosophic interest in that it is inspired by, and hopes to shed some light on, the notion of an ideal language. It is of interest to social anthropology in that its main subject is kinship structure. It may be of interest to mathematicians in setting a task.

IDEAL LANGUAGE

The notion of an ideal language played an important part in philosophy earlier in this century. The notion lacks clarity—though clarity is just one of the things an ideal language hopes to provide—but certain features nevertheless seem to emerge: an ideal language must be unambiguous. This means, amongst other things, that it observes the rule 'one thing, one name'; no two things may have the same name, nor may two names be given to one thing. Secondly, an ideal language is no deceiver, it does not mislead; permissible and impermissible inferences and transitions are clearly evident from the very notation. Thirdly, an ideal language does not distort the nature of reality; the notation clearly shows what is due to the notation and what is due to fact. It equally shows up the possibly related boundary between what is logically necessary and what is contingent.

The above is not clear. But then, nor are the reasons which led to the abandonment of this ideal. I shall return to both.

KINSHIP STRUCTURE

Kinship structure theory is an important and well-developed part of social anthropology. It is well developed for a number of reasons. The kinds of question originally asked about primitive societies were often connected with kinship; kinship structure is an aspect of society which is more tangible and stateable with accuracy than most; kinship lends itself to comparison between societies.

In fact, 'kinship structure' means two separate things, though, as will emerge, anthropologists are right in not normally separating them. *I* shall:

A society consists of people, male and female, *any* pair of whom can mate (with certain obvious qualifications concerning age) as far as biology is concerned. In actual fact, matings are not random in any society. In other words, actual matings are a sub-class of biologically possible matings. Kinship-structure in the *first* sense means the specification of how that sub-class is selected, in other words which matings, or rather which kinds of matings, actually occur. For instance in a strictly monogamous society with no pre- or extra-marital relations or re-marriage, the actual matings would be such that if A and B mate, then this precludes any mating of A with B' or of B with A'.

The *second* sense of 'kinship structure' is the correlation of social roles (which are not logically entailed by biologically-defined relationships) with kinship roles defined within the first sense of the term. For instance, the assertion that the provider or protector of the woman is ex officio her biological mate. Kinship structure in this sense specifies which roles, with what rigidity and to what extent, are so to speak functions of the biological kinship position of the agent (or vice versa). It will also contain negative assertions to the effect that such and such a role is not related to kinship. It is, for instance, often said that industrial society differs from most agrarian societies in that fewer roles are functions of kinship.

The first and second sense of kinship structure are logically distinct. Nevertheless anthropologists are right in lumping them together, this being inevitable. The reason for this is that many important limitations of matings (kinship structure sense 1) operate in terms of social roles; for instance, in one society I know a man may not marry a woman who was suckled by the same breast as he (though it belong to a mere wet-nurse of either/or both 'siblings of milk', as they are called). It follows that the tasks of the first and second kind of kinship study can only be carried out pari passu, and can be separated neither in the study nor in the presentation of material.

Contemporary social anthropologists, perhaps because they are anxious to assert the *social* nature and the autonomy of their discipline *vis-à-vis* physical or biological disciplines, tend to stress their concern with the second aspect of kinship, sometimes almost to the point of implying that the first does not concern them. But this cannot be so for the degree of overlap—admittedly incomplete—between social and physical kinship is precisely one of the most interesting things in the subject, and one to which the investigation of which social anthropologists are committed by the 'functionalist' theory that social kinship structure is explained by its serving the basic needs connected with procreation.

I shall now try to indicate what I think would count as an ideal language for kinship structure theory.

In many languages a man is named by some locution such as 'John, son of Peter'. Sometimes it is extended to something like 'John, son of Peter, son of Stephen'. There is no necessary upper limit to this kind of thing. Nor is there any reason why only the ancestors in the direct male line should be specified. All ancestors, male and female, up to a certain point back could be specified, and moreover specified according to a fixed order which would indicate just who they were, biologically speaking, in relation to the person to be named. No society, as far as I know, possesses anything like so complete a system of naming its members. That, however, is no reason why such a system should not be devised.

If such a scheme were devised, we should then have a way of naming human individuals such that their very name would promptly place them within their biological *logical* space. Is one justified in calling this a kind of logical space? I think so. The fact that man is born of woman and has a man for father is not a logical truth; it is 'merely' a synthetic, empirical truth of biology, though allowing for parthenogenesis as good a generalisation as ever we shall find. But for the purposes of the social sciences, it can be taken as a logical truth defining certain universal relations between objects they are investigating (namely, human beings). In certain contexts 'Mother's son' is indeed synonymous with 'man'; there are some languages in which 'son of man' is used in the sense of 'man'.

It is now worth specifying some of the difficulties that would have to be overcome in order that the above objective is attained.

(1) If an individual's 'name' in our ideal naming system consists of or at least contains an ordered list of his ancestors one has to take into account that the names of those ancestors, or at least some of them, will be similarly complex. Concretely, if John's name contains the sequence GHK, each letter of which names one of his ancestors, it is likely that G, H, and K may also in fact be ordered strings of names. Hence there must be some device for indicating whether a symbol occurs as part of a name other than the 'total' name, or whether it occurs atomically. Or alternatively, if the constituents of John's name build up from his ancestors' names so that the preceding distinction vanishes (every symbol occurring in both ways), then some rule must still be made specifying in what way one may

break up John's name and get the names of ancestors, rather than strings of symbols naming no one. If this system were ever applied to an actually existing group of human beings ancestors of a certain generation past would have to be 'primitive' ancestors and be assigned 'primitive' names. Though I do not think that if the present device were ever worked out, its use, if any, would be in actually naming people—people's names would be too impossibly long. On the other hand if the device is to be sound it is necessary that it should, however cumbersomely, be in principle so applicable.

Incidentally, the names would indicate the person's ancestors but never his descendants. After all, he may not have any, or he may acquire some after naming. The least a good name must do is not to depend on the empirical fortunes of the man named. This is what distinguishes names from descriptions. It is a curious fact that it is logically true (in our sense) that we all have ancestors, but not even factually true that we all have descendants. Those philosophers unfortunate enough not to be able to tell the direction of time, and who sometimes look for guidance in abstruse things such as entropy, may if they wish use this more homely fact to guide them.

(2) If the construction of an individual's name involved *nothing but* the ordering of the names of his ancestors the consequence would be that all siblings would have the same name. This would cause confusion in his and the next generation, and a violation of the principle 'one name, one thing' in both the first and the subsequent generations. Hence a device is again necessary for obviating it. It must in principle be possible. For instance, if GHKL is a string of names of ancestors specifying in good order the common ancestors of Paul and Peter, then Paul might be 1GHKL and Peter 2GHKL, Paul being the elder. Of course, a subtler device may be needed to prevent chaos when Paul's and Peter's name enter as constituents into their descendants' names. At each stage in this enumeration of difficulties the best I can do (and not always that) is to indicate possible minimal tricks that would do the job; to devise methods that would not lead to confusion when operating simultaneously is beyond both my ability and the scope of the present paper.

(3) The fact that there are two sexes is probably itself a nuisance in our scheme. I suspect that it would be necessary to treat only members of one sex as individuals proper in our scheme, members of the other sex being only admitted by courtesy but ultimately eliminable and definable in terms of the first (in a manner analogous perhaps to the one in which real numbers are ultimately definable in terms of rational ones). I suspect moreover that the basic sex should more conveniently be female, in view of the fact that it is harder for an individual to be ignorant of the identity of his mother than of the identity of his father. In other words, the basic language of kinship

structure would be matrilineal rather than patrilineal, though ultimately it would convey information about all the antecedent lineages of a named individual. A device for making men 'derivative' might be something like this; if Joan has three sons and Joan's name is J, their names would be J1X, J2X, and J3X where X conveys the necessary information about their respective fathers or father and in turn their ancestry. Perhaps this amounts less to making men 'derivative' than to ensuring that the sex of a person should be evident from the structure of his name. It would also mean that male names would never be primitive names in the above sense. Names constructed by making two people of the same sex the parents of an individual would then not be well-constructed terms of our language. The reason which makes me suspect that one of the other sex would have to be made 'derivative' is that if such a language were really constructed by a mathematician, it would probably owe something to set theory, which (I believe) presupposes that the individuals dealt with are homogeneous in the sense that if X is in a certain logical relationship with Y, then any Z can also meaningfully, if not always truthfully, be said to be in that relation with Y. (Is it not when this condition fails that the famous antinomies arise?)

It may be that our notation will require type-restrictions, for it must be made *nonsense* (not just false) for a man to mate with a man, or for a man to be his own offspring, etc. Biological impossibility must be made into a logical impossibility of our notation. Our notation must express the underlying biological presuppositions of kinship as logical truths inherent and manifest in the symbolism so that the *social* facts of kinship emerge against this background as asserted, synthetic truths. Note incidentally, that if this language were devised, 'individuals' in a logical system would for once mean *individuals*, rather than meaning nothing or anything.

If I may digress a little: I have always found it hard to think of systems of mathematical logic in other than kinship terms, with axioms marrying transformation rules to generate a fertile progeny of theorems in a timeless way, with formation rules guarding against the occurrence of miscegenation. Admittedly, in this world unnatural unions are not merely permitted but apparently fertile—for theorems and transformation rules are sometimes hard to distinguish. (I leave psychoanalytic interpretation of this fancy to others.) A possible answer to the philosophical question of what purely formal systems 'really are' seems to me that they are artificial systems of causation, imaginary worlds of which the initial elements are postulated and so are the 'causal' rules by which other elements come into being. This interpretation of 'what formal logical systems really are' seems to be supported by the fact that actually constructed and operating machines mirror logical systems. The consequence of such a philosophy of logic would be that logic would be a study of possible causal systems. It seems very paradoxical thus to make causation more fundamental than logical necessity . . .

One might add that if logic has sometimes borrowed its imagery or terminology from kinship (e.g. the 'ancestral' of Quine's), then my recommendation that it aid kinship theory gives it an opportunity to repay an old debt. (It will be sad if only the logical parts of this paper are tolerable to anthropologists, and only the anthropological parts tolerable to logicians. The life of a pontifex need not be an easy one.)

(4) No grave difficulty should arise from the fact that in real life many ancestors are not known. The system of naming should be so devised that it allows variables instead of actual names as parts of complex names.

So far, we have not a language but a system of naming (which is *not* a language). We must now add things that can be *said of* the things named. Now we are fortunate that in our logical space there is only one kind of logical relation. It holds, when it holds, between groups of three individuals of the system. It is a 'triadic relation'. It is the relation 'A (male) and B (female) begat C (either sex)'. Any individual in the system is either directly related, or indirectly related, or not related at all in this way, to every other individual in the system. If A is related (directly or *indirectly*) to B, and B is similarly related to C, then A is related to C. In other words our one logical relation in its *extended indirect* and *dyadic* sense is transitive. This second relation is definable in terms of the first and introduces nothing fundamentally new.[1] In view of this we are at liberty to say either that two elements in a system *may* be unrelated, or alternatively that if this is so, they do not form part of the same system. Which of these alternatives we choose will depend on whether we wish to make our 'system' correspond, in the real world, to 'relatives' or to 'society'.

Now if the above system of naming has been constructed to my specifications, *then there is no need for our one logical relation to exist in the basic vocabulary of the system.* Just this would be the beauty of our achievement, the attaining of what philosophers who wanted an ideal language had hoped for; namely, that logically necessary relationships should be 'shown', be evident, from the very notation, so that only synthetic, factual truths need actually be asserted. Note that in one sense, once people are named according to our scheme, they all have names with the same structure or 'form' irrespective of what their kinship organisation is; but just this provides the common logical form (mirroring the biological basis), and only reflects that we all have two parents, four grandparents, eight . . . etc. The first way differences in that common pattern arise—and hence information can be conveyed—is that in societies inbred to any degree, certain kinds of repetitive patterns will occur within the names. Secondly, information concerning, for instance, what counts as incest in a society will be conveyed by stating that people bearing names with a certain repetition-containing structure count, in that society, as offspring of incestuous unions.

One difficulty arises through so to speak the timelessness of our names. In using our naming system, the fact that a society permitted 'one man–many women' marriages would be conveyed by the compossibility of names whose structure revealed the same father but different mothers. But obviously such names are compossible even in a society which does not allow of such marriages, in view of the fact that one man may marry a number of women in succession. If something corresponding to the date of birth were introduced into our 'names' this would really undesirably complicate the names, by introducing something other than biological relation into the logical, necessary-connection-generating part of the notation. I think information of this kind would always have to be conveyed with help of 'synthetically' attributed sociological predicates, in addition to the predication 'occur' or 'there exist'. Names conveying one father but different mothers are, for instance, compossible in our society (owing both to illegitimacy and to successive marriages) and in a polygamous one. One might distinguish the two cases by asserting, synthetically, that in our society, when such two names occur this implies that either one or both are illegitimate or they are the offspring of successive marriages, whereas this entailment does not hold in the other society. (Note that it is no weakness of the notation that the names cannot convey whether their bearer is a bastard or legitimate. That distinction is indeed not a biological but a sociological one, and must be conveyed by the sociological predicates attributed to the names.)

IMPLICATIONS FOR SOCIAL ANTHROPOLOGY

How would the truths of kinship structure theory be conveyed in such a language (for the construction of which this article claims to be no more than a prolegomenon)? The truths of what I called the first kind of kinship theory—the specification of which of the biologically possible unions actually occur—would be conveyed by stating that, in a given society, only names of such and such structure actually occur. (For instance: such and such repetitions of the variables comprising a name would be barred, or favoured, or obligatory.) Truths of the second kind of kinship theory would be conveyed by attributing sociological predicates to names of a certain kind, or alternatively by denying connection between predicates of that kind and any of the permissible kinds of names. Truths of the first kind of kinship theory which can only be stated with the help of sociological predicates could also be stated, though in a slightly more complicated way.

Would all this be of any actual use to social anthropology? Almost certainly not in naming actual people, though it is just possible that we might one day name members of a society according to certain rules derived from our system, and then feed the names to a machine that would oblige by telling us the kinship structure. Unfortunately, by the time we had so named the individuals concerned we should know as much about their kinship structure as any machine could tell us. On the other hand, it is possible that the language devised might help analytically, by providing a guaranteed exhaustive classification of possible kinship structure and even bring out empirically unperceived similarities, as topology may show similarities or intuitively dissimilar knots.

Actual rules of naming and the inheritance of names in societies could be stated and compared by showing which parts of our ideal and complete names are left out, or on which parts or series within the ideal name the real name depends. Similarly inheritance rules could be stated and compared with the help of our language. In the case of what anthropologists call classificatory kinship terminology, (a name for a kind of terminology in actual use in certain societies) their functioning would be conveyed in our scheme by stating that all names (in our sense) of a certain structure are equivalent to one kinship term in that society's language. (For instance, in a classificatory terminology one term may serve for 'father' *and* for any 'paternal uncle'.)

It is also possible—I speak diffidently for my ignorance of demography is even greater than that of logic and anthropology—that it would facilitate a general theory of connection between demographic trends and kinship structure. There obviously is a connection between the fields. To take a simple example, on certain assumptions, a society in which one man may marry many women is more likely to grow in population than a society in which only women may marry a number of partners.

Of course, I imagine that demographers do in an ad hoc manner relate their analyses to kinship structure, but our language might make it possible to state an over-all theory. For instance, if the assumption were made that fecundity, childbearing age and perhaps some other variables are constant, a general theory might relate demographic trends to various kinds of kinship structure. (The *causal* connection between demographic and kinship facts may of course operate in both directions.) It might even be possible to devise general schemes for extrapolating into the past from the present size and structure of societies and thus obtaining an aid towards reconstructing the history of illiterate peoples and checking on their own often far-reaching kinship legends. Again, the scheme might be of use in genetics. Whether any of these possibilities would actually be useful

I abstain from guessing. There are, however, sufficiently numerous social scientists able and anxious to mathematicise their discipline and they might care to have a try. The actual working out of the rules of such a notation is a matter sufficiently complex, technical and difficult not to be usefully attempted in the same place as the verbal specification of what is required and the discussion of the implications of the attempt, which is essentially what is attempted in this paper.

PHILOSOPHICAL IMPLICATIONS

If the above scheme of an ideal language in the limited but empirical field of kinship theory were actually realised, or if even it were accepted that it is realisable, this would show that an 'ideal language' satisfying at least some of the specifications of that aspiration can be made to work over a limited but not trivial field. In a way the carrying out of the scheme could count as a 'formalisation' of a kinship theory; but as it would actually 'mirror' the subject matter of that theory, it would also count as an ideal language in the above sense.

As I have said, the reasons which led to the abandonment of the pursuit of an ideal language have not been made clearer than that notion itself. Historically, it seems to have been caused by the failure of the people originally inspired by that ideal to provide either samples of an ideal language or even satisfactory recommendations for constructing one. It was felt, perhaps rightly, that this failure contained a profound and important intimation of something— though I know not what. In consequence, philosophers of the relevant tradition turned their backs on ideal language and indulged in a study of 'ordinary language', a pursuit whose exclusive usefulness is not to my mind conclusively established. If the scheme propounded in this paper worked or were workable, reflection on the difference between limited fields or *the* limited fields where it can work and 'the world in general' might throw more light on why an 'ideal language in general' cannot be obtained. This device may be similar to Wittgenstein's 'language games' but perhaps superior in *not* being a game. This use of the idea gives it a certain philosophic interest even if it should not find other application.

NOTE

1 Strictly speaking, two steps are involved. We begin with our ordered triads. Then a dyadic relation of 'being directly related' is defined in terms of the triadic relation, quite simply: 'Any member of a triad is directly related to each of the other two. (Df.)' We then define 'being indirectly related' in the following way; 'If A is related directly or indirectly to B, and B is related similarly to C, then A and C are (at least) indirectly related (Df.)' This last definition is not circular.

12

THE CONCEPT OF KINSHIP

with special reference to Mr Needham's 'Descent systems and ideal language'

The purpose of this paper is not merely to reply to Needham's arguments[1] and to correct his errors but also, in the course of this, to throw some light on the anthropological concept of kinship. For simplicity of reference, it will be useful to number Needham's errors.

(1) Needham (p. 97): 'Biology is one matter and descent is quite another, of a different order.'

This is not so. This mistake of Needham's is particularly important, for two reasons: it plays a crucial role in the internal economy of Needham's argument, and it is a mistake which is not merely a personal idiosyncrasy of Needham's. It is a dangerous travesty of a valid idea, and a mistake which is perhaps shared by others: thus its discussion serves a wider purpose.

That it is a mistake can best be seen as follows. Suppose an anthropologist observes, in a society he is investigating, a certain kind of recurring relationship between pairs of individuals or of groups. (It may be a one–one relationship or a one–many or a many–many one. It may be a relationship of authority, or a symmetrical one of, say, mutual aid, or of avoidance, or whatnot.) Suppose the autochthonous term for the relationship is *blip*.

The crucial question now is: Under what conditions will the anthropologist's treatment of the *blip*-relationship fall under the rubric of kinship structure?

It will be so subsumed if the anthropologist believes that the *blip*-relationship overlaps, in a predominant number of cases, with *some* physical kinship relationship. Otherwise, naturally, the *blip*-relationship will be subsumed under some other rubric, such as of 'authority' or 'economy'. What, other than at least partial overlap with physical kinship, *could* conceivably lead a relationship to be classified as a part of 'kinship structure'? _{what does he mean by biology?}

The remark which Needham makes immediately after the assertion of his crucial error is important: 'They (i.e. biology and descent) will usually be concordant to some degree . . .' Needham believes this statement to be (i) a proposition which reports, as it were, a *de facto*

it seems that Gelner takes his notion of physical kinship as analogous to needham's notion of biology.

G. Sees Kinship terms as classifications of the rel. between social & physical facts.

164   *The concept of kinship*

usual concordance, and (ii) a minor concession which does not affect his main contention, namely that 'the defining character of descent systems is social'.

In fact, however, the remark about the 'usual concordance' of biology and descent unwittingly contains the operational *definition* of 'kinship structure', or 'descent system', giving away the condition under which a recurrent relationship can come to be classed under those terms. Far from it being the case that, as it were, *it so happens* that biology and kinship are 'usually . . . concordant to some degree', the fact that some social relationship is 'usually concordant to some degree' with physical kinship is, on the contrary, the main condition for that relationship being classed as 'kinship'. This is not primarily a discovery about societies, but rather about the anthropologist's use of terms. Moreover, it is not a minor concession compatible with Needham's argument, but a decisive refutation of it.

My point can be seen not merely from the consideration of what 'kinship structure' *could* possibly mean, but equally also from examining the actual use of kinship-structure classifications of anthropologists. Needham goes on to claim that *his* point can be 'seen in such institutions as . . . unilineal descent reckoning . . . adoption . . . leviratic marriage . . . ghost marriage'. But Needham's own examples and indeed the very notions conveyed by each of these terms in fact prove the very opposite from what Needham imagines they illustrate.

Let us take Needham's examples, sticking also to his own accounts of the meaning of the relevant notions:

'Leviratic marriage, in which a man marries a deceased brother's widow and raises descendants in his brother's name.' This is the simplest case of all: the leviratic relationship and its offspring are, as Needham's own definition clearly shows, a function of kinship. The anthropologist's kinship term 'leviratic' is only applicable when certain real kinship relationships obtain. The relationship, and its offspring, can only be identified by the anthropologist *as* 'leviratic' because the anthropologist knows that the fiction by which offspring are raised 'in the dead man's name' is indeed a fiction. If the anthropologist did not know this, if he too accepted the social fiction of the dead man's name, he would not be able to notice and identify the phenomenon which, as Needham's account lucidly shows (contrary to his intention) is defined in terms of a *systematic*, regulated disparity between physical and social kinship. The identity of the deputy for the dead man is also fixed in kinship terms.[2]

One of Needham's confusions (error 2) is the idea that a 'function' is always 'identity'. Identity is indeed *a* functional relation, and perhaps the simplest one, but of course there are innumerable others.

Take 'adoption'. Again, as with leviratic marriage, the very use of the notion, the possibility of classifying offspring as adoptive, depends on the observer's knowledge of the disparity between the social and the physical relationship, and it is this disparity which gives the term its meaning. It is true that in this case the social kinship relation is only negatively a function of the physical one: only a disparity is required, and the applicability of the term 'adoption', unlike 'leviratic marriage', does not also require specific physical kin relationship (e.g. the dead man's brother being the physical father). And note: it is not just contingently true that a physico-social disparity occurs in the case of adoption, but it is, roughly, what 'adoption' *means*.

With regard to 'ghost marriage' similar observations apply.

Finally, there is the example of 'unilineal descent reckoning'. (I have spent some considerable time studying one society of this kind, and can hardly be supposed to be as ignorant of the phenomenon or its implications as Needham supposes . . .) This, again, is a clear case. In such a situation, a person's membership of a lineage is determined by the lineage membership of *one* of his parents and theirs in turn similarly, and so on. Again, there could hardly be a clearer case of social kinship being a function of physical kinship. The 'function', the rule specifying the connection, is that a person's lineage is that of his male (or female) parent only, and physical and social parentage overlaps.

The situation can also be made clear as follows: anthropologists frequently say that, for instance, kinship is of great importance in simpler societies, or that in some societies of this kind a man's position in the social structure is determined by his birth. Suppose for a moment that Needham were right, and that this meant (merely) social kinship and (merely) social birth, and that the connection of these with physical kinship or birth were merely contingent and sociologically irrelevant. The meaning of the statements cited would then degenerate into saying something almost wholly vacuous, namely that simpler societies have some kind of structure of relationships, and that a man's social position is determined by *something* . . . These almost vacuous statements however would hardly differentiate one kind of society from another. The only content possibly left to these assertions *might* then be, that the structure of relationships or the social position of an individual in simpler societies are conceived by their members in terms borrowed from physical kinship. But the original statements meant far more than this, and in any case, this degenerate statement, to the effect that social relationships are described by participants in terms borrowed from physical kinship, would be highly suspect: for the ethnographer has to decide how *he* translates the autochthonous social terms, and the main reason he can normally have for translating them as *kin* terms is that their application does in fact overlap with physical kinship. If it did not, or if the overlap were contingent and irrelevant, the merely terminological overlap which, by implication, we should be left with on Needham's analysis, would be at the mercy of the vagaries of an inherently arbitrary translation.[3]

Needham's next error (3) is the assumption that if one thing is a function of another, it is a function of that other thing and of nothing else. Functional dependence may be complex. A thing may 'be a function of', i.e. regularly vary with, a number of other 'things' or variables.

To sum up this part of the argument: 'kinship structure' or 'descent system', and the more specific terms used in connection with them, are anthropologists' terms (not terms used by the people studied). Their meaning, as implicit in the actual practice of anthropologists, is that set of social relationships which largely, though not completely, overlaps with *some* of the physical kinship relationships of the people studied. They can be said to be those social relationships which are a function of physical kinship relationships, though the function (i.e. the rule specifying just which kinship relations correspond to which social ones) need not be a simple one, and indeed often is complex.

It goes without saying that social kinship relations are not the function of each and every physical kin relationship obtaining in a society. There are systematic omissions, and the manner in which the significant physical kin relationships are selected is of course just that which it is the job of the anthropologist to find out.

Moreover, the functional relationship between physical kinship and social kinship roles is such that it needs only hold in the predominant number of cases, whilst allowing of individual exceptions: for instance, an undetected infidelity on the part of a wife may lead to a disparity between the physical and the social relationship of fatherhood, without this having any social consequences and hence without being of any great interest to the social anthropologist.

It might be supposed—erroneously—that difficulties arise for this account of what 'kinship structure' means, from two kinds of sources: (*a*) the fact that, as stated, social kin relationships need only overlap with the corresponding physical ones in a predominant number of cases, but not invariably, and (*b*) from the fact that discussions of kinship structure also include accounts of *some* relationships which, *as* relationships, do not, at any rate directly, overlap with any physical kin relationship at all. In other words: not only may individual cases of a relationship be exceptions to the concordance, but a whole class of type of relationships may be exceptional in this respect. Neither of these difficulties invalidate the case, but they will have to be examined in detail.

(*a*) The issue may best be discussed with the help of an example. In our society, the (social) father of a child is generally also his <u>physical genitor</u>, and it may be said that the social role is a function of the position of the two individuals on the physical kinship map. But it is also true that occasionally there may be a disparity between social paternity and the genetic one, a disparity of which the persons concerned may or may not be aware. Does this possibility show that social paternity is not, after all, a function of physical kinship? *is there an exception*

Not at all. Suppose for a moment that our society changed: suppose promiscuity became so widespread that, instead of disparity between social and physical paternity being fairly rare, it became so general that it would be unusual for a person to know the identity of his physical father. At the same time, suppose the social institution of 'fatherhood' to remain unchanged. *to every rule*

If it were true, as Needham claims, that a descent system is a thing 'of a different order' from physical kinship, and has no connection, or only a contingent one, with it, we should then be forced to say that the kinship system of the second society is the same as that of our present one. For, ex hypothesi, nothing has changed in the social roles and relations.

But, on the contrary, the 'kinship structure', or 'descent system' such as our present one, in which social paternity generally is ascribed to the physical genitor, albeit with some exceptions, both conscious and unconscious, is quite different, and would by any social anthropologist rightly be counted as different, from a system in which physical paternity were unidentified or disregarded, and social paternity then ascribed in virtue of some fact (necessarily) other than physical paternity. It would count as different despite the fact that the social role of the 'father' vis-à-vis his 'offspring' and society might in all other respects be similar to that of a father in our society.

This *gedankenexperiment* shows that, although occasional divergences between social and physical kinship do not affect the principle that a social kinship role is a function of a physical kin relationship, a *regular* divergence results in a difference in what counts as kinship structure. The kind of convergence there is, or lack of it, is *part of* what anthropologists mean by the kinship structure of a society, and not something contingently true of it and sociologically irrelevant.

(b) There are other terms which one may encounter in discussions of kinship structure, such as, say 'clan' or 'godfather', where the independence of the meaning of such a term from physical kinship is of a different kind.

Let us take each of these terms in turn. The point about a 'clan' is this: its members may believe themselves to be descended from a single common ancestor, without necessarily knowing just how, whilst this belief is probably false and in any case irrelevant. We have here a case which seems to favour Needham's argument: a 'kinship' concept which has a social significance, defining a co-operating group, etc., by means of a kin notion, whilst the truth about the physical links does not correspond to the notion and is irrelevant to it. In brief, we cannot here give an account of the logic of this anthropological concept similar to that given in connection with 'leviratic marriage', etc.

The correct account of the logic of such terms is this: indeed, a term such as 'clan' does not correspond to a physical kinship reality. But: 'clan' is a concept essentially related to other concepts—they might be 'sub-clan' or 'lineage' or 'extended family'—which, in turn, do denote groups for whom some social reality (co-operation, co-habitation, for example) does have a reasonable and systematic congruence with some kinship affinity. A 'clan' will be a co-operating set (justifying or expressing or reinforcing its co-operation in terms of a kin myth) of sub-groups, which in turn *are* kinship groups in the sense analysed above.

The reason why 'clan' occurs within discussions of kinship structure is *not* because clansmen subscribe to the myth of a common ancestry, (although they do), but because the relationship of belonging-to-the-same-clan is one which, when spelt out, reads something like this: belonging to a $group_1$ of $groups_2$, where $group_1$ is in fact socially defined (whatever its possible kinship myth), whilst social $groups_2$ have cohesion-supporting kinship convictions whose claims *are* parallel, on the whole, with physical reality. Hence, the relationship of being-of-the-same-clan satisfies *indirectly* the criterion we set up initially for determining whether an unspecified social relationship, *blip*, does or does not fall under the rubric of kinship structure.

The case of a term such as 'godfather' or 'blood-brother' is different from cases such as 'clan'. Here, it is generally plain both to partici-pants and to the observing anthropologist that there is no physical kinship. What there is, generally, is the occurrence of some kind of ritual which establishes a relationship either similar[4] to, or system-atically parallel[5] with, relations dependent on physical kinship. Indeed, anthropologists are liable to refer to this kind of kinship as 'ritual kinship'. The point about calling this kind of relationship ritual kinship is not the fact that its establishment is accompanied by ritual, for that would not differentiate it from ordinary kinship re-lationships which are similarly initiated (though they are functions of the physical position, they *also* depend on the confirming ritual); the force of the expression '*ritual* kinship' is '*only* ritual kinship'—or 'kinship—but not really'.

There is of course an element of truth in the view Needham stresses (though this element, far from being in conflict with what I originally said, is *precisely* what my scheme was meant to bring out): namely, the fact that social kinship systems are not identical with the reality of physical kinship, but, on the contrary, systematically add to it, omit from it, and distort it.

The kind of situation which brings this out may be instanced by a tribe in which genealogies became untrue at, or after, the fourth generation: men will name correctly their grandfather and perhaps his father, but ancestors beyond that are simply 'arranged' so as to express, symbolise, sub-groups existing in the tribe now. There will, in the simplest case, be *one* alleged common ancestor for the whole tribe, who will be said to have had *n* sons, corresponding to the *n* sub-groups of the tribe. Each of these *n* minor ancestors may in turn find himself attributed a number of sons corresponding to the number of the sub-sub-groups of his sub-group, and so on, until these fictitious or quasi-fictitious genealogies are as it were tied on to the more accurate three or four generations deep genealogies of living men.

This is a fairly typical situation, and of course many complex variations of it occur. It is this kind of thing, amongst others, which makes anthropologists insist on *not* equating kinship beliefs with kinship reality. But: in order to see how the two diverge, and to say how kinship notions are 'manipulated' in the interests of the present group and of expressing its present alignments, one has to know *what* the physical kinship reality is which is being distorted and manipulated and *how* it is manipulated. Where there is a relationship, say *blip* again, which does *not* in any reasonably regular way distort some physical kinship relationship (i.e. is *not* a function of it), an account of its working will *not* fall into the account of a 'descent system'. In other words, relationships which *do* fit Needham's claim that they are of a wholly different order from physical kinship do not however fall under the rubric of social kinship (or 'descent system') either.

To sum up the position: 'kinship structure' or 'descent systems' are, by definition, systems of social relationships such as are functions of (are regularly related to) physical kinship, bearing in mind that the function is not identity; the rule relating the physical kinship and the social relation being generally complex, involving additions, omissions and distortions; and all this notwithstanding the fact that individual *instances* of the relationships may occasionally diverge from the rule (e.g. consequence of undetected infidelity), and also that individual *concepts* within the system of social concepts (e.g. 'godfather') may fail to be related directly by any rule to physical kinship (for they remain embedded in a system of concepts most of which *are* so related).

It must be stressed that this definition is not a prescription or recommendation, but an *explication* of what is implicit in the actual practice of anthropologists. Needham in all probability knows *how to use* the notion of kinship or descent. It is only when, as in his article, he attempts an explicit account of the concepts that he goes off the rails.

Kinship structure *means* the manner in which a pattern of physical relationships is made use of for social purposes—the way in which a physical criterion is used for the selection of members for a group and the ascriptions of rights, duties etc. Of course, the available physical facts are used selectively, distorted (but systematically), with *some* irregularity, etc. But: the elements of the physical pattern are essentially simple and universal, whilst the social patterns imposed on it are highly diversified and complex. And it is just this, the existence of the universal and simple physical substrate, which makes it possible to describe descent systems with some precision and to compare them meaningfully.

Once this central point about kinship notions is grasped, many of Needham's other numerous errors fall into place. I should add that, in one way, I have found Needham's article greatly reassuring. After I wrote and published the article which Needham attempts to criticise, I was somewhat worried by the fact that the point about the logic of kinship was something so obvious that it did not need stating. I knew that some anthropologists spoke *as if* they subscribed to something in contradiction with it, but it seemed charitable and reasonable to assume that this was merely a manner of speaking: and when discussing the matter with some of them, I found that this was indeed so. Needham, however, by coming out explicitly, and indeed with astonishing self-assurance, to assert the contrary viewpoint, has put me in his debt by showing that the point *did* need stating . . .

This brings me to Needham's error (4), concerning the motivation anthropologists have for adopting the misleading slogans about the alleged independence of physical and social kinship. (To Needham, of course, they appear not misleading but wholly true.) Needham: 'It has nothing to do with the alleged anxiety of social anthropologists about the social nature of their subject . . . but derives from the very nature of descent systems.' Needham gives no reason whatever for supporting this *ex cathedra* announcement; presumably, as he holds the misleading slogan to be true, no further explanation of why it is made is required. But in view of the fact that, as shown, the very opposite follows from 'the very nature of descent systems', one does need an explanation.

It is indeed true that what Needham says does sometimes, as he puts it, 'form an *early* part of *elementary* instruction in social anthropology'. (Italics and irony mine.) The valid insight which may be conveyed by means of this type of erroneous formulation, such as Needham's formula about physical and social kinship being of different orders, is that these two are not identical. It is necessary to train the student not to take genealogies at their face value, to put it roughly, and secondly not to accept myths of his own society, such as the 'natural' affinity of brothers, etc. (What people *say* about their own kin connections is not necessarily or generally true; and if there is an affinity or any other behavioural relationship between kin of given categories, then this is never a consequence of the physical kin relationship as such, but of the social arrangements sustaining it.) All this is true, and in order to stress it, slogans about the independence of social and physical kinship are used. But these slogans, or rather the true element contained in them, are not in conflict with the analysis of 'kinship' given above; Needham, however, unlike other anthropologists, takes them too literally and *is* misled.

Indeed Needham is right about this being the *pons asinorum* of the matter, if not about the identity of the *asinus*. It is true that those who have difficulty in seeing even the crude point—that physical and social kinship are not identical—will not see, and might as well not bother with, the slightly subtler point concerning their essential connection. One might add that those who see *only* the crude point, and not the slightly less crude one, may still perhaps do useful ethnographic work: at that level, conceptual self-knowledge may not matter (whilst a failure to see even the crude point, and thus to be unable to *operate* the concept, would indeed be disastrous). But if, like Needham, one also aspires to give an analysis or account of the anthropological notion of kinship, it does matter a great deal.

The next cluster of Needham's mistakes depends only in part on his misunderstanding of the concept of kinship or descent, springing also from his failure to understand the notion of an ideal language. The feature of an ideal language which is relevant to the argument is this: a logically ideal notation is one such that, when a statement is made in it, it is easy to see what is contributed by the rules of the notation itself, and what depends on the particular object of the statement. The elements 'contributed by the notation itself' may be said, roughly, to be those features which are true of the subject matter of a statement simply in virtue of it being described, or being describable, in the notation at all. To give a simple example: suppose one describes an area made up of regular squares by giving the co-ordinates of each square, plus some additional property of each square, say its colour. '4·7; yellow' would then be a statement in a language devised for describing the area and its constituent squares. This language would have the desired logical property. The fact, for instance, that each square is bounded by four other squares, that it is characterised by two numbers, and no more than two, and that no pair of numbers can designate more than one square, is clearly seen to be not so much a property of any particular square, but of the notation. It really specifies the conditions which a 'world' must satisfy before it can be properly described by this notation. (For instance, a more than two-dimensional continuum would not be describable by this notation.)

My application of this to kinship systems in anthropology was based on the observation that the subject matter of the anthropological treatment of kinship could be made in some measure to satisfy such conditions.

The subject matter in question is people plus, as shown above, the nature, overlap, interdependence and divergence of their physical and social kinship and *not* social relations alone, as Needham argues). But the physical (kinship relations of people are, ultimately, very simple: these 'elements' of the system, i.e. people, are either not related at all, or related by one and only one relation, a triadic one (A and B begat C). They may be related by this relationship either directly, or indirectly by its reiteration (in the course of which, naturally, the same individual may occupy different positions).

problematic |

This provides us with, as it were, the substrate of the co-ordinates of physical kinship whose basic pattern is, for the purposes of social sciences, *given*.

according to our biological model |

Superimposed on this pattern and corresponding to the colours in our simple examples above, are the social predicates, i.e. the kinship terms actually used by the society under investigation, the rights and duties allocated, etc. The subject matter of an investigation into a society's kinship structure or 'descent system' is a specification and understanding of these terms and roles, etc., *and* the nature of their overlap with physical kinship: the manner, and extent, in which they are selected out of the physical kin substrate of the society. The type of notation suggested would, if devised, bring out more clearly the elements which are being related.

Strictly speaking, the situation is rather complex, for three levels are involved:

(*i*) The basic pattern is determined by the *given* fact (given to social studies by biology) that every person has two physical parents, one of each sex. The same point of course again applies to these parents, and so on. All this is, for social studies, 'necessary' and not a result of some findings. (If it were not so in some cases, it would not, ex hypothesi, be *social* anthropology that had found it out.)

Furthermore, it is a part of this basic pattern that other people may and do in fact exist, who will either be unrelated, or related to the initial person either by his mating, or the mating of one of his ancestors, either as a partner or as offspring; and again, by a kind of transitive 'contagion', if, for any of the kinds of reason stated above, A and B are related, and B and C, then of course so are A and C.

This and only this gives us the basic physical map, so to speak. In as far as the notation of our proposed language would have to mirror it, the 'structure' of all names, at this level, would be identical. (The great practical difficulty for devising the notation would of course be in connection with specifying the type of relations indicated in the second paragraph. The *necessity* of ancestors makes a notational device for their formal specification easy; the *contingency* of descendants, mates and collaterals makes it difficult.)

(*ii*) Within this universal form of every person's name, there could and would be similarities and divergences of structure, in another but still physical sense. Suppose, to take a simple case, a person were the child of parents who were themselves full siblings: this would manifest itself in his 'name' by the repetition of the same (incorporated) name in the place reserved for paternal and for maternal grandfather, and similarly for paternal and maternal grandmother. In this sense, the 'structure' of a name would *not* be invariable.

(*iii*) Having this 'map', the ascription of social kinship terms, roles, duties, etc., to points on it can be expressed in terms of the additional, 'synthetic' predicates ascribed to each type of name, relatively to the name of 'Ego'. ('Ego' would not have to be supplied with a name, but the ego-name would be a kind of permanent 'origin' of the system.) If, for instance, Ego's name is A, a rule of our notation would enable us immediately to infer, or rather construct, the 'name' of his physical father, say B. The fact that in our society the physical father is also the social one might be expressed by saying that, for the society, F(B).

The occasional occurrence of adoption could be conveyed by saying that, in some cases, 'G(X) leads to F(X)', where the *variable* X shows that this social ascription is independent of the physical kin position, and where G, like F, is a social predicate, and in this case means something like 'performed acts necessary for adoption'.

The job of describing further each of these levels is at present generally done—satisfactorily enough for practical purposes—by the diagrams used by anthropologists to sketch kinship systems and of course by the accompanying prose.

The theory which Needham finds so surprising in my article—that I should start my analysis with a reference to names and not categories—corresponds to the fact that anthropologists' diagrams of kinship also start with an individual (typical) 'ego'.

The ordinary anthropological manner of doing all this is of course satisfactory for practical purposes. But it fails to bring out the difference in logical status of truths of the three levels, and the manner in which they are related. The anthropologist, his intuitions trained and formed by familiarity with his subject matter and his habitual techniques for handling it, knows how to interpret the information despite the logical untidiness of its presentation. An 'ideal notation' would however distinguish *explicitly* between information of differing logical status. This might or might not be of practical importance. Perhaps not. But, in any case, it would assist anyone interested in the logic of anthropology to avoid confusions such as Needham's.

As indicated, the central figure of an ideal notation is that it separates, in any statement, that which is provided by the notation itself and that which reflects something in the particular object described. The central feature of 'kinship structure', on the other hand, is that it is an account of how social ascriptions—kinship terms, roles, etc.—are superimposed on to, or recruited in terms of, a pattern of physical relationships which are biologically given; once these two facts are grasped (and both evade Needham) the relationships of the two subjects become clear. The basic rules, co-ordinates of an ideal kinship notation, would utilise the universality and basic simplicity of physical kinship; what would be *said* about each society's own and possibly idiosyncratic manner of arranging its affairs on this basis, would be conveyed by means of the further predicates, contingently attributed to various relative positions or 'names' in the scheme.

Needham's specific errors can now be brought out. He believes (p. 1) mistakenly (error 5) that it constitutes a refutation of my argument to say, as he does, that 'descent systems do not simply regulate marriage, but are as importantly concerned' with other matters. Quite so; but the remark connecting kinship structure with the specification of possible mates was, in the context, bringing out that the relationships making up the physical substrate of kinship consist only of the presence, reiteration, or absence of one and only one relationship (the triadic one of mating–procreation), and that the only choice which exists at this level[6] concerns the identity of the partner. Hence, at this level, the kinship structure is exhaustively determined by the rules governing mating. All else on this level follows. The social relationships, the consideration of which become relevant later on, are superimposed on a pattern which is moulded, exclusively, by the pattern of mating, for there is nothing else which can affect it. The social predicates which are then imposed on the pattern, and which also (to complicate matters) enter into the rules determining that pattern itself, were discussed later. This criticism of Needham's is a misinterpretation arising out of his failure to consider the context of the remark.

Error 6: Needham credits me with the view or assumption that kinship terms are names, individual designations of single human beings. He rightly finds such a view 'almost incomprehensible', and one may only wish he had found it *wholly* so. But I am aware, oddly enough, that 'uncle' is not a name, like Harry S. Truman. But an ideal language of the kind envisaged would indeed have to begin with names, i.e. with unambiguous devices for picking out single individuals. It does not however follow in the least—nor was it supposed, nor is there any evidence in the relevant article to make it seem so—that these names were to replace kinship terms. On the contrary, kinship terms were to be defined in terms of the relation between *types* (and classes of types) of names in the ideal notation, just as in normal anthropological practice kinship terms are defined in terms of the relation between types of position (and groups of positions) on the diagrams. (Needham himself later notices conclusive evidence in the article itself against his interpretation, when he notes that all names in the scheme would have had the same structure.) Kinship terms are indeed classifications relative to an individual, and the intention of my scheme was that a kinship term of a given society would be definable in terms of the *kinds* of names that were to be related by it. (For instance: suppose the names were constructed by including a list of ancestors' names in a certain prescribed order. Then the concept of 'cousin', as occurring in our society, would be defined as the relationship ascribed to people whose names contain the identical sub-name at certain places, i.e. the places in which grandparents are named.)

Error 7: Needham supposes he can refute the contention that 'for the purposes of social science it is a logical truth that a man has a man for a father' by pointing to phenomena such as a woman becoming, socially, the 'father' of a man, etc. I am not unaware of these phenomena. He has, of course, completely misunderstood the assertion: the point is that the presupposed biological truth is given to social anthropology (and is a 'logical truth' for *it*), and is *used* by it, and not that there is some common universal pattern of *social* paternity (which would indeed be absurd). Needham, who fails to see that a sociological account of social relationships such as marriage involves plotting their relationships against the existing physical facts (or, in marginal cases, against the lack of physical facts), consequently also fails to see why and how the truth imported from biology plays a part in anthropology. (The same error reappears later in connection with mating.) Needham's confusion here, as above, springs from the failure to see that the very identification, description and explanation of these phenomena requires one to see them for what they are, i.e. as involving a disparity between a social term x and physical kinship category, and to be able to say what the disparity is and how it is sustained. If one were not aware of the disparity with physical fact, about which we are informed by the *given* truths of biology, we should be unable either to note or to categorise these phenomena. Physical kinship categories are universal, as human biology does not vary sufficiently to make this otherwise; the social recognition of physical kinship, the distinction and classifications made, the kinds of physical relationships utilised for group-membership recruitment, and the social attributes predicated of the recruited classified persons, may and do vary from society to society. But Needham supposes (error 8, p. 98) that the existence of these social diversities, rather pompously indicated by him by the ill-understood phrase (borrowed from yesteryear's philosophic fad) that each 'has to some extent its own logic', constitutes a further objection to my argument. On the contrary, the purpose of my scheme was to have an *orderly* manner of examining and comparing those diversities, which do indeed form the subject matter of anthropological studies of kinship. (Shapes vary; to express comparisons amongst them, one needs a constant system of co-ordinates. The universal facts of physical kinship were to be used to provide these co-ordinates in terms of which the diversity was to be expressed.)

Needham's complaints that a system of naming which remains the same cannot capture the distinctive characteristics of varying kinship systems again misses the point. (Error 9): a system of co-ordinates is not incapable of expressing different areas or shapes just because the system of co-ordinates remains the same and consists of points whose structure is similar. On the contrary, just this is the condition of its doing the job of expressing the diversity of patterns within it.

Needham misinterprets (error 10) the difficulty raised in connection with the existence of two sexes. The difficulty arises because whereas, say, a system of co-ordinates defines a *homogeneous* set of points, the 'points' of my system would have to contain individuals of *two types* (male and female), whose differentiation is relevant to what is subsequently said of them. This difficulty arises only at the initial level of specifying the points on the 'logical space', and not in connection with what is subsequently said about the points on it, and thus has nothing whatever to do with whether there are 'unilineal, cognatic or bilineal' societies.

A similar misconception underlies error 11, expressed by Needham's jibe about Victorian anthropologists, to the effect that no one since then has argued for the primacy of matriliny. The point that it is harder to be ignorant of the mother's identity than the father's, as indeed it is (maternity is not in doubt, as the deceived husband remarked), was, unambiguously, not a premise for any kind of conclusion about what kind of kinship systems actually occur in simple societies, but only for deciding what kind of logical framework would be most useful (assuming we want one at all) for anyone attempting to construct a formal scheme for the study of kinship systems.

Needham's next error (12) is in connection with what he calls the third misapprehension. He credits me with a failure to realise that what is important about members of kinship groups is what they do. Far from being unaware of it, the scheme as expounded in the original article is intended to bring this out, and is quite unambiguous in this respect. After kinship categories had been picked out from the bio-logical logical space, the social truths about them would be conveyed by 'sociological' predicates, *synthetically* applied. (Necessarily so: for what people do is *not* entailed in their physical kinship position as such. The social, and not logical or biological, compulsion making them do what people of the given kinship category habitually do in the society, is a central part of the subject matter of social anthro-pology.) Needham grotesquely misinterprets a phrase referring to social characteristics, which he quotes from me: '*only* synthetic factual truths' (italics Needham's). The force of the 'only' was *not* 'merely'—I do not consider these sociological attributes to be un-important—on the contrary; the force of 'only' was 'exclusively'. The whole point of the exercise was to *separate* clearly, and not to dis-parage, what is logically distinct, i.e. the physical kinship position and the social predicates (including social kin terms) attributed to it. There is no excuse whatever for Needham's complete misinterpreta-tion of my meaning. He proceeds to speculate about what else I might suppose or mean in order to make sense of my alleged dis-regard of the social characteristics: needless to say, these speculations are as false as they are unnecessary, as the problem they are in-voked to solve (why I should underestimate social facts) does not arise.

The curious thing about some of Needham's errors and conclusions is that they are not even mutually consistent. His opening charge is that I fail to distinguish biology and social function; where he does come across evidence that in fact I *do* distinguish them, instead of seeing that this shows his earlier charge to be wholly misguided, he proceeds instead to invent a further one: he treats my distinction of the physical from the social as evidence for another crime of his own unwarranted invention, my alleged disregard of the importance of the social . . .

Needham is of course right in supposing that the social character-istics are analytically contained in the very meaning of the *autoch-thonous kinship terms*; and they are of course *not* so contained in the physical kin positions of the individuals as such [7] (as he realises). It is the connection between the former (i.e. roles plus local kinship terms) on the one hand, and the physical kin position on the other, which constitutes much of the study of 'kinship structure'. The category used *by the anthropologist* to describe the kinship structure of the society is itself, in effect, a report on the manner of this (synthetic) connection, and hence *both* the physical and the social kinship posi-tions are (analytically) implicit in the *anthropologist's* classification. Needham's confusion is complex: seeing (as in a glass *very* darkly) this connectedness, which however he cannot state as he does not consciously believe in the relevance of one of the terms related (i.e.

the physical kin position), he stresses instead the near-vacuous connection between native kinship term and social role. But that connection, though indeed it obtains, doesn't amount to much: naturally, a term means what it means. Naturally, 'brothers' are expected to be 'fraternal' (and this tells us little unless we know *which* people are expected to behave 'fraternally', i.e. that they are *also* 'brothers' in some other—e.g. physical—sense, and which). In any society (terms such as) 'being-an-X' and 'behaving X-wise' are to a considerable extent defined in terms of each other, and we do not get much further by connecting them. We do get somewhere when we discover how (for example) those whom we call 'brothers' *and* expect to be 'fraternal', are *selected*, relatively to a given individual, from the total population. This gives us the connection between a role and its recruitment. The true and important generalisation that in simple societies the identification of important roles is 'in terms of kinship' only escapes vacuity because we can specify just how in each society 'kinsmen' are picked out in terms of physical kinship in general. But 'brothers act fraternally' or 'kinsmen are kinned (kind)' says very little, if 'brother' or 'kinsmen' are emptied of their *physical* meanings.

Misunderstanding as he does the nature of anthropological studies of kinship (at any rate, when he attempts *to give an account* of them, though perhaps not when he actually *practises* it), Needham has absurd and self-contradictory expectations of what a systematic notation for this study would involve. He seems to expect it to be just one further (native-type) kinship terminology, doing the same kind of work as *one of them*, *and* yet serving to compare them all, and to fuse rather than distinguish the social and the physical as *they* do in their various ways, and yet at the same time to serve for comparing their different ways of doing it . . .

At one stage he complains that the ideal language could not be used by any society as its kinship terminology. Of course it could not, nor was it so intended. When, however, *he* comes across evidence that it was not intended for such a role (the fact that the general structure of the 'names' remains constant), he treats this as one further complaint against it, rather than, as he should, as a corrective of his first interpretation . . .

There is a further set of heterogeneous errors of Needham's, not all of them specifically connected with his failure to understand what is involved in the notion of a descent system or of what is involved in an ideal language.

There is, for instance, the issue of tangibility. Needham denies (error 13) that kinship relationships are more tangible and stateable with accuracy than most aspects of a simple society. On the contrary, for the very reasons which led me to suggest the schema for a formalised language, they *are* stateable with considerable precision and *are* tangible: the connotation of an autochthonous kinship term can be ascertained *just* because we can plot its denotation against the physical kinship map of the people in question. To take another of Needham's own examples, his account of the Kuki term *tu*: it 'covers members of three generations, two distinct descent lines, and both sexes'. This, plus of course further specifications concerning how these *tu* are to be picked out, (and what they do and what is done unto them), gives us much of the meaning of the term. Some shadowiness may enter with regard to the rights and duties of *tu*, but even there, matters such as their inheritance claims, the relative disposition of their habitat, etc., can be ascertained by the observer. Compare this with the practical difficulties of giving a concrete and accurate account of a people's values or beliefs! Things such as values, important though they clearly are for the understanding of a society, are very intangible and hard to assess. With regard to them, the situation which Needham mistakenly supposes to hold with regard to kinship, the possible absence of an equivalent 'thing' in our language, does hold. (There is no third, common, universal and given factor, such as the physical facts of kinship, to *mediate* and thus to facilitate comparisons.) Kinship terms may also not be directly translatable, but the very fact that they are essentially related to physical kinship (in a way which varies from society to society—but the idiosyncratic way in which it varies is fairly accessible to observation) which in turn *is* built up from universally identical elements, is what makes them inexplicable in a language other than that of the people themselves. Needham proceeds to offer some speculations as to why I 'appear to think' (mistakenly, according to him) that kinship systems are tangible. These unnecessary speculations of course represent neither what I think nor what I might be supposed to think on evidence found in the relevant article.

The point can also be seen from the fact that anthropologists avoid, in their accounts, convenient shorthand terms such as 'cousin' and use instead long-hand expressions such as 'father's brother's son'. Apart from the elimination of ambiguity, the relevant feature of this explicit longhand is that it fixes the relative position of the individuals on the *physical* kinship map so that, subsequently, a society's habit of attributing kinship terms, roles, etc. to the individuals so related can be explained. (And the reason why this anthropologist's longhand is unambiguous is not merely that it breaks up the relationship into its links, so to speak, but also because in this usage the term 'brother', 'father' and so on are used in a purely physical sense, purged of any of the fraternal, paternal etc. role-connotations which of course vary from society to society, and which can then, like the native terms, be ascribed to the individuals previously identified by the physical, de-socialised terminology.) For instance, with regard to our society, it may be said that 'cousin' covers father's brother's, and father's sister's offspring, and similarly for the mother. In a schematic notation this information about the range of people or 'names' covered by 'cousin' would be conveyed in a more condensed and perhaps manipulable way by simply giving or specifying the range of 'names' of people to whom cousin-hood, relative to Ego, is attributed.

It is equally wrong to say (error 14), as Needham proceeds to do, that the term *tu* could not be dealt with in my scheme. If a naming scheme such as I proposed were designed, then of course, given the schema for Ego's name, the necessary and sufficient conditions of being Ego's *tu* could be expressed in terms of what types of names (in the devised language, not their own) the *tu* would have to have. (In *their* own language, *tu* are *tu* . . . and behave *tu*-wise . . .) This would merely convey, in a systematic way, the kind of information which Needham in fact gives us in English.

There are also (error 15) Needham's remarks about functionalism. My own observations, to the effect that functionalism should bring home the connection, including *systematic* disparity, between physical and social kinship, a connection which is in any case already entailed by the very notion of kinship as used by anthropologists, were primarily an *a fortiori* argument directed at those who, like Malinowski, attempt to isolate specific needs and directly relate them to features of a society. I am not unaware of the fact that this extreme kind of functionalism is not shared by other anthropologists, having elsewhere commented on this fact in print. But in any case, the argument applies, in a different form, even to the functionalism which *is* very widespread amongst anthropologists, and so Needham's objection remains invalid. Given the fact that mating always is regulated and needs to be, and given the fact societies have kinship structures, it is virtually certain that the latter institution plays some part (though perhaps neither exclusively nor exhaustively) in serving the former need. Given this, there will, in any given society, be some regular connection ('function') between the two, and Needham's crucial separation of the two cannot obtain. In any case, functionalism as a widely accepted *method* (and not as a doubtful and widely doubted *doctrine*) does commit the anthropologist to *finding out* the extent to which social kinship arrangements do assist in the regulation of pro-creation, of the assigning of offspring to groups, and so on—and all this can only be ascertained if one has some knowledge of the physical kinship facts. The remark in my first paper claimed no more.

Needham also accuses my system of being cumbersome (error 16). Though normally shy of openly claiming merit, I assert categorically that my system is *not* cumbersome. My absolute confidence springs from the fact, which inexplicably escaped Needham, that there was *no* such system in the article, which explicitly restricted itself to trying to show that such a system should be possible, and what general conditions it would have to satisfy. A system which lacks existence cannot be endowed with cumbersomeness . . . In this way, as in the others indicated, Needham completely and unnecessarily misunderstood what was stated in the text.

Finally, there are Needham's expressed doubts about the usefulness of the intellectual exercise which I was recommending and which he misunderstood; in these doubts he is quite possibly justified, and I am sometimes inclined to agree. But nothing he says actually supports his doubt or sheds light on the issue. There are, I imagine, many criticisms which may justly be made of my paper (not least that it was pompous): but none of those actually made by Needham are amongst them, or have any validity.

There are also certain criticisms of Needham's which are wholly unanswerable—namely, the unspecific ones. He darkly hints at 'other erroneous or questionable points', and later at mistakes in another work of mine. (For my own part, I do not wish to suggest that Needham committed any errors other than the sixteen which I have explicitly indicated.)

In one society which I know, a rule is known which calls upon a man to pay *half* the usual blood money if he fires at another and misses, but to pay the *full* 'dia' if he takes aim and does not shoot. The reason given is that, as one does not know where the bullet would have gone, the amount of the compensation must be determined by assuming the worst. Given the quality of Needham's marksmanship, I should gladly forgive him the half-price for his misfired actual shots, but feel some sympathy for the rule which would penalise him for waving his gun about in this manner.

Needham's error when analysing the anthropological notion of kinship is important, in as far as it springs from an anthropological manner of speaking which is indeed liable to lead to this kind of error (though I do not think others commit it when they think about it explicitly, as Needham *has*). Needham's other errors are partly corollaries of it, partly unwarranted attribution of positions to the article he attempts to criticise. Failing to see that anthropological kinship terms are classifications of the relation between social and physical facts, he interprets my remarks about the universal physical relation as though they were about the social (thereby of course turning them into absurdities). Of the three charges presented in his summary, (*b*), the confusion of individuals and categories, and (*c*), the confusion of specification and function, are simply misrepresentations, whilst (*a*), concerning the relationship of biology and descent, does show a genuine disagreement, but it is he who is in error.

but are these fundamentally related to biology, and if so, who's biology?

NOTES

1 See *Philosophy of Science*, **27**, 96–101.

2 There is one complication here: it might be objected that the brotherhood relation between the deceased man and his substitute-genitor might itself not be physical but a consequence of an earlier social 'fiction'. In individual cases, certainly, but if it happened regularly, this would itself affect the classification of the kinship structure in which it happens.

3 For instance: in a certain society, the same term is used by a woman to describe her husband's father, and (by everyone) to describe the chief of the clan. Of course there is a tenuous connection between the two notions, but one would *not*, on the strength of this terminological overlap, place an account of clan chieftaincy (which in this case is *not* a function of the kinship position of its holder) in the chapter dealing with kinship structure. *If* the overlap or otherwise with physical were really irrelevant, one would then have to deal with chieftaincy under kinship in this context, for one *could* say that the term is borrowed from kinship.

4 A blood-brother may have to behave like a real one.

5 A godfather does not do the same things as a father, but to every father there may correspond one or a fixed number of god-fathers, performing duties complementary to the father's.

6 Disregarding for the moment things such as infant exposure, abortion, etc., which affect the quantity of surviving offspring.

7 Although, conversely, (to complicate matters), a *view* of the physical kinship position—correct or otherwise—*is* contained in the meaning of the autochthonous kinship term.

13
NATURE AND SOCIETY IN SOCIAL ANTHROPOLOGY

This paper is concerned with the way in which social and physical elements both enter into the accounts given of societies by social anthropologists. To discuss this is, in effect, to discuss the manner in which human society is, or is not, part of nature, and vice versa. In a rough kind of way, it is easy to grasp the distinction between social and natural events. For instance: if a man dies, an autopsy can establish the causes of death *qua* natural event. It cannot, however, establish its nature *qua* social event: was it an execution, a ritual murder, private murder, homicide, a part of a feud, etc. ? Such classifications, of utmost interest to the social anthropologist or any student of society, do not necessarily presuppose any corresponding physical, natural differences in the causes of death. Social events occur within physical nature, but they do not appear to be identical, in some way, with the events which interest the natural scientist.

Interesting methodological and ethical issues hinge on this general relationship between social and natural facts. One extreme but possible position is to assert that social facts are wholly distinct from natural ones. It may be argued that an event acquires social significance only through social recognition of it and this recognition is both necessary and sufficient: without it, a physical event is irrelevant, and with it, it is redundant. If this is true, it has as its methodological consequence a kind of declaration of autonomy for the social sciences, and as its ethical consequence a gratifying liberation from the fear of physical determinism.

An area in which society and nature overlap conspicuously, or seem to, is *kinship*. The analysis of the notion of kinship from this viewpoint has recently caused some discussion.[1] Dr Needham and Professor Barnes have claimed, in connection with kinship, that the social anthropologist is not concerned with the natural, biological aspects of kinship in its physical sense proper (though not denying, and indeed, in the case of Barnes, rightly stressing, that he is concerned with 'physical' kinship in the sense of the beliefs of the members of the society in question about the physical processes involved).

My own view is that the denial of the relevance of the physical-

proper to the social anthropologist's concern is mistaken, both as a recommendation and as an account of actual past practices in social anthropology; and I wish to argue this, particularly against Barnes' refined version of the opposed view, having argued against Needham's version of it earlier. At the same time I wish to highlight the wider issues about the relationship of nature and society which depend on the arguments invoked specifically for kinship.

It is of course both a pleasure and an honour to evoke a contribution from Professor Barnes, even if it is only one written 'under a sense of obligation' arising from the fact that he discussed the matter with me in 1955. Professor Barnes remarks:[2] 'It appears that I did not make myself clear to Gellner (in 1955) and I shall try again.' But I think I do quite clearly understand the position which Professor Barnes now records in print, and I *still* disagree with it. The issue is: the nature of the connection between physical and social kinship.

The question whether there is a connection between social and physical kinship, and of what kind, is inherently interesting and would by itself justify a further contribution as long as there is room for disagreement: but in addition, some of the points raised by Professor Barnes are of extreme interest for the appreciation of the general logic of anthropological theory.

My own position was (and is) as follows: for the relevant anthropological purposes a society can be seen as sets of relationships between people. Not *all* of these relationships are studied or described at the same time. Sub-groups of them are isolated in various ways and dealt with one at a time, not because they are supposed to exist in isolation (on the contrary), but because one cannot say everything at once. One such sub-group, and one which of course is much favoured by anthropologists, is called 'kinship'. On what principle is this sub-group isolated from the total mass of relationships? Answer: by selecting those relationships which systematically overlap, in the anthropologist's view, (without being identical with) physical kinship. It is for this reason that he translates the indigenous words, which he finds used to denote these relationships, as 'father', 'brother' and so forth. What other principle *could* he conceivably employ for selecting 'kinship' relations?

This, in substance, was my position, and the rest of my article on 'The Concept of Kinship', was concerned, apart from clearing up misrepresentations, with showing the invalidity of apparent objections to it. There is nothing in Barnes' article which undermines the argument either. Nevertheless, a mere reiteration of the position would not be adequate because it would fail to show why it *seems* to Barnes that his points do undermine this position; and moreover, as stated, his points do seem to me to have a very great intrinsic interest quite apart from their bearing on the previous issue.

I

To begin with, I have some doubts about the correctness of what Barnes says about the past anthropological use of terms connected with kinship. The point concerning which I have my doubts Barnes expresses in his article as follows:

'The usual brief definition of genitor may well have led him [i.e. Gellner], as I am sure it has led others, to infer that the genitor is identical with the physical father, genetically defined, or the genetic father, as I shall call him for brevity. This is not so.'

In opposition to this alleged mistaken identification of 'physical father' and 'genetic father', Barnes argues (rightly), that the two are to be distinguished: the distinction is, in substance, between the person to whom physical paternity is *ascribed* in the society in question (the socially-physical father, so to speak), and the person to whom it is 'rightly' ascribed (the physical-physical father, as it were) i.e. the person to whom it would be ascribed in the light of modern genetics in those cases—rare, in Barnes' view—in which the genetic facts can be reliably ascertained. My first doubts concern *not* the validity of this distinction (with which I agree), but the claim that the distinction has in the past been properly observed by anthropologists.

Now this point is not of importance for the main issue: for if this distinction is drawn (and I agree with Barnes that it should be, though not that it really has been), my point about the falsity of excluding genetic (physical-physical, so to speak) kinship from the concern of anthropology still holds, as I shall try to show in the main part of the argument. But in the meantime, it is also of some interest to establish whether indeed this distinction *has* been drawn, as Barnes claims. In order to throw some light on this, it is worth confronting Barnes' claim that the distinction has been drawn with his own definitions in his rightly celebrated article on 'Kinship' in the recent edition of *Encyclopaedia Britannica*:

Writers on kinship therefore distinguish between physical parents, *genetically related to the child,* and the foster parents who care for it while it matures, and between both of these and the social parents in whom it acquires rights and privileges, duties and obligations, who, as it were, give it its social personality. . . .

Following L. H. Morgan, anthropologists refer to the social parents as the pater and mater, in contrast with the physical parents, the progenitor and progenitrix. . . .

The study of kinship is the investigation of how social ties of descent and marriage are established, elaborated, fabricated, modified, forgotten and suppressed; how these ties are related to other manifestations of personal and social action; how carnal connection is distinguished from social kinship. (Italics mine.)

Here Barnes speaks of the 'physical parents, *genetically related to the child'*, and of the fact that in the study of kinship *'carnal* connection is distinguished from social kinship'. (Italics mine in both quotations.)

Now if this is an example of the 'usual brief definition' of genitor and physical parent, as Barnes would now have it, then indeed not only have I and others been misled, but I think that I and others could legitimately complain that we have been misled unnecessarily: allowing for the fact that definitions have to be brief, need they have been *quite* so misleadingly brief? Need we have been told that the 'physical parents' were 'genetically related to the child'?—and that 'social kinship' was to be distinguished from 'carnal' connection? Surely it would have been possible to say, as Barnes now does say, that the 'physical parents' were genetically related to the child only *in the eyes of the society in question*, and that social kinship is distinct from carnal connection *as ascribed by the society in question* (in addition, of course, to *both* of these being distinct from genetic kinship proper). This would not have lengthened the definitions unbearably: we should expect it in an article which is otherwise a model of careful formulation. If the distinction which Barnes now stresses was already clear in his mind, it was hardly forgivable not to make it explicit, especially as this could be done at the cost of so few words, as what he actually said then plainly contradicts what he now says is the true situation, and as the failure to be explicit must most legitimately tempt me and others, as he says, into the error with which we are now credited.

I do not wish to deny that the distinction which Barnes now stresses was already present to his mind in some less-than-fully explicit manner, in part because I certainly do not hold him guilty of deliberate misrepresentation, and partly because the general form of this distinction (i.e. between social ascription and physical reality) is so inherent and pervasive in anthropology (and rightly so), that it can easily be applied to the notion of 'lover', for instance, just as it has in fact been explicitly applied to the notion of 'father'. But it is one thing to say that a distinction is implicit in a general approach (as in this case) and quite another to say that it has been explicitly and consistently applied.

This point is of some interest and importance, in as far as it is a general mistake in the philosophy of science to suppose that fully-fledged definitions of concepts exist, in some latent way, prior to the emergence of the problems which lead to the explicit formulation of those definitions. This is false even for mathematics, supposedly the home of clear and distinct definitions established prior to the use of the defined concepts in argument.[3]

A fortiori, it is false for anthropology, in which definitions are ever in need of refinement in the light of new arguments or material.

Hence Barnes misrepresents the past of anthropological concepts (in all good faith, certainly), when he retro-rejects a distinction, whose importance has only been highlighted by the dispute about the relevance of genetic kinship to anthropology—a distinction which has only been drawn clearly and explicitly in consequence of that dispute or at any rate after it. It is misleading to claim that the distinction was present prior to this discussion. Potentially, no doubt, in some sense it was: but to say this is not to be confused with the (false) claim that it was consistently observed, even implicitly. That this is so is amply shown by the quotation from Barnes' own *Encyclopaedia Britannica* article.[4] This article is authoritative, and not merely in view of the status of the volume of which it is a part or of the pen from which it springs: for instance, it is classed among the *very* small number, (two and three, respectively,) of *essential* texts in both the Introductory and the Advanced courses on Kinship at the London School of Economics . . .[5]

This side-issue is of interest in itself, despite its independence of the central issue to be discussed below. Anthropologists make a habit of showing how human societies retro-ject current arrangements onto their own past, e.g. onto their genealogies. As Barnes himself says, in the *Encyclopaedia Britannica* article, the study of kinship includes the investigation of how 'social ties of descent . . . are . . . fabricated, . . . forgotten and suppressed . . .'. Similarly, a study of anthropologists themselves must include an account of how occasionally, as in this case, a currently essential distinction has been retro-jected onto the past . . .

II

It is now possible to state the general form of Barnes' argument to be centrally considered here. He concedes that the study of social kinship is (at least in part) a matter of relating it to something else. He thinks however that I have failed to identify correctly what that something else is. On his view it is socially-physical kinship, and not genetic kinship. He thus agrees with Needham on the crucial question of whether or not the anthropological study of kinship is concerned with genetic kinship, answering it, like Needham, negatively. Thus his position is in substance identical with Needham's. But there is a refinement, namely the distinction between socially-physical and genetic kinship. Barnes also believes that this distinction was already present in Needham's article and the work of other anthropologists, including his own. (This is not quite how he puts it. He says that all anthropologists he knows admit their concern with physical kinship, and he adds that from his reading of Needham's article, he thinks that Needham does so too. But at the same time he denies that anthropologists are or can be concerned with genetic, physically-physical kinship; it follows that those who *are* concerned with the former but *not* with the latter *must*, of course, have drawn the distinction between the two.)

As against this, I maintain that anthropologists are and must be concerned with genetic kinship—('must be' in the sense that it is entailed by what they do in studying kinship), and that this is in no way affected by Barnes' refinement, which I fully accept and indeed never denied. The explicit formulation of this refinement, with which I do and did wholly agree, I welcome. Barnes remarks (p. 298), somewhat anxiously, that 'the distinction I [i.e. Barnes] make between the genetic father and the genitor, the culturally-defined physical father, is no mere quibble'. I entirely agree: it is not a quibble at all but a valid and important distinction. Concerning the claim that it was already present in his own past work I only have the partial reservations stated above, based in part on the evidence of his own *Encyclopaedia Britannica* article.

Various extremely interesting issues hinge on Barnes' refinement, and apart from contesting his main conclusion, which he shares with Needham, I also wish to bring these out. The main issue is: is anthropology (or can it be) concerned exclusively with social matters, or is it inherent in anthropological method that it studies society as located in and limited by a physical environment, which also enters essentially into the anthropological accounts? The first alternative—social facts only—is a corollary of the Needham–Barnes position (elaborated by them *only* with special reference to kinship; but, by symmetry, the conclusion would have to be extended to other spheres of social life). It is the second alternative, however, which seems to me demonstrably true.

Barnes in effect employs two arguments. The first could be called epistemological (or negative), and the second structural (or positive). The first argument is epistemological and negative, in as far as it hinges on the contention that physical or genetic kinship proper cannot be the concern of anthropology, because it isn't accessible to anthropological knowledge. The second argument is structural and positive, in as far as it strives to show that what *is* of concern to the anthropologist, for instance the ascription of physical paternity in a given society, is itself a *social* event in the society in question, rather than a physical one. It is the structural and positive one which is more important but I shall deal with the epistemological, negative one first. In any case, the two arguments complement each other neatly.

The substance of Barnes' negative, epistemological argument is that anthropology cannot be concerned with the genetic father because his identity cannot be established.

Who is the genetic father? It is he who supplies the spermatozoon that impregnates the ovum that eventually becomes the child. Evidence for his identity is rarely conclusive. Even copulation, among most peoples most of the time, is a private affair, whilst human impregnation is always unwitnessed and unrecorded (p. 297).

And he goes on to add that when we try to identify this genetic father

We admit circumstantial evidence as to time and place and fall back on eliminative procedures such as blood groupings.

But all this merely proves that it is difficult to know the genetic father with certainty, and perhaps, impossible to know him with absolute certainty. But it is a strange conclusion that we cannot know him at all, or that we cannot know with sufficient confidence to be concerned with his identity. In practice, we often have no doubts at all about the identity of genetic fathers. Now if Barnes wishes to adopt, as a general position, an epistemological scepticism which refuses scientific consideration to all facts or putative facts which possess no higher certainty than this, then I, for one, will not try to beat him with the stick of what 'in practice' we consider adequate evidence: I have no reverence for practice and common sense, and I do not consider it legitimate or sufficient to invoke them against someone whose critical standards are more severe. *But he will have to do it consistently.* If Barnes wishes to exclude events and identifications for which the evidence is circumstantial and eliminative from the concern of anthropology, he will find both its subject matter and its range of evidence disastrously curtailed.

Consider, for instance, *murder*. It is generally more private than copulation, with the added disadvantage that only one of the two partners survives, and he has strong incentives not to disclose the truth. It would be absurd to conclude that students of society are only concerned with the 'social' murderer, so to speak, i.e. the person socially credited with the physical act of killing, and not with the physical perpetrator as such. Yet by parity of reasoning, Barnes would be committed to such a conclusion. Yet I do not suppose for one moment that comparative criminologists, or those concerned for instance with questioning whether the death penalty for murder has never been applied in error, would accept Barnes' recommendation to concern themselves with 'social' murderers only, and never with 'physical' ones, and to refrain from any investigations concerning the closeness of their overlap, on the grounds that the circumstantial and eliminative grounds for identifying the latter do not allow of certainty.

Barnes really comes close to the doctrine (though I don't think he realises this) that the physical world is unknowable, and only the social world accessible to knowledge. What leads him in this direction is this, I think: the physical links in the chain of causes leading to birth are, at least in part, microscopic and take place inside human bodies, and, as such, not accessible to direct observation by the anthropologist. *Some* social facts, on the other hand, are so to speak demonstrative: it is of their essence that they are conspicuously displayed and hence directly observable. Notoriously, the point of wedding festivities, public trials, ritual conferments of office, etc. etc. is to make plain and visible a given social fact.

But equally notoriously, social life has not merely its 'daylight', so to speak, but also its 'night-time', the events and relationships which the participants are not anxious to advertise, and which indeed they may be anxious to dissimulate and forget. No modern anthropologist would dream of excluding this dark side of social life from his purview (certainly not Barnes, whose *Encyclopaedia Britannica* definition of kinship goes out of its way to include the suppressed and forgotten facts within the concern of anthropology, and who has contributed a most suggestive phrase, 'structural amnesia', to anthropological language). Indeed this is the premiss of the rejection of anthropological work based only on uninterpreted informants' reports: it leaves out the un-public, un-stressed parts of social life. The point of field work is not so much that the anthropologist can, like an Invisible Man, perform a kind of social surgery and witness that which is normally hidden: if he is lucky he may do a little of that too. But even then he will see not much more than does an average member of the society himself, which is not very much. The point of field work is that, from participating in the local life in the round, the field-worker can see, by use of circumstantial and eliminative evidence, how to fill in the lacunae and correct the inconsistencies or falsehoods of the 'official', overt self-image of the society which is more easily accessible from informants and public rites and activities. A consistent implementation of severe epistemological rigour now advocated by Barnes would de-bar anthropology from any concern with the 'dark' side of social life. I cannot imagine that Barnes, once he sees this implication of the epistemological position he has now adopted (ad hoc, I hope) in defence of a Needham-ian account of kinship, will wish to continue to hold it.[6]

Barnes himself partly sees this difficulty, when he makes a concession in connection with *maternity*. As he says, 'the identity of the genetic mother is readily known'. This has the odd and unsymmetrical consequence that whilst he comes down in favour of a Needham-ian analysis of the notion of paternity, he is willing to concede a Gellnerian one of maternity.

But I am afraid that such a half-a-loaf will not do: here we must play, or argue, doubles-or-quits. It seems to me that the *same* kind of analysis must apply in the case of both notions. The difference between them is only one of degree. It is of course true that maternity is *harder* to conceal or simulate than paternity, but it is not impossible. Dynastic disputes of succession have hinged on such matters, and a plausible case of simulated maternity, carried out without even the conscious co-operation of the 'mother', is described in Stendhal's *Lucien Leuwen*. And until recently in England, the Home Secretary had to be present at Royal births, precisely in order to make this possibility more difficult.

The general point one must make about Barnes' negative-epistemological argument is this: both in society and in nature, much exists which can only be known or identified by 'circumstantial and eliminative' procedures. (Plausible epistemologies exist which maintain that even 'direct observation' is never as conclusive as Barnes appears to suppose, and that some interpretation is *always* involved: but I shall not urge this against Barnes.) The negative argument, applied consistently, does not favour the social as against the physical. A consistent application of the criterion of certainty, used by Barnes to exclude genetic fathers, would exclude not merely them, but also many 'social' matters, and leave anthropology empoverished and transformed out of all recognition. Heavens above, in villages people often know the identity of genetic fathers as well, if not a good deal better, than they know most other things. And how much can a single participant observer actually know from direct observation?

III

It is Barnes' second argument, the structural and positive one, which raises really fascinating issues. The argument runs, in substance, as follows: it is not merely *pater* that is a social role, but so is *genitor*. They are systematically connected, though not identical.[7] But: neither is it identical with or systematically related to the genetic father except accidentally and, from the viewpoint of anthropology, irrelevantly. With this latter point I disagree.

I agree with Barnes' premiss: it is the conclusion which does not follow. It is true that (for instance) 'lover' is a social role, just as 'husband' is, though possibly a somewhat less 'formal' one. One can easily imagine, for instance, a society in which it is customary and mandatory for a married woman, after some years of marriage to take a lover. Such a lover would have certain expectations, and certain things would be expected of him: in brief, a 'role'. A character in Somerset Maugham's *The Razor's Edge* claims that a pattern of this kind in fact obtains among the French upper class:

> In France, which after all is the only civilised country in the world, Isabel would marry Gray without thinking twice about it: then, after a year or two, if she wanted it, she'd take Larry as her lover, Gray would install a prominent actress in a luxurious apartment, and everyone would be perfectly happy.

Given that this is an expected pattern (and clearly, it could be, for the qualification 'if she wanted it' in the above passage, sounds like a mere manner of speaking), it must happen not infrequently that people are canalised into the occupancy of even such a relatively informal role without particularly liking it, and that at the same time they are not sufficiently motivated or determined to resist the social pressure leading them to their social destiny. For instance, everything about the position and accomplishments of Madame X and her husband might make it socially expectable that young Y, Monsieur X's subordinate, should become Madame X's lover.[8] At the same time, through personal idiosyncrasy, neither of the 'lovers' feels much inclination for the other, yet neither will go against the social pressures making for this relationship. So, 'lovers' they are, whilst Madame X, going against custom, takes a kind of meta-lover with whom she deceives young Y.

My point is: the performance of the duties expected by Madame X of her meta-lover is *also* a social role, albeit less formal than that of lover, which in turn may be less formal than that of husband. There is often a hierarchy of formality in roles (or a multiplicity of hierarchies), and even the most informal is a kind of social role, though it may approximate more closely to a mere performance of a physical act. The category of 'the social', like that of 'knowledge', can easily and plausibly be made omnivorous—everything it touches comes to be subsumed under it.

In a sense I think Barnes would agree with this—it was he who stressed that genitor was a social and not a physical role—yet I think he has failed to notice just how *very* omnivorous 'the social' is. He appears to think that there can be a residual category of purely physical acts, which, as such, are then irrelevant to social anthropology. His criteria for delimiting this residual class of acts, which is quite essential for his arguments, are not very well worked out, and in any case are quite unworkable. The only example given is copulation and fertilisation, and the criteria appear to be a relative lack of witnesses (just how many witnesses make an act social? three?), and the fact that microscopic or hidden processes are involved. (Is poisoning another person not a social act? Poison also works unobserved.) Any attempt to make such criteria work must break down: there will be too many borderline cases, and the boundaries themselves will fluctuate most uncomfortably with technical innovations and changes in the fashion for doing things publicly or privately. (For instance, a telephone conversation would not be a social event by Barnes' implicit criteria, but would become such when tapped . . .) In any case, there is something very odd indeed about saying that copulation is not a socially meaningful act.

Concerning the spectrum of formality/informality of roles, this can be said: highly formal roles (those which are much advertised, socially recognised, consecrated by ritual and terminology) may or may not correspond to reality: the formal owner may or may not really control the property, the father may or may not be the genetic father. The very formality of roles gives them a kind of independence, for they can survive without a corresponding 'reality'. The situation is different at the other end of the spectrum: roles of maximum informality, so to speak, will overlap with 'reality' to a remarkably high degree, for the very absence of formality means just that there is little other than the real performance of some role which is to keep that role—or its occupancy by a given individual—in being. Performance of these roles is indeed a 'social' event, but it is one which, owing to the lack of formal ratification, can only be identified through knowing, or guessing, what 'really', physically happens. The informal margins of social life are indeed parts of social life, but they constitute the area where the social and physical necessarily overlap to a high degree, and where the disassociation argued by Barnes cannot obtain. However much is incorporated in 'the social'—and I agree with Barnes that even informal roles are still roles—this will not thereby exclude 'the physical', for there is and must be an area where the two overlap.

These hierarchies of formality of role are of course by no means restricted to the sphere of kin and sexual relations. They are prominent in other spheres, such as the political. For instance, a country may formally be ruled by a monarch. But informally, power had passed into the hands of a court chamberlain, a mayor of the palace or whatnot. This situation may crystallise into a stable pattern and continue over generations. In due course a weak or politically uninterested successor may also arise in the informal dynasty of palace stewards, and real power pass on to a kind of second-order informal power-holder. As in the sexual case, nothing but unmanageable complexity sets a ceiling to the number of such possible levels of formality. This type of situation is of course not uncommon: the Merovingian or Abbasid dynasties, or recent Nepalese history, might provide examples.

One can see now how Barnes' two arguments converge: the

epistemological argument is to show that the physical is outside the anthropologist's ken: the structural one shows that anything done in society, including activities normally contrasted with more formal ones, is itself social. These two pincers as it were converge against the position which I hold, namely that a good deal of anthropological work (including studies of kinship) consists of relating social *and* physical reality.

In opposition to Barnes, I assert the following: however ramified the hierarchy of formality of roles, roles only come to be subsumed under a given rubric ('kinship', 'politics', 'economy') in virtue of overlapping in a reasonably systematic way, directly or indirectly, with the real facts of procreation, of power, or of usable commodities. A social pater may be distinct from the social genitor, and he in turn from the genetic father: but unless there is a reasonably regular link[9] between each of these two pairs, the former could not be classed as kinship roles. Imagine two such 'detached' roles, an alleged social role X (say: protector and provider) reduplicated by another related role Y (defined in any way you wish, but *not* one which creates a presumption of genetic paternity). If indeed one had no reason for identifying either of them as literally physical fathers of a given child, would any anthropologist really call the occupiers the child's *father* or *genitor*? So, the basic objection against Needham's position applies equally against Barnes' refined version—though the refinement is in itself both valid and interesting.

IV

The matter can perhaps be brought out most clearly if we consider the application of these points to the *feud*. In a sense, the feud is a kind of kinship in reverse: both feuding and kin relationships are of course complex and ramified, (and of course they overlap) but essentially, when we are concerned with feuding, we are concerned with those relationships centred on the systematic elimination of individuals from the world, just as when we are concerned with kinship, we are interested in those relationships centred on bringing people into the world. Kinship studies concern the social allocation of new entrants *into* the world, studies of feuding the social selection of people to be expedited and to expedite, *from* the world. (Feuding is of course distinguished from individual murder or from war with its anonymous unselective killing. Persons killed in a feud are killed neither for individual idiosyncratic reasons nor anonymously *en masse*, but in virtue of their social role: just as people's kinship relations are not those they acquire *qua* individuals, nor those, like class, attributed to whole masses, but those generated by their birth and birth-producing relationships.)

Now it is illuminating to re-enact the disagreement about kinship in terms of the feud. Somewhat pompously, one might begin by defining the feud as follows: The Feud is a relationship between two groups such that it involves from time to time the violent elimination of individuals from this world, and such that the selection of individuals *for* elimination, and the selection of the agents *of* elimination, can both be specified in terms of the principal role system of the two groups involved.

At this point, someone might raise a Needham-like objection [10] (i.e. one corresponding in its logic to Needham's points about kinship) and argue as follows: 'This position is a complete misunderstanding of social anthropology and its handling of the feud. Feuding cannot be defined in terms of physical killing at all, for social anthropology is only concerned with social relationships, even if these happen to be more or less concordant, sometimes, with physical ones such as killing. But the latter do not concern us. Killing is ascribed in various societies in accordance with the concepts of those societies, which have, each of them, their own logic, and do not necessarily correspond to any physical fact. (Consider killing by witchcraft, etc.) Hence any concern with the overlap between the social and physical aspects of feuding, or any attempt to define the former in terms of the latter, is profoundly misguided.'

In reply to this, one is forced to observe that the indisputably social nature of feuding (in one sense) in no way precludes the fact that we can only define feuding, and identify feuds, by the fact that from time to time members of the two relevant groups do really and physically kill each other, notwithstanding the fact that some killings may be ascribed rather than real, and that sometimes the killing is performed by hired assassins whilst being socially ascribed not to them but to the person hiring them, etc. If members of a group neither kill nor are killed, nor are in any reasonably systematic way connected with deputies or proxies who do, we cannot and would not really speak of a feud, though we might perhaps speak of ritual or simulated or mock feuding, precisely in order to distinguish it from real feuding.

At this point, someone might come in with a Barnes-like position, and argue as follows: 'Yes, it is true that in feuding there must be at least a systematic connection between roles such as a person-in-feud and the hired assassin. Nevertheless it is wrong to say that feuding can be or is defined in terms of a certain systematic relation between a social role or activity and physical fact. It is false for two reasons: the hired assassin is one further social role (this is the structural-positive argument); whilst the actual physical killing often takes place in private and in the dark, there are only two witnesses and one does not survive, we can never be sure of the actual cause of death and can only establish it inconclusively by appealing to eliminative considerations such as that the killed man was not at the time suffering from this or that fatal disease, and so on. In brief, the social cause of death can be established, but the physical one cannot, at least with certainty, and cannot be held to be systematically connected with the former. (This is the epistemological-negative argument.) So, the anthropological study of the feud remains within the realm of the social, but we must distinguish between at least two kinds of social roles involved, the being-in-feud and the (social ascription of) being the agent of death.'

A person arguing along these lines would of course be entirely correct in his facts, though not in his conclusion. He would however have one advantage over the person arguing the analogous position with respect to kinship, that he would not even have to concede that in the past anthropologists have failed, at least in their general formulations, to recognise clearly enough that roles such as being a hired assassin are indeed social roles and not just physical performances. For anthropologists are quite clear that hired assassins are indeed an *institution*.

Consider the following remarks:

(Chez le tribu des Beni Ouriaghil, de la région du Rif) . . . à propos d'un chien tué, une lutte de sept ans éclata entre deux villages, qui fit 50 morts d'un côté, 70 de l'autre. Les vaincus émigrèrent . . . et vendirent leur biens. Ils louèrent avec cet argent, les services d'assassins à gage pour tuer leurs vainqueurs.
. . . signalons que l'horrible *institution* des assassins à gage, qui n'a pas disparu, existe chez les Kabiles de la Grande Kabilie. (Emphasis mine, pp. 106 and 109 of H. G. Bousquet, *Les Berbères*, Paris, 1957.)

Or again,

The fact that a chief may do few of his revenge murders himself matters little in this connection. As the responsibility falls on him who paid for the murder, it is he who requires the courage . . . to live permanently under the threat of revenge from an increasing number of people. (F. Barth, *Political Leadership Among the Swat Pathans*, London, 1959, p. 85.)

Now the hierarchy of formality of role could occur here as much as it does in kinship. For instance, guns-for-hire might run in families, and probably sometimes do. One can imagine a man born into such an assassin lineage but wholly disinclined for his calling. He might, for instance, loathe the sight of blood, be frightened of the dark, and detest the violent impact made by a rifle butt when the rifle is fired.

But let us suppose that our reluctant assassin is also unwilling to go against the social pressures making him stay in the ancestral profession, and that he is intelligent and resourceful. So, naturally, he sub-contracts the assignments which his inherited reputation and goodwill bring him, to a kind of meta-assassin.[11] But does this possibly show that feuding is socially and not physically defined? No, for the meta-assassin in turn is a social role, and so on ad infinitum, should the regress continue. At some point or other, the role must systematically overlap with a physical act: it is the nature of this act —a copulation or birth, killing or violence, production or exchange of goods—which determines the rubric (e.g. kinship, politics, economy) under which the role in question is subsumed by the investigator: and this rubric then as it were carries over to the more formal roles which are systematically tied to it, by one or more steps.

V

A good number of further interesting issues hinge on all this, which it is only possible to indicate briefly.

1. Not all anthropological categories can be defined along these lines, though I think kinship, politics and economy can. Religion, ritual, and play activity probably cannot. There is, perhaps, in these latter cases no universal activity, definable without invoking so to speak culturally specific concepts, which would seem as it were to provide a nucleus by reference to which these spheres could be defined. Religion, for instance, tends to be defined either by reference to the transcendental (which involves the difficulty that the distinction between the mundane and the transcendental may be relative to cultures, and indeed to the personal view of individual anthropologists), or negatively (e.g. ritual activity is that which does not have any practical purpose, a kind of residue after technical activity has been abstracted), or speculatively (e.g. religion is the symbolic expression of the social order—which might even be true, but is hardly so manifest, or so clear in its meaning, as to be justly incorporated into the very definition of religion . . .).

Spheres of social life such as these, not anchored to a necessarily universal feature such as procreation, violence or the production or accumulation of goods, present special difficulties of interpretation, more so perhaps than do spheres such as kinship. Hence different considerations perhaps apply in those spheres: I have attempted to discuss the general form of these considerations elsewhere.[12]

2. There is a dead or moribund approach in anthropology which attempts to correlate institutions with 'basic needs' served by them. There is no need to rehearse here the reasons which have led to the abandonment of this approach. But one can see the kernel of truth

underlying it: the categorisations 'kinship', 'economy', 'politics', etc., are naturally imposed by observers, who have to proceed from certain easily identifiable features of any societies—the reproduction and allocation of children, or power and control, or the procuring and distribution of necessities. This does not mean that these 'needs' are necessarily satisfied by discrete isolable activities: societies, unlike committees, do not have neat agendas.

It is I suppose conceivable that anthropologists may one day replace existing categories such as politics, economy and kinship by others with other boundaries, just as historians may revise periodicisations of history. It might be found that by re-drawing the boundaries of categories of social relations, more important insights or generalisations are arrived at. We have seen Homans (n. 7) recommending a reform of this kind. If such a reform did take place, it is conceivable that there would be no single category, such as 'kinship' is now, which was only identifiable and definable through its overlap with genetic kinship. The argument for concern with genetic kinship based on the need for identifying an existing category might *then* lapse. But it still would not be true that genetic kinship was of no concern to social anthropology: for we should still be left with the set of considerations that it must be the job of the social scientist to see institutions, etc., not merely in relation to each other, but also in their physical setting. This brings us to the next point:

3. The doctrine that anthropology is concerned exclusively with the social and not with physical reality makes nonsense of a great many of the attempts at functional interpretation, i.e. at specifying how one activity or institution is conducive to the maintenance of others. Physical reality (including biological aspects of man) provides the milieu, the obstacles as it were, within which social life goes on. The perpetuation of groups and institutions, the achievement of individual and social ends, takes place within the limits and difficulties imposed by nature. A functional account shows how, given this physical environment (plus the social environment of other institutions), a given institution manages to overcome the obstacles and utilise the opportunities to survive and aid the rest of the social structure to survive. If we excluded physical nature and the difficulties and imperatives it imposes, functional accounts which merely related purely social features to each other would get rather close to logical vacuousness.

They might escape complete vacuousness: something might be left. There is perhaps a sense in which one social institution, belief, etc., can aid, sustain, make possible another without this relationship of support being, so to speak, routed through the medium of the physical. But a very large proportion of 'functional' connections *is* so routed. For instance, if we say that an inter-tribal religious sanctuary is functional in that it makes possible inter-tribal trade which in turn is necessary for the tribes in question, we pre-suppose the *physical* fact that the material resources of the relevant region are such that neither tribe can be economically self-sufficient. We must know or presuppose this physical fact if the functional explanation of the frontier shrine and sanctuary is to make any sense.

Many anthropological explanations presuppose physical facts in this manner, by showing how a practice or institution operates in the physical world and helps solve a problem set by that world. Hence to offer such explanations is to make or presuppose some assertions about the physical environment, which consequently cannot be ruled out of bounds for anthropology. Anthropological monographs in fact do take ample notice of it, of course, and tell us about the geography and ecology of the relevant region (and *not* merely about the indigenous *view* of the geography, ecology, etc., which of course, as in the case of kinship, is not always identical with it . . .). Some aspects of this physical environment are more accessible to the anthropologist's inspection than others, and some can only be worked out inferentially: but then, *just* the same is also true of the social world . . .

The assumption of the validity of the Western view of nature may or may not be justified, and it may be a piece of arrogant hubris: this question I do not propose to discuss. What is certain is that as anthropology is actually practised this assumption is in fact made, and must be made. For instance, it would be a strange anthropologist, and one unacceptable to the anthropological community as at present constituted, who explained the Ifugao belief cited by Barnes, to the effect that a child can on occasion have more than one genitor, by saying that indeed this does occur. *This* explanation is excluded by the canons and norms of anthropology. An acceptable explanation will offer an account of how the belief is sustained, what social effects it has, how it is squared with counter-examples (which in this case does not arise), etc. Having done this, the anthropologist may perhaps commend such a belief as salutary for the society in which it occurs, and hence, in that pragmatist sense, as 'true'. But the whole pattern of his explanation will in fact hinge on the fact that the belief, though 'true', is not true. Anthropologists are sometimes tempted by such pragmatism, and indeed one of them has claimed,[13] that pragmatism was a decisive influence at the very start of modern anthropology. But the trouble with such pragmatism is that, by linking truth and social usefulness, it makes it impossible to say that something is socially useful *just* because it is false: whereas, in reality, many anthropological explanations have *precisely* this form! Consider how fond, quite rightly, anthropologists are of showing how tribesmen 'manipulate' beliefs about ancestors in order to express or reinforce current social alignments, doing this with the help of, for instance, 'structural amnesia', in Barnes' own celebrated phrase. This is so, but in order to say it, one must (a) be willing to say that what the tribesmen say and believe is indeed false, and (b) one must have some idea (arrived at, if you wish, by circumstantial, eliminative, etc., means) of what the divergent real truth is.

4. The mistaken doctrine that only social matters are of concern to social anthropology provides a prop for a quite unnecessary kind of social and conceptual relativism, to the effect that every society can only be understood through its own concepts, etc. (I don't think Barnes intended this, but there is some evidence in Needham's article that *he* did.) If one retains a firm grip on the fact that to give an account of a society is, among other things, to situate its activities in and against the background of natural fact, one sees that such relativism can be at least to some extent avoided. Western science is involved in anthropology not merely as a cultural feature of Western society, but as a premiss shared by all anthropologists as such (whatever their culture of birth). One does *not* interpret an indigenous society in terms of its own concepts, though one *does* interpret those concepts. For instance, an indigenous belief or concept which is contrary to Western genetics simply cannot be invoked to explain goings-on in the society in question. What in fact one does is try to explain the goings-on *and* the concept itself against the background of a physical-biological reality seen through Western eyes. (Again, when it comes to religion, the situation is more complex. All anthropologists accept Western genetics as opposed to local indigenous beliefs when it comes to biological phenomena: concerning the transcendental, there is no Western consensus, either in general or among anthropologists. There is an interesting question concerning whether this apparent diversity among Westerners is real or merely superficial.)

There may be forms of relativism which cannot be refuted. But it simply is not true that anthropology, as actually practised, is relativistic in the sense of being committed to explaining each society in terms of its own concepts only. On the contrary, it sees every society as coping with and functioning within a natural environment. Thus, the natural environment does enter into the account and explanation: and it is seen in an identical non-relative way (i.e. through Western eyes) for all societies.

5. The hierarchies of 'formality' of roles etc. are in reality often extremely complex. I have refrained from a proper definition of 'formality', letting the notion emerge from such series as husband–official lover–unofficial lover, or Monarch–Court Steward–informal Eminence Grise. A proper working out of the notion might be interesting. Given roles often move up and down along this scale, and

may have different positions on it in different contexts. (The Brigade of Guards has a formal role of protecting the Royal Family, a role so formalised that it cannot be properly carried out, the real task falling to the more-than-semi-formal police force, which has to protect the guardsmen themselves from importuning tourists. In different context, in wartime, the Guards, but not the Beefeaters, revert to a real physical rather than a formal role. Associated with their over-formal role as 'guards', the guardsmen have at the same time a semi-formal but perfectly recognised role in connection with social stratification, etc.) In the context of Western societies with a sense of cumulative history, one is tempted to say that roles begin their careers at the bottom of the scale of formality and end it at the top: for in Western contexts, we tend to think of ritual as ossified practical action. But there are probably many variant possibilities.

6. My general position may be summed up thus: societies are situated in physical nature (which of course includes the biological natures of their members); anthropological explanations give accounts, amongst other things, of how societies cope *with* nature, and indeed of how they cope *in* it. Hence anthropologists cannot claim to indulge in a kind of social *epoché*, to be professionally oblivious of physical and biological facts (as opposed to their social images). For they are concerned with the social impact of physical facts as they are, and not merely as they appear.

Formulated thus, my general position seems a trivial truism. So it is. What makes it worth asserting, and working out in detail with reference to institutions such as kinship, is that there is a persistent temptation to deny it. The denials of it are not mere by-products of careless formulation. Apart from the relativism and pragmatism already mentioned, there is a certain kind of Idealism which appears (not always under that name) from time to time in the social sciences,[14] and the denial of the relevance of physical nature to social understanding is a corollary of it.

Such idealism has various roots, but two are specially worth singling out. One is connected with the work situation of the anthropologist: his specific competence, not shared by other groups, lies in observing social institutions and assessing their consequences. On the other hand, he is not specially equipped to deal with the natural environment of the society he is studying. He may be trained in primitive technology, but when it comes to surveying fields, doing demography, etc., he is not necessarily more than an amateur. It is naturally tempting to suppose that such investigations into the environment as it is, rather than as it socially appears, are not his professional concern.

The second factor making for the kind of idealism mentioned springs from philosophy: if only social phenomena were wholly

202   *Nature and society in social anthropology*

autonomous, if only their explanations never had to invoke extra-social realities, this would have the gratifying consequence of obviating disagreeable possibilities such as physical determinism. (I should say that, in the case of Barnes there is no evidence that his particular argument in favour of the autonomy of social kinship is motivated by a desire to support such a generalised position.)

I feel the utmost sympathy with such aspirations: but social phenomena are not fully autonomous in the required sense, and the vindication of the desired philosophic consequences cannot, unfortunately, be obtained in this way.

NOTES

1   In *Philosophy of Science*: E. Gellner, 'Ideal Language and Kinship Structure', **24**, 1957, 235–42; R. Needham, 'Descent Systems and Ideal Language', **27**, 1960, 96–101; E. Gellner, 'The Concept of Kinship', **27**, 1960, 187–204; J. A. Barnes, 'Physical and Social Kinship', **28**, 1961, 296–9.
2   Op. cit., p. 296.
3   For this assertion, I accept the authority of Dr Imre Lakatos and his work on the history of definitions in geometry, 'Proofs and Refutations', *Brit. J. Phil. of Sci.*, **14**, 1963–4, 1–25, 120–39, 121–45, 296–342.
4   That the distinction was not very clearly perceived can also be seen from Needham's paper. Needham observes (p. 97) that 'they (biology and descent) will usually be concordant to some degree . . .' If Needham were here conscious of Barnes' distinction between socially-physical and physically-physical kinship, he would have had to specify just which concordance he had in mind.
    This also shows that though Barnes and Needham agree on the central point (irrelevance of genetic or physically-physical kinship), their analyses are otherwise not in harmony. In speaking of contingent concordance 'to some degree', Needham is, from Barnes' viewpoint, saying either too little or too much. For Barnes concedes that there is a systematic and regular relationship between social and socially-physical kinship, whilst he denies any relationship at all, or adequate knowledge on our part of a relationship, between social and genetic kinship, at any rate in the case of paternity.
5   London School of Economics and Political Science, *Calendar 1961–2*, 397–8.
6   In a certain sense, Barnes is (unwittingly) reviving the doctrine of primitive promiscuity *and* extending it to all humanity. For if

Barnes' contention concerning our ignorance of genetic paternity is taken literally, it follows that we possess no information with which to counter the *prima facie* plausible supposition (plausible in the alleged absence of all contrary evidence) of a random distribution of partnerships in copulation. Barnes is either committed to such a view of his argument, or at the very least deprived of any means of contradicting someone who holds such a view. For any positive counter-argument to such a view (as opposed to mere general scepticism) must *eo ipso* be a claim that these partnerships follow certain patterns, and to make such claims is to say that one has access to information which, according to Barnes, is inaccessible.
7   On this point Barnes agrees with me. This point is of importance, in case there is someone still tempted to hold the extreme position, i.e. one to the effect that anthropological kinship terms can be analysed in purely social terms and involve no reference to physical kinship of any kind.
    Note: if this were true, why should anthropologists, when giving accounts of the kind of matrilineal society in which the mother's brother takes over the duties assigned to the father in our society, refer to him *as* the 'mother's brother' and not simply as 'father'? On the extreme theory, they should!
    It is interesting however that at least one distinguished anthropologist tentatively recommended just such a reform (though he was quite clear that this *would* constitute a reform, and not a perpetuation of current practice). G. C. Homans, in *The Human Group*, (London, 1950, p. 258) suggests that in certain respects Trobriand and Tikopia kinship systems are identical 'if we forget about biological kinship . . . and look at the working group instead.'

This plainly implies that we should first of all have to forget something which according to Needham we never cared about, and according to Barnes we never knew in the first place, namely 'biological kinship'.

S. F. Nadel quotes the remark (*The Theory of Social Structure*, London, 1957, p. 105), and observes about it that 'we should say, perhaps more correctly, that . . . what we "forget about" (should be) the different human and role material . . .' This correction of Homans by Nadel seems to be very close to Barnes' position.

8 In his fascinating study (*Les Officiers*, 1958), of the French officer class, Vincent Monteil gives the rules governing the loves of officers: 'Jamais avec les femmes des inférieures: avec celles des supérieurs, *c'est un devoir*, pénible parfois . . .' (p. 51, italics mine).

9 Allowing for the various provisos elaborated in my previous article.

10 Cf. op. cit., pp. 96–101.

11 Unfortunately I cannot think of an actual example of this, but there can be no doubt but that this is socially plausible. Mr Colin Rosser reports a thief lineage in a Himalayan village—so why not an assassin lineage? Professor J. Berque (*Structures Sociales du Haut-Atlas*, Paris, 1955, p. 271) reports the subcontracting by hereditary saints of the proceeds of their ancestral shrine—so why not subcontract assignations of murder? Subcontracting of killing must be common in urban criminal or terrorist organizations.

12 See 'Concepts and Society', pp. 18–46 in this volume.

13 E. R. Leach, 'The Epistemological Background to Malinowski's Empiricism', in R. Firth, ed., *Man and Culture*, London, 1957.

14 Cf., for instance, P. Winch, *The Idea of a Social Science*, London, 1958.

14

THE ALCHEMISTS OF SOCIOLOGY

The eagle never lost so much time as when he
submitted to learn of the crow.
William Blake, *Proverbs of Hell*

The pretentiousness and verbiage which in some measure mar the
social and psychological sciences are at last identified, and Professor
Sorokin is well qualified to castigate them with much wit. He is also
concerned to cure, not merely to diagnose: but it is possible to disagree with his positive suggestions, and yet to enjoy and appreciate
his critical castigation. Sorokin's diagnosis of the ills which he pil-
lories[1] is that they 'are largely due to their faulty philosophy and
theory of cognition' (p. 279). What is true is that, for the first time in
history perhaps, we are faced with a (pseudo) empiricist scholasticism. By scholasticism, generically speaking, I mean an active but
barren tradition whose barrenness is somehow ensured by its organisation, ideology and practices. What is novel here is an official
adherence to the slogans, images and even practices of empiricism.
But these practices are a kind of ritual, the performance of magical
incantations and movements. Such a methodological ritualism, with
its initiations, arcana and the whole works, should not be confused
with empiricism.

It is true that what underlies this methodological ritualism is a kind
of self-consciousness, which manifests itself in thinking more about
method than about subject-matter. Preoccupation with method can
be a kind of evasion of reality. 'Method' calls forth a strange world
of its own, separated from both the inner world of ideas and outer
social reality. Indeed this alienation appears to be its function. The
inner life is then atrophied and/or handed over to the psychiatrist,
and outer reality ignored as un-amenable to true science. Method is
conceived less as a tool of discovery, than as a kind of *ersatz* tabula
rasa, or as a means of approximating towards that state of purity . . .

Instead of what he considers the empiricist fallacy, Sorokin commends a new approach both to cognition and to the social reality
cognised. But if in his constructive views Sorokin takes one into a
somewhat slapdash and extravagant realm, that is only a small part
of the book; in its major part, devoted to the Fads and Foibles, his
touch is sure, his aim accurate and deadly.

What then, if not its positive contribution, makes this a significant book? In brief, it accurately portrays an important subculture within psycho-social science. These are no random fads and foibles; they clearly have common social and ideological roots. It would be difficult, and presumptuous, for anyone who is not a careful student of the American sociological scene, to assess how widespread the participation in them is. But without presuming to make such an assessment,[2] and stressing that there are many untainted by it, and that many of those who are also produce distinguished and valuable work and are men of the highest ability, a casual observer is nevertheless in the position to confirm with conviction that such a subculture exists, and that Sorokin has hit it off.

All one can add is that if some of us are freer of these fads and foibles, it isn't for any lack of trying; we don't often have the opportunities. And there is a real glamour in the genuine vitality and *drang* associated with this Scientism.

But having made, repeated and stressed the qualification that this is only a portrait of a subculture within the larger world of American psycho-social science, the fact remains that it exists,—filled with feverishly active men with very curious horizons, lacking any past, history, or philosophy; within those low horizons of a few decades, a curious Daliesque world with a few simple kinds of things: some spindly statistical concepts, rickety structures of struts rising high upwards: a few psycho-analytic cumulus-cloud-concepts in the sky, and the rest a flat, flat plain strewn with a mass of indistinguishable and disconnected 'empirical studies'. Plus some indigenous 'theoretical conceptual frameworks', like the old isolated cupboards with half-open and empty drawers, standing alone, unconnected with the strewn objects or with the spindly structures which cast no shadow. In this strange world, lit with a cold light, a population of over-active and over-anxious eager men, who, no wonder, can only bear it by having recourse to those shamans of the Western world, the psycho-analysts. (Symbolised perhaps in the picture by a huge all-seeing eye attached to nothing in particular.)

This world exists, curiously hygienic in its lack of historical and philosophical vistas. Its inhabitants, though anxious, are extremely confident and yet curiously touchy; often equipped with psychic deafness and a methodology instead of a mind. Between the aridity of statistical ritualism and the tropical lushness of psycho-analytic imagery, they wend their way to scientific truth, something like this: 'Night follows day'. Footnote: Cf. McAllister and Finkelstein, *Society in its Temporal Setting*. Or rather, 'The functional sequentialisation of diurnality by nocturnality has been established for a wide range of social structures.' (I can't really do this kind of thing properly.) The best footnotes, too, are at the end, just as in real science, simply: McAllister and Finkelstein, 1952*b*. Whatever else the psycho-analysts have not achieved, they have exorcised the logical super-egos of their wards.[3]

It simply won't do, as some very distinguished visitors have tried, to defend this kind of stuff by suggesting that those who object to it are wedded to a dilettantish, belle-lettristic conception of social study and fail to allow technical expression for new truths. For one thing, there are no new truths here, and the expression is not more but less accurate: these neologisms are generally a case of *l'art pour l'art*. It is not an effete aestheticism which makes one protest: the aesthetic criteria applied to expressions of thought are *not* independent of the logical criteria applicable to the *content*.

In his chapter on 'Obtuse Jargon and Sham-Scientific Slang' Sorokin refers to Schopenhauer's views on obtuse and foggy speech. Indeed, Schopenhauer's classic abuse of Hegel will ever remain the model for those who fight academic pretentiousness. But let us be fair to poor Hegel: whatever his defects, by being turned up-side-down he gave rise to one of the most important sociological theories. So much cannot be said for the contemporary version: a ball of fluffy cotton-wool looks exactly the same *any* way up.

There is, however, if Spinozists will forgive me, a certain similarity between it and Spinozism. Spinoza was awed by the very ideas of the possibility of rational explanation and of the unity of the world and the interdependence of things within it. He confused the assertion of these formal possibilities and the elaboration of related formal concepts with substantive theory. Some modern sociological theory confuses the assertion of the possibility of sociology, the elaboration or repetition of its most general concepts, and the idea of unity of and interaction in society, with a genuine sociology. Spinoza was described as a *Gottbetrunkener Mensch*, and these theorists may equally merit the description of *Gesellschaft-betrunkene Menschen*. But: Spinoza had a good head for abstract concepts, and his intoxication led to no relaxation of logical control, no unrestrained release of conceptual *id*.

Those who doubt the existence of such a world must read Professor Sorokin's book. That is its merit. Its demerit, or rather its incompleteness, curiously similar to that of Khrushchev's speech to the XX Congress,[4] is that it leaves unanswered the question of how the critic or anyone else could remain untainted, or indeed unabsorbed by that world; and it fails (despite illuminating obiter dicta) to provide a *social* explanation for the ills castigated: and this *is* required, for an erroneous epistemology, like the wickedness of one man, is not a sufficient explanation for ills so widespread and so institutionalised. If the indictment contained in Professor Sorokin's book were only partly true, how could he or anyone else escape the consequences of living in a world where such things go on? I do *not* mean that he too may be guilty of some of the fads and foibles: in fact, he rather nobly pleads guilty to this in the preface. It is not for me to say whether indeed he is, but it seems to me a small matter. All or most of us in the academic profession are guilty of some humbug some of the time. If only the innocent could cast stones at humbug few stones would ever be cast (the present reviewer would have to retire at once) and there would be little hope of progress. No: the issue is not individual innocence, but the very possibility of an individual escaping an atmosphere which seems so diffused and so well rooted. There is, after all, such a thing as Gresham's Law of Ideas. What happens to genuine ideas in a world in which so much that is vacuous has to be taken seriously? (One is puzzled by this just as one is by Khrushchev's speech: one doesn't doubt that there were intelligent and honest men in Stalin's Russia, but one wonders how and to what extent they could remain so.) It is perhaps no accident that the most striking work on contemporary America has come from one who is not an academic social scientist at all, but a journalist: W. H. Whyte. And similarly, that when a really interesting work appeared, D. Riesman's, eyebrows were raised—we have the authority of the leading academic theoretician for this—amongst the pukka scientific sociologists . . .

One explanation which suggests itself is that we are in the presence of a *Cargo Cult*. The successes of the natural scientists have been so overwhelming, so manifest and so impressive that they can hardly be considered to be the same species with their colleagues. Non-scientific subjects may indeed illustrate the wit, the elegance, the courage of the human spirit, but they also illustrate the Faustian awareness of the futility of the quest for knowledge. How many professors of non-scientific subjects—excluding men buried in the minutiae of their disciplines—do not sometimes feel like Faust's opening speech? '. . . und leider auch Theologie . . .' Let's be frank, *und leider auch* any other damn subject. But scientists are no longer Faustian men.

We know what may happen to cultures which are too suddenly brought into contact with the overwhelming wealth and technological superiority of another civilisation. They may develop a hysterical Cargo Cult, a desperate attempt at a short cut to the benefits of the superior technology. The pseudo-scientific features of the Fads and Foibles seem to me strictly analogous to the technological primitive who builds himself crude wooden imitations of western mechanical tools and then expects miraculous Cargo to arrive. The empiricism of American psycho-social science is sometimes attributed to the pragmatic temper of the American nation, but surely the striking feature of some of those pseudo-scientific gadgets is their practical irrelevance, cumbersomeness, indeed obstructiveness. This is even noticed by their users, but they don't mind: the miraculous Cargo will not arrive at once, one must have a little patience ... The magic will work, but not just yet. No deadline is set for the demonstration of its efficacy. Now I am not saying that social and human studies cannot be 'scientific' in the sense that there is no room for accuracy, neologism, system, quantification, any more than I doubt the capacity of Polynesians to learn Western techniques. But one can easily tell a Cargo cult from genuine adaption, by a certain hysteria, an uncomprehending concentration on the externals.

A different explanation which is sometimes put forward for the phenomena described by Sorokin is McCarthyism. As an explanation this is wearing a bit thin now. It is however true that the tendency either to float in extremely abstract conceptual schemes,[5] or to bury one's nose in the sand of statistically camouflaged, very factual fact, does tend to have total innocuousness as its consequence—which surely ought to be a danger signal. *Wertfreiheit* is all very well, *Gedankenfreiheit* is too much. It is a strange thing when *sociological* statements become quite such milk-and-water.[6] The most quicktempered policeman, in any regime you care to name, is unlikely to reach for his truncheon on reading them. I suspect that few if any of the theoretical books are even on the Index, and if they are not republished in the Soviet Union, it is not because they are dangerous.

Of course it may be said that the near-triviality and innocuousness of the propositions discussed is deliberate and desirable.[7] Such appears to be the view of Professor Homans. No doubt it is true of Homans himself, clearly a man of genuinely impressive intellect, that when what he says is obvious, it is so because, rightly or wrongly, he subscribes to a methodological view which requires it. He has interesting ideas too, but, methodologically, he values them less, perhaps. But a very pretty picture emerges if we generalise this. Are indeed all the authors of those theoretical frameworks, etc., full of interesting ideas which they keep back in order to build the unexciting groundwork first? If so, one can only take off one's hat in humble admiration for their truly iron self-restraint.

There is another way, more specific than general innocuousness, in which the Fads and Foibles perhaps serve current social trends. The ideas and values implicit in the study of small groups may reinforce the conformist trends of the time; the general theory, with its image of roles, interaction, equilibrium, etc., though in one sense tautological, also suggests a concrete picture, a society of status rather than contract, and may help provide a rationale and a favourable state of mind for an emerging social order. If so it would be curiously analogous to classical economic theory, which also sets out to be a universal descriptive theory, is also tautological in its stricter interpretation, and also in effect helped create some of the phenomena in its own image, nature imitating science as well as art.

One can only suspect and vaguely discern the social explanations. Psycho-social studies have boomed in the United States, presumably with the expansion of higher education. Lacking firm traditions, they have been easier prey for fads than other subjects, and needed them more to simulate achievement and attract attention and financial support. The expansion created a vacuum, intellectually and institutionally speaking, which had to be filled: sociological theory, like God, had to be invented if it did not exist. Those who invented it made more of a hash of it than did the prophets and priests who invented God, and they never attempted the *via negativa*, at least not knowingly. I suppose borderline sciences or disciplines can be divided into (a) *Misgeburten* and (b) test-tube babies: on the one hand nature's errors, subjects which logically have no right to exist, which no one would have put on an *a priori* list, but which have a curious vigour nonetheless and resist attempts at liquidation (philosophy, psycho-analysis, perhaps even social anthropology as an autonomous discipline). On the other hand, scientifically planned and designed creations, which logically must exist but into which the breath of life has only entered feebly if at all . . . Self-conscious sociological theory of the Action Theory kind, carefully designed from the best methodological recipes, appears to be amongst these.

The milieu and atmosphere in which fads and foibles come into being would require the skill of a Budd Schulberg to describe them. *What makes psycho-social science run?* For run it does, in a world of total anomie, especially intellectual. Some of the foibles can only thrive where no one is sure of his intellectual standards and violent and unbridled competitiveness combines with a sad conformism, a mania for massive production with lack of genuine cumulativeness and criticism. The big prizes available to the truly successful, the insecurity protracted late into academic life for the majority, the doubtful competence of the external adjudicators in the strife—all these perhaps, contribute.[8] These factors presumably help to explain why such genuinely great ability, such numbers, such unquestionable energy and hard work, not to mention the financial facilities, lead generally to such uninteresting results. Since the appearance of *Fads and Foibles*, some of the sociological problems inadequately pursued in it have been implicitly answered by *The Organisation Man*.

One of the questions arising from that book is whether we must choose between conformism and a 'Protestant Ethic' (whose attractiveness and perhaps reality it retrospectively exaggerates). University departments in the psycho-social sciences seem doubly hit: in terms of their internal competitiveness they are still in a nineteenth-century stage, tough enough for the requirements of the most stringent of Protestant Ethics, whilst at the same time the values and outlook of the bureaucrat have come to dominate the content and style of research. In addition to the pseudo-scientific ideology, it is the influence of the bureaucratic norms which is probably an important factor making for the thinness of results, the appalling verbiage, the deliberate prolixity and tedious presentation, and so on. There is, after all, a well-known sociological law about him who pays the piper calling the tune. The piper is generally paid by the Foundation.

Now if the well-known multi-millionaire, Mr Cheeseburger, were to take a fancy to social scientists and encourage and aid them, the chances are that he would end up by supporting quite a few phoneys. One thing, however, he would not support, and that is *dullness*, for Mr Cheeseburger personally, like most people, doesn't like being bored. But Mr Cheeseburger has not taken a fancy to anyone. He created a Foundation so as to keep control of the Cheeseburger enterprises. The Cheeseburger *Foundation* is run by highly competent, responsible administrators. *They* do not mind dullness: on the contrary, if it is the right kind, they welcome it, insist on it. The essence of a good administrator is that he is accountable, and behaves as if he were, even if not called to account: he honours his trust. Having handed out some money, he wants to see results: he may not understand them, he is not expected to be a specialist in everything even if he was himself once in the academic field. Now what could be better evidence of work done, of money well spent, than the number of pages covered, the number of questionnaires filled up, the number of calculations made, the number of variables considered, etc., etc. The prose and style of work widely adopted is simply not explicable[9] without the fact that its standards have evolved with an eye on the Foundation bureaucrat, to the specifications of the middlemen of the intellect, who need *weight* to justify expense. The bureaucrat is almost ex officio debarred by his impartiality from assessing merits of rival ideas, but he can count pages.

The interesting and ironic thing is that this happens even when a Foundation is sophisticated and strives to go against the dangers it discerns in the current scene. One distinguished Foundation, with a good reputation, distributes grants to individual scholars and, according to its pamphlet, wishes the grants to be used for thought, orientation, reflection, and not for the completion of specific *projects*, etc. So far so good: but despite this being the official ideology of the thing, the Foundation sees no contradiction in placing the holders of such a grant under the supervision of advisers, whose advice comes at the same time as the money, the supply of which they control, and who (1) know little or nothing about the subject, (2) have no inhibitions about offering advice none the less, concerning for instance the precise limits of the general thinking that is to take place (!) and (3) giving weight to that advice by financial pressure. The only effects this kind of situation can have is either a cynical and superficial adaptation by the Thinker, or a partial acceptance of those criteria of academic work which seem so self-evident to the bureaucrat that he doesn't know he holds them; or a mixture of both.

Of course, the main consequence of the manner of financing research is the development of what may be called managerial, entrepreneurial research.[10] The managerial Professor is now as familiar as the managerial General. Here again, we are faced with something that seems to flow inevitably from the social realities. A successful academic generally reaches the highest available rank, full professor, some time fairly early in middle age, with many energetic years yet ahead of him. Leaving aside academic administration, which involves him in abandoning his subject, what is open to him? Of course, he could content himself, as he often did in the past, with the informal rewards of an intellectual influence. But intellectual influence can only be exercised through ideas, and in the fads-and-foibles atmosphere ideas have little prestige: few would recognise an idea under the jargon if they met one, and if they did they would not care. (Are we not turning social studies into a *science*, and hence obliged to despise mere *speculation*?) This being so, there is one way conspicuously open: bigger and bigger *un*speculation, large-scale *research*. The money for it is of course not misappropriated by the successful research-entrepreneur. But it gives him patronage and hence power, and money actually owned would not be usable in any other way. We can all think of some of the great Czars of research, sometimes men of no particular intellectual distinction. A research empire, once established, has a vested interest in the research paraphernalia, in self-justifying quantity, and often in unintelligibility. The size of the research, the complexity of the tools, the abstruseness of the language, are a kind of Conspicuous Display which is essential to the prestige of the enterprise and its further expansion. They are also a protective smoke-screen. It can no more confess failure than can any other political organisation. It can hardly grope through trial and confessed error. Defeats are not admitted, and the premium is on the kind of question and technique and language which appears to give some answer anyway. The supervising bureaucrat is happy, he has something massive with which to balance the money spent, and the Czar is happy, for the Empire prospers. Their symbiosis is interesting. The sociology of *the gift* has been explored, but the equally fascinating sociology of *the grant*, with its profound implications for donor and recipient, awaits its investigator. Of course, there are many techniques which may be genuinely useful or essential, and there are many problems which can only be answered by organised large-scale

212   *The alchemists of sociology*

research: the autonomous research-for-its-sake, or for the sake of the Empire to which it gives birth, flourishes amongst and to the detriment of its genuine rivals.

The merit of Sorokin's book is that it establishes beyond doubt that there is a world of Fads and Foibles of some size, and not merely the product of a jaundiced observer's eye. It portrays the world of men who think they are the Newtons of the Royal Society of psychological and social science, and who in fact are its alchemists. Sorokin's witty account of them will live as a historical document long after those works themselves are forgotten.

NOTES

1 Pitrim A. Sorokin, *Fads and Foibles in Modern Sociology and Related Sciences*, Chicago, 1956, London, 1958.
2 We are all looking forward to Professor Wright Mills' forthcoming book on this.
3 I was once assured, in praise of psycho-analysis, that one of the leading sociological theoreticians used to be merely a scholar, of the old European kind, until he underwent analysis, after which he acquired wings and was freed of his shackles. This is undeniable.
4 I owe this point to Mr P. Stirling.
5 'The repellent recipe' as Mrs J. Floud has appositely called one of them.
6 I own a respectable *Introduction to Sociology*, printed in 1948, officially used for teaching by a reputable university, whose competent chapter on the history of the subject manages to avoid mentioning the name of Marx.
7 Cf. some very interesting comments on this by Mr A. H. Halsey in 'British Universities and Intellectual Life', *Universities Quarterly*, 12, February 1958, 141–52.
8 I am pleased to have my superficial impression confirmed by Mr N. Birnbaum, in 'America—a Partial View', *Commentary*, 26, 1958, 42–8.
9 Cf. Mr H. J. Gans, 'Informal Sociology', *American Sociological Review*, 23, August 1958, 441–2.
10 Cf. Mr B. Moore's letter in *The Times Literary Supplement*, 3 October 1958, 561.

15
THE SOCIOLOGY OF FAITH

In principle, there would seem to be some tension between believing in, accepting, a religion, and investigating it sociologically, as one object amongst others. Hence one must welcome a study which attempts to resolve this tension, and explore the manner in which others have attempted to do so. Dr W. Stark's *Sociology of Knowledge* is such a study. This book, which incidentally is too long and would have profited from some pruning, is at its most interesting when it discusses and describes the views of various people who undertook substantive or analytic studies in this field. I shall, however, not concentrate on this, the picaresque aspect of the book, its wanderings amongst the highways and byways of gnosio-sociological thought, but shall extract and discuss the central thread of continuous argument which, camouflaged by prolixity and many digressions, is to be found in this work.

One of the ways in which the author believes himself to be advancing the subject is by drawing a distinction between sociology of knowledge proper and the theory of ideology: the failure to make this distinction has, he thinks, bedevilled the past treatments of the subject. But what differentiates them? It appears (p. 46) that the doctrine of ideology '. . . is . . . different in its nature because it is a *psychological* rather than a sociological discipline' (italics mine). It is true that the study of *individual* prejudice, the psycho-pathology of *self-deception*, is not a part of sociology, but who uses the term ideology to designate it? On the contrary, although the term may be used pejoratively in the sense of *false* consciousness, it definitely implies that the illusion in question is collective, institutionally supported, and quite compatible with individual, psychological normality, rationality and freedom from self-deception. That is both the customary and the useful employment of the term 'ideology'. I find it hard to see any merit in Stark's re-definition, other than the dubious one that it helps him attain certain favoured conclusions.

The picture which he presents is: on a more specific level there are 'ideologies', factional, false and motivated by concrete interests and behind them 'perspectives, vantage-points of whole societies', all of them true and mutually complementary, and transcendental (for rigorously testable subjects are exempt from this schema). Only the latter, the vantage-points, are the proper objects of sociology of knowledge. Dr Stark attempts to support or establish the distinction by an example, but the example seems to me to show merely that we all hold or presuppose views of differing levels of abstraction, that opponents may share the same presuppositions at one level and not at another, and that where our views have social roots, different ones may be relevant at different levels.

What Dr Stark is trying to do also emerges from his definitions. He maintains (p. 49) 'If all men could and would come to control their subconscious and rise superior to the insinuations of selfish or sectional interests, the doctrine of ideology would die off, because there would be no more raw material left in the contemporary world for it to study.' But (p. 80) 'the whole truth—will include *no* ideology and *all* socially determined knowledge (Dr Stark's italics): . . . socially determined knowledge is part and parcel of it (truth), indeed, constitutive of it—only . . . different aspect-structures . . . must be fused . . . to give the full truth . . .' But this attempt to define ideology in terms of both falsehood *and* of factional or selfish motivation, and the object of sociology of knowledge proper in terms of truth *and* of the whole or 'supra-functional' society, must break down. Not all factionally motivated convictions are false (on the contrary, the closeness of convictions to some practical interest gives them a better chance of verification). Not all outlooks of whole societies can be true, unless we have a truly amazing faith in some remarkable synthesis or mishmash of all apparent contradictories. The background outlooks, just because they are about transcendent or categorial matters that are not easily checked, are in fact particularly liable to be swayed by interest. How large or supra-functional must a group be before it is above 'factional' interest? What is a society, what is a faction, in, for instance, our contemporary world? In a society with a ruling class, how does one distinguish the society's outlook and the biased outlook of its ruling class, especially when the others do not attain articulateness? If they are not to be identified, are we then, when talking of the social outlook, speaking merely about something latent, an ideal but unrealised synthesis, or are we talking about some common presuppositions, something wholly inexplicit? But may not these too have motives, or be false, or inconsistent? Thus not only does Dr Stark smuggle his conclusions into his definitions, but also these definitions turn out to be unworkable ones.

Another questionable distinction introduced by the author is between what he calls macro- and micro-sociology of knowledge. His official definition of their difference (pp. 20 and 21) makes micro-sociology the study of 'the narrower world of scholarship and art', whilst macro-sociology 'fixes its attention on the inclusive society and its influence'. He considers both to be useful, but the latter to be more fundamental. When however we get a fuller picture of the two kinds, in the course of refutations of writers who preferred micro-sociology (J. Kraft and F. Znaniecki, p. 28), it emerges that Dr Stark thinks of micro-sociology as so to speak an internal study of who believes what and why in a given society, whilst macro-sociology concerns itself with societies *as units*. But either this distinction is entirely relative, a matter of degree or numbers, or, if a fundamental difference is allowed, Dr Stark will come up against two things: the charge of reifying abstractions, and the problem of how non-arbitrarily to delimit his units for analysis and comparison (see below). The possibility of the former, nominalistic criticism he dismisses in extremely cavalier fashion as '. . . materialism so crude as to rule itself out of court'. By under-rating what he calls micro-sociology of knowledge Dr Stark in effect turns his back on what makes sociology of knowledge important and interesting, namely the institutional and organisational aspect of ideas: something that both 'ideologies' and 'vantage-points, perspectives' of whole societies, have in common. This brings out that Dr Stark's correlation of ideology with falsehood and motivation, and of perspectives with truth and freedom from faction, is untenable.

So having dismissed the study of ideology as a psychological concern, and partly dismissed the institutional aspect of ideas as the subsidiary subject of 'micro-sociology', we are left in the dizzy heights of outlooks of whole or 'supra-functional' societies. Why—*cui bono*? It is difficult to resist the temptation to indulge in some speculative ideological analysis oneself, and seek the motive. Notoriously, the kind of sociology of knowledge conceived by Dr Stark often leads to relativism and despair of the attaining of true knowledge. But Dr Stark is not led to this. On the contrary: we are led into a strange night where all cows are, for a change, white or off-white. Dr Stark in effect believes that although knowledge is socially conditioned, *all* societies grasp the truth, though only partial aspects of it. On page 155 we are sternly told that 'We are far from anxious to indict, secularise, ironise, satirise, alienate, devalue: these pastimes are for the market-place, not for the study, for the propagandist, not for the scholar.' I should have thought that the combating of error, delusion and superstition was the work of both study *and* market-place, and easier in the former.

His doctrine that 'every society, and every other supra-functional subsociety as well, can lay claim to truth, the substance of truth, though only one aspect of it' (p. 155) is later given the name *metectic*. But allowing this even for *sub*-societies; Dr Stark's view comes up sharply against the problem he would in any case have had to face in view of the difficulty of delimiting societies: is then the doctrinal conflict between subsocieties (and societies) a mistake, an illusion, or even a necessary illusion *à la* Hegel? Are disagreements between groups only apparent, waiting for sociology of knowledge to illuminate an underlying harmony, or is even the conflict a part of a deeper unity? For, contrary to what the 'metectic' view seems to imply, holders of rival views generally consider those views incompatible both logically and in their concrete implications, and not without reason; and even whole societies sometimes change their outlooks in the belief that they are exchanging a falser for a truer one. The problem is also high-lighted by the fact that Dr Stark's universal tolerance is not *quite* universal, some cows retaining their more habitual nocturnal greyness: 'Positivists of the nineteenth century, having cramped their style of thought, were in no position to tackle (the issue of theism versus atheism) successfully, or even sensibly' (footnote, p. 159). All (sub)societies have a partial grasp of truth, but some less so than others, it appears.

Like many of those whom the diversity of outlooks led to a sceptical relativism, Dr Stark exempts from his own—quite different—conclusion the more rigorous kinds of knowledge: '. . . the absolute truth of the multiplication table need not be brought into doubt—nor that of the more recondite propositions of the mathematical kind' (p. 161). No partial truths here—only one truth, and outside it error. Where superficially this does not appear to fit there is a way out; '. . . their mathematics was like ours, but was overlaid with magic: the physics underneath their metaphysics was in no way different from any rational physics.' Possibly so: but the sharp separation, of the rigorous kinds of truth, universal and unique, on the one hand, and on the other, the metaphysico–religious kind, where the 'metectic' view holds and *all* ideas have a measure of truth, really makes the general argument too easy: '. . . when primitives make statements which seem to deny a basic law of formal logic, they are not acting otherwise than the most modern logician who is at the same time a good Christian. He, too, asserts that in the Godhead Three and One are identical, but that does not mean that he denies the absolute truth of the law of contradiction. He has merely decided not to carry it from physics into metaphysics, and this is quite legitimate . . .' (p. 162). Quite a lot appears to be legitimate *in* this field, but not the denial of the field altogether: 'To us it seems clear that positivism . . . cannot provide a true representation of the facts in their entirety because it presses the methods appropriate only to the study of one sector of reality (nature) beyond their proper sphere, and we should always unambiguously condemn it . . .' (p. 181).

Dr Stark notices the inconsistency, the arbitrary asymmetry, of condemning just this view, and exempting it from 'metectic' tolerance. On the next page (182) he says 'This . . . is an opinion as legitimate as any other . . . But the curious fact is that men have never been able to live with it.' He then proceeds to prove the practical untenability of total relativism, of a complete acceptance of flux in all things and truths, implicitly confusing this with positivism. But positivism is not identical with it, unless it be proven that no way out of total flux other than a transcendental one exists, *and* that the transcendental escape route is a possible one—and he proves neither. On the contrary, the grandiloquent title of the last chapter, 'The *Conquest* of Social Determination' (italics mine) turns out to be an empty boast—*such* conquests would make Alexanders of us all. The conquest appears to consist of a very mild recommendation of the metectic theory, the view that different societies perceive differing, incomplete aspects of one unique but transcendent and unknowable higher reality. The rival 'pragmatist' doctrine is condemned because 'useless as an epistemology . . . does not so much as conceive of the possibility of absolute truth where man and his society are concerned' (p. 339). The corresponding defect of the metectic theory is frankly admitted: '. . . it contains an irreducible element of faith' (p. 342).

Wondering what Dr Stark would make of one of the earliest doctrines of the extra-individual determination of important knowledge, namely the doctrine of Grace (which, be it noted, did not 'conquer' but accepted such determination), I looked up St Augustine in the index. The reference, page 270, did not lead me to an answer to that question, but shed light on the concrete implication of the metectic view:

> Is Christianity not in fact a set of ideas come down from heaven? The present writer would be the last to deny it. [continued in footnote on the same page:] . . . though the divine message is a revelation . . . of a higher reality, it was . . . presented in a form which fitted . . . its day and place. We need only think of the parables of our Lord . . . To get at that meaning, we must penetrate the outer crust of socially determined : . . . ideas to reach . . . the generally human and . . . the divine. The social environment in which it worked . . . appears highly significant for the understanding of the divine message itself.

Clerics of various denominations in the United States are nowadays often graduates of the social sciences. Dr Stark has, for the future, provided them (barring, as he explicitly does, Fundamentalists) with a reason for being sociologists *of knowledge*. Sociology of knowledge is for him, if not identical with theological exegesis, at least its necessary prerequisite and its support.

Thus the essence of Dr Stark's general argument is this: he excludes the possibility of error in social outlooks by a definition consigning false consciousness to the study of ideology and throws out such a study from the sociology of knowledge proper. He reinforces this by a mistake through which he misses the whole point of sociology of knowledge, namely the mistake of the attributing of falsehood to individual self-deception. He further strengthens the claim that various outlooks are true by excluding the positive and corrigible sciences from them, and by stressing the transcendence, the inaccessibility of this residual truth, and wards off the possibility of the rejection of this kind of truth *in toto* by an appeal, for a change, to a practical consideration. Whether he holds all transcendental views *equally* true, equally metectic, or whether the Christianity to which he subscribes is *more* so, or whether he thinks that other outlooks are a lisping or crypto-Christianity, is not fully clear. Dr Stark's idea that there might be a world without ideology reminds one of the Marxian hope of a society without alienation: but in the Starkian version, man free from faction, egoism and delusions might also find himself in a society crowned with a *mélange* of all possible religions and metaphysics, for they are all claimed to be partial views of the truth. Some have preached universal harmony through eclecticism and watering down: others, for instance in anthropology, have claimed to find the universal transcendent truth held in strange clothing and social contexts. Dr Stark has provided both these activities with a gnosio-sociological rationale, and he has reintroduced as 'sociology of knowledge' the shallow optimism, familiar from time to time in philosophy, which hopes to have *and* eat all possible cakes. It is a metaphysics of faith rather than a sociology of knowledge. But this rationale of Higher Eclecticism is logically ill-founded, it travesties the religion which it seeks to defend, and it is unhelpful in sociology.

SOURCES

The following are the original places and dates of publication of the chapters in this volume:

chapter 1: *Proceedings of the Aristotelian Society*, suppl. vol. **30**, 1956, 157–76; the appendix first appeared in P. Gardiner, *Theories of History*, Chicago, 1959; chapter 2: *Transactions of the Fifth World Congress of Sociology (Washington)*, Louvain, 1962, **1**, 153–83; chapter 3: *British Journal of Sociology*, **11**, 1960, 170–2; chapter 4: I. Lakatos and A. Musgrave, eds, *Problems in the Philosophy of Science*, Amsterdam, 1968, 377–406, 426–32; chapter 5: *The Times Literary Supplement*, 5 April 1968, 347–9; chapter 6: *Mind*, **67**, 1958, 182–202; chapter 7: *Transactions of the Sixth World Congress of Sociology (Evian)*, Louvain, 1967, **2**, 49–83; chapter 8: *Universities Quarterly*, **13**, 1958, 86–92; chapter 9: *Oxford Magazine*, **5**, 17 June 1965, 417–19; chapter 10: *Beaver*, 12 November 1970, 6; chapters 11, 12 and 13: *Philosophy of Science*, **24**, 1957, 235–42; **27**, 1960, 187–204; **30**, 1963, 236–51 respectively; chapters 14 and 15: *Inquiry*, **2**, 1959, 126–35, and **1**, 1958, 247–52 respectively. The author has made occasional slight alterations in the texts.

INDEX OF NAMES

Italic page numbers indicate an especially important reference; *n* indicates the reference is in a footnote, *q* in a quotation.

INDEX OF SUBJECTS